Barbara,

Life is gift.
Enjoy it

Agnes Chowadi
12/14/2020

ME
WITHOUT
I

Agnes C Chawadi

BALBOA.PRESS
A DIVISION OF HAY HOUSE

Balboa Press books may be ordered through booksellers or by contacting:

Balboa Press
A Division of Hay House
1663 Liberty Drive
Bloomington, IN 47403
www.balboapress.com
844-682-1282

Because of the dynamic nature of the Internet, any web addresses or links contained
in this book may have changed since publication and may no longer be valid. The views
expressed in this work are solely those of the author and do not necessarily reflect the
views of the publisher, and the publisher hereby disclaims any responsibility for them.

The author of this book does not dispense medical advice or prescribe the use
of any technique as a form of treatment for physical, emotional, or medical
problems without the advice of a physician, either directly or indirectly. The
intent of the author is only to offer information of a general nature to help you
in your quest for emotional and spiritual well-being. In the event you use any
of the information in this book for yourself, which is your constitutional right,
the author and the publisher assume no responsibility for your actions.

Any people depicted in stock imagery provided by Getty Images are models,
and such images are being used for illustrative purposes only.
Certain stock imagery © Getty Images.

Scripture texts, prefaces, introductions, footnotes and cross references used in this
work are taken from the New American Bible, revised edition © 2010, 1991, 1986,
1970 Confraternity of Christian Doctrine, Inc., Washington, DC All Rights Reserved.
No part of this work may be reproduced or transmitted in any form or by any means,
electronic or mechanical, including photocopying, recording, or by any information
storage and retrieval system, without permission in writing from the copyright owner.

Print information available on the last page.

ISBN: 978-1-9822-5801-6 (sc)
ISBN: 978-1-9822-5802-3 (e)

Balboa Press rev. date: 11/11/2020

Dedication

To Amma,
my beautiful mother,
my inspiration,
my fire and wind.

Contents

Acknowledgements

Like a child gestating in the womb, this book has been forming inside of me for what feels like forever. I described it for nearly a decade to my friends and acquaintances, and it is finally ready to come to life! While I am probably not going to remember everyone, who nourished me along the way and encouraged me to follow my intuition, I would like to say "thank you" to those who hold a special place in my heart for helping me give birth to this book. I will not forget you!

First, I want to thank Ellen Geerling, who provided me the needed impetus to start turning my ideas and experiences into words. Thanks, Ellen, for editing my writings, for supporting and encouraging my views, and for giving your best to the flow of the spirit world in the book. You breathed life into my words and together we grew in a friendship that made our presence real in the book. To Patty Eversole, my kindred soul, friend and a teacher, thanks for offering your proofreading. Although this is a technical undertaking, you brought yourself into it, feeling the pulse of the words and continuing to appreciate the written work. Thank you so much for being generous with yourself and your gifts! Thank you, Kathryn Messner, for scanning through the pages of this book with a critical eye. You offered some valuable suggestions and raised questions on behalf of every reader so that they can now enjoy the clarity of insights expressed here-in. Thank you, Julie Harig, for your punctuation work. You were extremely generous with your time, talent and appreciation of the written work, stories and incidents mentioned. Thanks a lot, and I know the readers unknowingly will gain from your contribution to the book.

Thanks to James Taff, who volunteered to design the cover page and did an excellent job. He managed to bring to life the reconciliation of the two worlds that it is possible in and through each human person, when they release the power of love contained in their hearts. Thank you, Jim, for working diligently and incorporating the spirit of the book in the cover page.

Thanks to Martha Desloge for nudging me to pursue my desire to write. You were very gentle in reminding me to get started, by way of inquiring every now and then. You are a friend everyone should have in life. Thanks to Brother Jeffrey Callander, CFC, who kept pushing me to pursue writing and constantly supported me with prayers.

I can't imagine this book without the love, lessons, and experiences provided to me by some of the great personalities like Ross Isbell, Patricia Newman, James Messner, Wally and Joanne Lewis, and their families. They taught me to love simply and that transformed me inside out. Thanks, Joanne, for listening to my stories and feeling their spirit in your heart. Thank you Fr. Xavier Jeyaraj SJ, for boosting my literary energy and encouraging me every step of the way. Some of the names mentioned here are now my angels in heaven, and the rest of you continue to support, to love me, and to ignite the fire of love dormant in me. You are God's gift and His presence. Much appreciation to you all!

Undergirding this book is a group of my supportive and loving friends who call forth the best in me. You know that your names are inscribed in my heart and my sentiments of gratitude will find a home in your hearts!

Finally, I also remain grateful for the team at Balboa publishing group, who brought this book into its final form and delivered it to the world! I am grateful for their professionalism and for taking a chance on a new author.

I went through a journey without I

There my heart opened up to joy without I

The beloved who always hid his face from me

Suddenly showed his beautiful face to me without I

I died from the pain of not finding you

A new birth came, and I was reborn without I

Now I am always drunk without any wine

Now I am always happy and joyful without I

Do not ever remember me for who I was

I am the remembrance of me without I

I say happy and loving words without I

It is I who is always alive without I

All the doors of fortune and joy were closed on me

Suddenly they were opened to me without I

With I, even if I am a king, I am a slave of time

Without I, there is no slavery in all my kingdom

I am drunk with the wine from Shams Tabrizi

May this drunkenness of love be always without I

—*Rumi*

Introduction

There once was an eagle who thought he was a chicken. When the eagle was newly hatched, he fell from the safety of his nest. A chicken farmer found the eagle, brought him to the farm, and raised him in a chicken coop among his many chickens. The eagle grew up doing what chickens do, living like a chicken, pecking in the farmyard, and believing he was a chicken. A naturalist heard the story about an eagle acting like a chicken and came to the chicken farm to see if the story was true. He knew that the eagle is king of the sky and was surprised to see the eagle clucking around the chicken coop, pecking at the ground, and acting very much like a chicken. The farmer explained to the naturalist that this bird was no longer an eagle. This creature was now a chicken because he had been trained to be a chicken, and he believed that he was a chicken. The naturalist knew there was more to this great bird than his actions showed as he "pretended" to be a chicken. He had been born an eagle and had the heart of an eagle, and nothing could change that. The man lifted the eagle onto the fence surrounding the chicken coop and said, "Eagle, thou art an eagle. Stretch forth thy wings and fly." The eagle moved slightly, only to look at the man; then he glanced down at his home among the chickens in the chicken coop where he was comfortable. He jumped off the fence and continued doing what chickens do. The farmer was satisfied. "I told you it was a chicken," he said. The naturalist returned the next day and tried again to convince the farmer and the eagle that the eagle was born for something greater. He took the eagle to the top of the farmhouse and spoke to him: "Eagle, thou art an eagle. Thou dost belong to the sky and not to the earth. Stretch forth thy wings and fly." The large bird looked at the man, then again down into the chicken coop. He jumped from the man's arm onto the roof of the farmhouse. Knowing what eagles are really about, the naturalist asked the farmer to let him try one more time. He would return the next day and prove that this bird was an eagle. The farmer, convinced otherwise, said, "It is a chicken." The naturalist returned the next morning to the chicken farm and took the eagle and the farmer some distance away to the foot of a high mountain. They could not see the farm or the chicken coop from this new setting. The man held the eagle on his arm and pointed high into the sky where the bright sun was beckoning above. He spoke: "Eagle, thou art an eagle! Thou dost belong to the sky and not to the earth. Stretch forth thy wings and fly!" This time the eagle stared skyward into the bright sun, straightened his large body, and stretched his massive wings. His wings moved, slowly at first, then surely and powerfully. With a mighty screech, the eagle flew. (Story from *Walk Tall, You're A Daughter of God*, by Jamie Glenn, 1994, Deseret Book Company.)

For fifty years, I had been that eagle acting like a chicken. I had confined myself to a tribal mentality and its limitations, thinking that was the best deal in my life. Like the eagle, I simply did not know any better. Though I had the capacity to fly like an eagle and had felt deep in my heart that I could be better, I remained in the chicken coop and tried my utmost to be a good chicken. This life approach provided safety and comfort along with the rest of the chickens in the coop who were comfortable with their state in life, but the circumstances of my life, and the difficulties and suffocation experienced in the coop, became the natural factors that provided wind beneath my wings. Deep within I was tired of what I had always been doing—tired of my attitudes, my safe-seeking, my fear. I had little courage and no guts to venture out of the coop. The barnyard and chicken coop were my reality, and I had never known any life beyond that. It was not the life beyond the coop that summoned me, but the choking I experienced in the coop that finally pushed me out.

For nearly two decades I had a recurring dream in which I attempted to fly. With each attempt, my wings were clipped. Little did I realize that the life I was leading was the wing clipping keeping me from flight. Society around me revered the type of life I had chosen. Seemingly I had it all: I was a nun in full religious outfit, with respect, safety, security, meals and shelter, and meaningful work. What Catholic would not respect the life I had chosen? My religious sisters and I were appreciated and valued for the work and spiritual knowledge we provided to those whom we served, so I continued to superimpose meaning onto my life's activities despite experiences that made me feel otherwise.

When you are conditioned to think in a particular way, you think that is reality. You embrace it with all your heart, and you give your best to it. You ignore the difficulties experienced along the way and hope they will pass away. You use the terminology given to you to justify your situation and keep hoping against hope that your feelings of emptiness are just an illusion—or vanity, or ego. For a long time, I thought that my gnawing urge to leave the conditioned way of life and embrace my inner beauty was nothing but a passing temptation. I kept ignoring and pushing it away by adding so-called spiritual practices. This inner turmoil tortured me for almost twenty years. Every now and then, I tried to share my struggle with close friends and relatives. They were very well meaning and would push me back into the same hole—the low-lying chicken coop—with encouraging, supportive words or kind deeds. Nothing really provided relief. When I could no longer tolerate a lifestyle that had become suffocating, I decided to call it quits and embrace a new path. I am grateful for that moment of decision and for all the additional difficulties that followed. Through each of them I grew stronger and clearer in realigning my values and way of life. I had to work much harder than I ever had in my safe, protected institutional life, but in the end, the rewards were exponentially greater.

There is a magnanimity of life and beauty in breathing fresh air into one's life goals and purpose. From a few weekly hours of spiritual practice, life itself has become a spiritual practice. My seeking of God that took me away from ordinary life has—paradoxically—brought me right back into the middle of it. It is here that I have met God as never before. I no longer need to strive for rigorous and conventional religious practices. Life itself has become a tapestry of ongoing, spontaneous spiritual practices. It has changed the way I see myself and the world and breathed new energy and deep inner freedom into everything I do.

Each of us struggle for that inner expansion of self for which we are created. Each of us is an eagle with an immense capacity for soaring the skies. When we restrict ourselves to a conventional way of life, we put ourselves into the chicken coop and behave as lesser creatures than we really are. This book is an attempt to share my life experiences of this wonderful transition from the coop to the sky. This book is not intended to change anyone's thinking or beliefs, nor to indoctrinate anyone or force them to take a path they do not want to take. Rather, this book and the insights shared are intended to inspire anyone who is seeking, who may suspect they are stuck in the chicken coop, who may have the nagging feeling they were meant for more and who may want to spread their wings and soar.

Life is a journey and a dance. Many people shrink against the wall and fail to join the dance. They are afraid. They ignore the urge to spread their arms and twirl. What will people say? Will I look ridiculous? What if I fall? This book is the story of my own dance. I have questioned every belief I ever held, every teaching I was given and all the cultural norms and ways I had absorbed to assimilate myself into larger structures. This self-inquiry helped me rethink and give voice to the Spirit that was calling me to live a new life. May the same Spirit find voice in your heart and a fuller expression in your life and choices. Life is continuously evolving in and through us, if we dare to give ourselves to the process. My sharing will generate different responses among the readers of this book. Those responses have less to do with what I am sharing and more to do with what you are going through. I pray that you will use this book as a springboard to venture into a new inner journey that will free you to live up to your fullest human potential. A whole new world blossoms when we abandon small, individual self-seeking pursuits and join the Spirit of humanity. Let me illustrate this with a personal example.

My mother has been bedbound for the last fourteen years. She has declined gradually over time following a cerebral aneurysm. According to her doctors, from a medical context, she is a living miracle. No scientific research accounts for why she is still alive. And yet she lives, most likely due to the attentive and loving care of my siblings. Each time I look at her frail body I ask, who is she? Is she my Mom? The answer is yes and no. Where is the person who once had so much vigor, fire, drive for life, motivation, energy, and action? What has happened to her beliefs, convictions and habits that once made her my Mom? I see none of these. She does not know her name, her family members, or if she is alive or dead. Her person is no longer present, but her body is. At this point, I wonder if there is a difference between her body and the body of another person in a similar condition. The only difference I can see is that we can identify them by their names. Does that identity mean anything to them right now? What is the essence of human identity? Is it the sum of our memories, perceptions, attitudes, desires, hopes, fears and relationships? Is that what sets us apart from one another? In that case, all these individual psychological traits are quite individual and are in constant flux, as is the identity we call "self." While our physical body may appear the same, these other factors continually change and appear very different in each human being.

Across the span of our lifetimes, we continue to chase happiness, success and meaning. Like a hamster running on the wheel in his cage, we keep racing the little self that we created in this human body. We suspect that there is more to our lives than daily chores and concerns. There are many mysteries attached to our lives and we try to find answers or at least make sense of these mysteries in a variety of ways. Some are drawn to and find comfort in religion and religious practices handed down by their families, while others seek answers elsewhere. Religion provides a great deal of help to satisfy the human seeking for meaning and purpose. For many people, however, being "a good religious person" means a few hours a week at a service or in private prayer at home. But what happens to the rest of the moments that consume our lives? Is being a good person or living life with meaning just "punching a ticket" or timecard? If we practice religion or spirituality for just a small amount of time, it will leave something lacking. If we are to experience a difference—a real spiritual transformation—then our whole life must be spiritually oriented. We can make ourselves, and every breath we draw, *a living prayer.* Jesus said, "I have come that you may have life, and have it more abundantly." This book is intended to share with you the possibility of living your life abundantly by integrating spiritual practice into every moment, every breath, every act, every thought that measures your lifetime.

It has been said that "no man is an island," and surely no one benefits from a compartmentalized existence. Organizations discuss the negative effects of the "siloed approach" to doing things. We are all connected. Although a series of events or experiences, our lives, too, are one whole that can be aligned into a right order that merges with the vastness we call God. It is my hope that this book will help readers to pay attention to the present moment even in the most ordinary of situations, to live in creative harmony with the divine presence, and to bring the quality of spiritual life to everything we do. We will then free the constricted "I" to realize its full potential and its highest expansion to "Me." We will then, like the eagle, leave the chicken coop and soar the vastness of the sky.

You are the message of wholeness

A parish church made an announcement that went like this: "Everyday Stewardship—Living an Extraordinary Life, Parish Mission with John Smith." Many from my circle of friends decided not to participate in the event. After inquiring, I realized they were afraid to attend the mission lest they be asked to shell out more money, time or talents, but the mission had nothing to do with this fear. The mission had been organized to help people get more out of their daily lives.

What made people pre-judge and opt out of such a helpful event?

The word "stewardship" of course! Over the past few years, churches have used this word to run fundraisers or to recruit volunteers to build and lead active ministries. From these past experiences of the use of the word "stewardship," my friends had assumed this meaning of the word, and had made clear choices based on this assumption. Their reaction came from the concept they had formed based on past experiences and the underlying fear of being asked for more.

Don't we do this all the time? We have so many pre-conceived notions, perceptions, definitions and beliefs about life, self, and others and, at any given moment, we seldom take time to explore the real meaning.

I have similar fixed ideas in my mind about everything and everyone in life, particularly about the word "wholeness." I will never know why I was enchanted by this word, and I fervently desired to be whole. Ever since I got acquainted with my inner desire to be whole, I have tried very hard to invest every ounce of my energy and resources to become whole. In the pursuit of wholeness, I said multiple prayers, practiced virtues, did acts of service, attended retreats and set goals to arrive at wholeness. The inner sense of lack has haunted me and pushed me to seek. Seek intensely, in everything and everywhere.

But of course, I did not bother to explore or question the meaning of wholeness; rather, I succumbed to the hidden feeling that I am not whole. Deep down in my heart, the nagging sense that I was not whole consumed me. Where did this come from and when did I develop this feeling? I guess it came from years of conditioning by my family, school, church community, culture and society. Somewhere along the line I had absorbed and accepted the idea that I was not whole.

Through the process of seeking wholeness, I have questioned the very desire and watched the word change its meaning. It has been a fascinating experience to notice how I have evolved and shifted my understanding of wholeness as faith and unity consciousness to feeling complete from within. I believe I have unconsciously held definitions of wholeness as success, name, fame and doing something spectacular and out of the ordinary. I assimilated these meanings from the people I watched and stories I read.

Across the years of seeking wholeness, there have been several moments of insight, inspiration and the deep need to write about these experiences. Revisiting all past notes, journals, practices and rituals helped me realize that wholeness is nothing but projection of my ideas and concepts. The seeking can be so intense that it consumes you from within and no matter what you do, you keep looking for that thing which will provide you inner satisfaction and a sense of deep connection. I am not here to provide you with a new definition of the word or make a statement of arrival. Rather to share a story of experiences of daily transformation—an attempt to share how life has evolved in my effort to seek and find the wholeness.

Today I view "wholeness"—or the quality of being whole—as total acceptance: accepting everyone, everything, and life as it is in the given moment. There's nothing out there that will bring us the sense of wholeness. I might think that possessing this or that will satisfy me and help me feel whole. That's far from the truth. The wholeness is more a matter of how your mind processes the definition of wholeness and perceives life and related activities. Everyone and everything are whole as they are. I am at rest with life and open to receive it, as it wants to reveal itself to me. My beliefs and concepts that I once thought were strengths and guidelines, have in fact kept me away from experiencing the wholeness of life. I have come to realize that until I embrace life as is, I will never become all that I am created to be. Beyond the identity formed by concepts, I have come to be at peace in my heart. I feel as if I have come home and can now put my feet up and enjoy all of life as it is. I am not looking for something more or different. I am content with the way life is and I am. All race and definitions have come to a standstill, and I am beginning to flow with life.

Recently, on one of my regular walks, I experienced an awesome sense of expanse and vastness, realizing that within my being I held fifty years of investment of family, society, culture and universe. In my DNA I carry the investment of years and years, of the eons, since humanity came into being. I am a repository of volumes of wisdom, and through my daily life experiences, am continually evolving into wholeness. It turns out that I did not need to imitate someone or box myself in with some societal, cultural or other external definitions of what it means to be whole. Wholeness is ever fresh and ever new. Life's unique experiences provide a way for wholeness to manifest in and through me. I did not need to force myself to experience life as someone else does. So, what is my understanding of wholeness? Wholeness means standing on the firm foundation of wisdom embodied in my being and evolving through daily experiences. They need not be similar to anyone else's experience or be better in any way. Each of us experiences life in a unique way and we are whole in that experiences.

What does wholeness mean for you? The whole universe invests itself in you and in me, so that we become the fresh revelation of life. You are the wholeness and so am I! Together we are expressions of wholeness that uniquely manifest through our daily life experiences. When I abandon all given concepts about life and open my heart to live from life as it happens in the given moment, I notice a sense of inner freedom. Everything comes together and everything starts making sense. Our life experiences are the vehicles for our wholeness. They are at the service of our journey to wholeness. You and I are unlimited and whole at this very moment!

> *"You don't need another person, place or thing to make*
> *you whole. God already did that. Your job is to know it."*
> *Maya Angelou*

Life seeks you to express itself abundantly

The word "life" might conjure up differing ideas and thoughts from one person to the next. The synonyms for the word "life" as used here are: God, Universe, Allah, Kingdom, Higher Self, Love and Consciousness. Some people call it the Force of life. It is that force or energy which moves in and through us. At different times it takes different shapes over the course of one's lifetime. This energy and drive are hidden in every human yearning, desire and seeking, and it manifests uniquely in people. While in some it shows up as a desire to do something daring and different, in others it is hidden in a simple desire to move up the social ladder or to care for someone. Some seek it in the name of love and happiness, while others look for it in money and power. Such seeking is not hidden solely in human beings but in the whole of creation. In fact, everything in the universe is in dynamic movement toward its next and higher self, along the lines of Romans 8:22 (New American Bible Revised Edition): "We know that all creation is groaning in labor pains even until now." Life does not happen at birth and end at one's death, like a switch turned on and off. Life happens at every single moment. Through life's experiences, we go through birthing contractions and allow life to take newer forms in us. The word *life* is used in that context, where the living dynamism is operative through a complex and mysterious combination of events and happenings. This is an invitation to leave behind the fixated ideas, pre-conceived notions, stereotypical definitions, concepts, goals, and beliefs about life and to open up to a myriad of ever-new possibilities for greater life. Each day is new and exciting if we are willing to experience the freshness it brings.

It is normal human behavior to set ideas and goals for life. These may make us feel more safe and secure—that life is under our control. Most of us know that the feeling of control is ultimately an illusion. How much of life is under our control? Even though someone thinks that they are willfully choosing a career or life partner and planning details of married or working or parental life, one never really knows what spouse, career or children will go through or turn out to be. Much of life simply happens, and the more we open to this ever-birthing creation, the more we open up to an experience of vastness and spaciousness within our hearts. As much comfort as we find in the known, there is much more joy and enthusiasm living the mystery of the unknown. We need to dare to be open to live life however it shows up on each day.

Life is full of creative energy, wanting to pour itself out into the world, through you and me.

———————————

During a recent episode of "America's Got Talent," a 35-year-old performer, Marcelito Pomoy, blew away viewers and judges with his male and female singing voice. The show offered a heart-rending introduction before his performance. At the age of 7, Marcelito had been abandoned by his Mom while his father was in jail. The desire to reunite with his family drove him to find ways to do so. He began singing to overcome his rejection and abandonment. He wanted to find the very people who had left him to his fate. While living on the street, he happened to watch a TV show, "Pilipinas Got Talent," and he decided to use this platform to find his family. Perhaps, he thought, his family might see him on national television and would contact him. With that desire, he entered the show and won it, in 2011! Ultimately the show did indeed unite him with his family and helped him find his soul mate, too. Not only did Marcelito re-unite with his family, he is now a contestant on the popular television show in the U.S., "America's Got Talent." Who knows if he will win the show and have his own studio and show in LA?

Consider the case of Ranu Mondol. A year ago, Ranu was a beggar who made her living singing at the Ranaghat Railway Station in West Bengal, India. Ranu lived in poverty and had been disowned by her only daughter ten years earlier. Her daughter, ashamed of her mother's humble circumstances and need to sing for her supper, had cut off all contact ten years earlier. One day, software engineer Atinda Chakraborty was walking by on the way to his train and noticed the middle-aged woman's beautiful voice. He took a quick video of Ranu's singing and posted it to social media. The video went viral and Ranu became an international sensation! She developed a following among the general population and celebrities alike. Because of her growing popularity, TV producers called to cast her in their shows. She even had offers to sing backup in Bollywood movies. Her sudden, rags-to-riches fame eventually united her with the only daughter who had once failed to acknowledge her existence. Ranu's daughter had been ashamed of her mother singing at the railway platform, but the social success and positive attention had taken away that stigma and they reunited.

Why do people disconnect with others when they are at their worst, and come back together when they are at their best? Shouldn't the worst times in our lives—or when we are at our worst—be precisely when we need our loved ones' support? Learning about Marcelito's and Ranu's stories may understandably give rise to feelings of anger and outrage. We can view such cases from multiple angles. The very people who disown you in your weakest moment, start recognizing and connecting with you when you are at the highest point in your life.

But there is another message. Could it be true, too, that sometimes one needs to go through such tough experiences in order to find their purpose or vocation in life? It is hard to accept that this could be true—that one must go through dark moments to find the light. It seems very cruel of life! Both Marcelito and Ranu were forgiving and opened their hearts. As a result, they are now happily enjoying their newfound relationships with their family members. They did not allow themselves to be caught in the social drama of paying it back or living from the wounds of past rejection or abandonment. We are supposed to disown those who disown us in hard times. Ranu and Marcelito did not dish out such taught responses to life experiences, rather they let their heart be true to their feelings.

Why do these two individuals—and many like them—continue to seek light even in the darkest moments of their lives? Why were they able to be loving and forgiving and seek out loving relationships with the very individuals who had abandoned them? The light within them refuses to react from the dark moments they had gone through. Were they able to recognize the flow of life through these tough times and surrender themselves to the current? Why were these individuals able to give birth to greater life while some would succumb under the pressure of hard times? Jesus was able to do the same on the cross when he said, "Father, forgive them for they do not know what they are doing." Jesus was able to dine with—and even kiss—the very person who betrayed him and handed him over to his enemies.

It is difficult to accept that life may put us through painful, trying situations to help us become the best version of ourselves.

What if Marcelito and Ranu had not gone through the rejection they experienced? Would they have developed their potential if they had lived comfortable lives in normal circumstances with ordinary supportive families? We may never know the mystery of life or have answers to questions like these and others. We will have to humbly bow before the flow of life and say yes to the unknowable. Marcelito made the conscious effort to develop and use his voice to find his family, while singing was the only thing Ranu could do to make her living. Both were united with their loved ones because of their newfound fame, and today they are both celebrities in their own rights. More important, their loving and forgiving hearts said "yes" to life and, as a result, they live happy lives, reunited with their loved ones.

Rich or poor, black or white, male or female, Christian or Muslim, American or Russian, every human being goes through similar experiences of challenging times. Each of us can recall many such moments in our lives. Every such experience, if handled well, takes us to the next stage of our evolution. When difficult experiences are accepted as gifts from life and unwrapped well—with inquisitive and loving hearts—they help us arrive at our fullest potential. Every time we go through a difficult experience, we come out stronger and more mature, provided we do not allow ourselves to become consumed by it.

When we get stuck in the negative energy of difficult times and are not able to move through them and beyond them, we experience problems and consequently suffer. Sometimes there's such an innate tendency to limit our perspective by focusing on others' actions and reactions, that we forget to realize our own hidden potential. If Marcelito and Ranu had reacted negatively to their families' past rejection, they would not be able to enjoy the love with their families in the present. When we let hatred grow in our hearts, we fail to give love a chance. For every instance in which we can view life from a larger perspective, we receive the gift of greater energy of life. Life's toughest moments release in us the gifts that otherwise lie dormant and undeveloped. Without such experiences, we might live mere mediocre lives. This is not to say that life evolves only through tough times—it also happens through experiences of beauty, love and happiness. But by default, we humans tend to see life's meaning in good experiences more than in bad ones. We feel entitled to good experiences and want to gain immunity from all bad experiences. Sometimes our religious practices seem nothing but a sort of security plan to help save us from bad times. However, life is not a one-trick pony and has its own flow and rules. The way to allow life to flow like a river through me is to accept life as it is, and to unwrap its gift and potential. Life will flow on after me as it has before me. I am not here to achieve my goals and establish my kingdom, but I am here to momentarily hold and let life evolve. We are instruments of life.

The perspective that life is constantly seeking us to live abundantly will help us rise above labeling the events of our life as good, bad or ugly. When we label an event, we limit the power of life within us and our own power to choose how we think and what we believe about the event. While labeling comes naturally to the conditioned mind, it takes courage and effort to see life beyond the established concepts through which we perceive life. The irony is that we have no time or interest to get to the core of each experience in the given moment. When we have fixed concepts and labels in our minds, life seems to be easy. Such a stance gives the impression that everything is under control. After all, in our busy and stressful lives, where and when can we find the time, interest or energy to stop and question each idea? Fixed ideas and pre-conceived notions seem to be the best way to get through life. As illustrated with the earlier example of the women pre-judging and avoiding the parish mission, it's easy to take a stand based on our pre-conceptions and then to move on. Stopping, probing and making up our mind anew each time is both energy and time consuming. And who wants to deal with a new experience each time? It is much faster and easier to travel the beaten path.

Psychology, science and medicine have provided us with many readymade definitions that make life much easier and provide clarity and language that serve as a quick frame of reference. If "such and such" is the symptom, then "such and such" must be the disease. Tell Alexa your symptoms and she gives you the diagnosis and treatment. Who has the time to observe one's own body and find out how your symptoms might be different from the definitions available on Google? But pre-determined or obvious solutions are not always the best way to go. For example, if you are running a fever, your raised temperature may not be impending flu, but merely your body's way of saying you're overworked and need some extra rest. In the context of Covid 19, it could be an indication of virus contraction. For a few months the country ran out of thermometer because everyone wanted to have one in their pocket to monitor their body temperature. We humans have a tendency to see life from provided answers that keeps us from exploring life.

It would not be right to assume that tough times alone lead us to explore the best in us. Life is constantly and continuously seeking to take us to the higher ground. Tough times do hasten the process as we put all our efforts to seek ways out of it. The problem is when most people have come to accept a pre-determined view of life, success, happiness and health. These pre-determined expectations tell us that if one has "X" amount of savings, a good spouse, children/grandchildren, vacation and leisure time, decent housing and choice of food, one should be satisfied. Most people settle for things that our society and culture define or determine as measures of success and happiness. And those who have a stronger need for fame and power invest their resources and energy in going after them. But it is not these worldly, pre-determined measures of success, happiness, money, fame, or power that ultimately will help us to live abundantly in life. Life has an inherent power wanting to express itself in and through us that does not fit into any of the definitions we have developed so far. Life pushes its boundaries in and through us and breaks forth in new expressions and manifestations.

Tough times are opportunities - A Case Study

Rani was the envy of her friends and neighbors. She had it all. She was married to a handsome professional for 30 years and together they had raised four intelligent, successful children. They had enough money to enjoy and celebrate life daily and to travel internationally for vacations. In addition to having all the latest consumer gadgets and a lovely, comfortable home, they had the pleasure of eating at upscale restaurants in the city. When the children had left home to pursue their college studies and careers, there was an unexpected turn of events: Rani's husband thought it was the right time for him to pursue some of his plans that he had put on the backburner. In order to do that he needed a divorce. Rani was shocked, aghast and devastated upon learning her husband's plans. She found it extremely difficult to understand the turn of events. "What? Don't you love me anymore?" she cried. "How is that possible?" You were the one who waited for me at the bus stop! You were the one who pursued me! You were the one that proposed to me. You were the one who professed that I was the perfect woman for you. We have four adult children and over thirty years of life together. We have made a home and a family, and you say you are contemplating divorce?"

Rani sought marriage counseling and, for a time, tried every tool in her kit to save her marriage. When her husband eventually separated from her and she discovered that he was living with one of her best friends, she could not take it anymore. After many months of grief, she moved to the final stage of acceptance. Rani came to terms with her ex-husband's new choices. But she still wondered how the love they shared for thirty plus years had faded in a moment. This episode broke her from deep inside, and it took almost a decade for Rani to finally accept that she was divorced.

While she was going through the process of divorce, one of Rani's friends optimistically suggested that there could be a positive new life awaiting her beyond this marriage. That didn't sit well with Rani, who could only accept sympathy from friends who joined her in blaming her husband. She wanted nothing to do with a friend who saw the potential for new direction, and so it took her an additional three years to realize that her friend might very well be right. Ten years after her divorce, Rani finally stepped out of her box and became involved in local issues of social concern and started a non-profit to fight human trafficking. In the process, she discovered herself a new person— she had evolved from being an empty nester, mid-life mom looking forward to a comfortable retirement with her spouse, to an activist who was making a global difference and helping millions. Rani had been through a very tough and trying time and at her lowest point, she could not have foreseen this new path. From time to time since then, Rani stops to wonder whether she would ever have recognized her new and fulfilling calling if she had continued along in her comfortable, planned path in married life.

———————

Allowing life to express itself abundantly could become an adventure in growth—but for many people, also a real struggle. For those considering the journey, the evolution, and the transformation that may be awaiting them, some questions for reflection might be helpful:

- Do I intentionally let life express and flow through me, and how do I do that?
- Do I become passive and abandon all my plans?
- Am I just going to live, not knowing how my day is going to be?
- Will life express itself with or despite me?
- How can I get out of life's way as it expresses itself abundantly through me?
- What can I actively do to be in touch with the life force?

As we navigate through life, in the first few decades of our lives we are offered help from various social agencies, for example, churches and schools, to develop our potential and use it to advance our own interests as well to promote others' welfare. We complete our studies, we make a career and a we raise a family. But often the goals that kept us busy in the first half of life start nagging us from within. The family that helped us find our way, friends who contributed their suggestions, jobs that helped us meet our daily needs become redundant. The needs and dreams of life and people who seemed to become a stepping stone to the next step in life--sometimes it becomes necessary to leave these and embrace new relationships, jobs and even move to new places so that we are able to let life flow anew. The movement toward abandoning that which keeps us contracted and embracing that which expands us from within, is the natural and organic movement of our second half of life.

Once I ran into a monk and we were talking about our plans for the coming year. I shared with him that I wanted to work two jobs and save a particular amount in my retirement fund. He replied that I should reconsider my plans and not push myself hard toward these goals. He described his adventurous expedition into the mountains with a small backpack, and he advised that I should consider something like this.

13

I was somewhat reluctant to follow this advice. "Well," I responded, "Since you are a monk, people in the mountains might offer you some shelter, and if not, you can rely on your religious community for all your temporal needs. It is easier for people to live by the wind when their basic needs of life are taken care of."

But I understood his message. While we spend our earlier years worrying about needs such as shelter or food or savings or raising children, in our later years it is not a bad idea to seek more meaning, to have a carefree life and to have the luxury of following life's promptings. To have an adventure. And part of this means one must learn to live in the mystery of the present moment, welcoming and unfolding life as is.

———————————

What's wrong with using pre-determined, expected concepts of life, and living in a traditional way, if that's what someone wants to do? Well, there's absolutely nothing wrong with going by the beaten path and singing the old songs. There can be joy and abundance in doing so!

But it's been said that "tradition makes a good guide, but a poor master." Letting life express itself anew is for those who feel called, who feel the nagging desire to surrender themselves to the ever-creative universe—the Life Force who seeks to create and renew the creation. Only when an apple seed allows itself to be freely worked upon can there be a new breed of apples. We can all be satisfied by the apples we have. But it is human nature to be drawn to the new and the fresh. Our markets are flooded with new items, our electronic gadgetry evolves with new apps being produced every single minute by people asking questions and finding answers. Variety is in the DNA of the human fabric.

It is the random ant that moves away from the rest of the hardworking ants, only to find new sources of food and sustenance for the rest of the ants. Perhaps you and I could be that random ant that lets life find its new way through us!

It has been said, "Life is not about me, but I am all about life." Our small plans for life's comfort and joys are limited. Those plans are more from our ego-based needs than the magnanimity of life itself. That's not at all to say planning is bad. Planning is very good and helpful. It is not the plans in themselves but the energy behind those plans that matters most. Am I writing this book for name and fame or am I surrendering myself to the writing because something new wants to be born in me? In the secret chamber of one's heart lies the answer to this question, and that answer will determine the flow of life and its purity.

Two students planning to pursue the medical profession could harbor very different motivations. One wants to make good money in order to have a comfortable life, while the other might want to research and find a cure for terminal illness. Both doctors will have needed professional knowledge, but the quality of treatment given by these two doctors will be very different because it all comes from their intent. In the first case, it serves the self needs and in the second case, it serves the need of life being fulfilled. No doubt both types of doctors are needed, and both are fulfilling a need. There is a difference between a teacher completing her lessons and a teacher ensuring that the students learn from their lessons. The priority for the first teacher is that her job is done, whereas the second one wants to make sure that all her students have learned and understood the lesson.

> *"Teaching is not about information. It's about having an honest intellectual relationship with your students."*
> *Paul Lockhart*

15

If I am all about life, what would happen to my life? Will I become an outcast and not be able to enjoy the little pleasures of life? Decidedly not! Becoming a vessel for life to live through me and express its fullness does not mean giving up the joys of my life. Rather it would mean something like Jesus' advice in Matthew 6:33: "But seek first the kingdom [of God] and his righteousness, and all these things will be given you besides." When you make seeking life—in all its messy, creative abundance—your primary focus to let life live through you, then all that needs for you to live life in fullness will come as a byproduct. So often we live in so much fear of meeting our lives' needs that we put life itself on the back burner.

Somewhere we have imbibed the idea that I will be happy when life is free of conflicts, sickness, and tough times. I am blessed and in good books with God if I have enough money, health, love of family and friends. Labeling life as good and bad, happy and sad, confine us to see life from restricted views. Those views affect our mental status and emotional wellbeing. For those who love life, everything works out for their best. The Book of Romans 8:28 notes this: *"We know that all things work for good for those who love God, who are called according to his purpose."* There cannot be anything better than the excitement of letting life happen through you. It's an enchanting and ever fulfilling experience. You are so taken over by the force of life that you do not need small superficial events to entertain you. Life starts producing deepest joys in you.

Are you resistant? I have been. My own beliefs, concepts and doctrines have made me so. Resistance to what life offers only delays our evolution. Resistance blocks our path to fulfillment. Failures to let life evolve in newer forms and shapes sometimes turn into illnesses and problems. The stuck and stagnated energy has the potential to even cause physical and mental harm, and perhaps many of us have been there.

Like my friend Rani, her resistance deprived her of ten years of happiness, because she was not able to see divorce as life sent. That's understandable. It is difficult for humans to reach the place where they can accept both painful and joyful events with similar serenity. Stressful events take more out of us than the joyful ones, but they also build more intensity needed for our next step in the spiritual and creative evolution of our lives.

There is a beautiful story about Jonah and the big fish in the Bible that beautifully depicts this kind of resistance and how life fulfills its plans despite our resistances. Jonah 1:17 describes how God called Jonah one day and told him to go preach to Nineveh because the people were very wicked. Jonah hated this idea because Nineveh was one of Israel's greatest enemies and Jonah wanted nothing to do with preaching to them!

Jonah resisted and tried to run away from God in the opposite direction of Nineveh, heading by boat to Tarshish. God sent a great storm upon the ship and the men on board decided Jonah was to blame, so they threw him overboard. As soon as they tossed Jonah in the water, the storm stopped.

God sent a big fish, some call it a whale, to swallow Jonah and to save him from drowning. While in the belly of the big fish (whale), Jonah prayed to God for help, repented of his resistance, and praised God. For three days, Jonah sat in the belly of the fish. Then, God had the big fish vomit Jonah onto the shores of Nineveh.

The big fish is a metaphor for difficult people and circumstances in our life. They consume us. But in the belly of those difficult experiences, life pushes us to where we are meant to be.

Why do some people have multiple experiences of being in the belly of the big fish, while some seem to have it easy? We will never know those answers. Everyone's life purpose is so unique. The only reality we can know for sure is that we can choose to be open to that call and offer ourselves fully to the experience of being in the belly. Do we want to delay the process or surrender to life's call? We cannot battle life's tides for too long. Life has an inbuilt system in each one of us, to push us to our next phase. A baby cannot help but grow into an adult. No power on earth can stop that process.

Times of despair can become potential for intense suffering when we question, "Why me?" There's a hidden sense of entitlement that no bad things should happen to me because I have been a very good person. My goodness becomes a passport to earn immunity towards life's troubles, we think.

A tree withstands all the seasons and allows them to pass through its substance and being; the tree is able to grow into a full, mature and abundant form, producing new leaves, flowers and fruits. There's a difference between being in difficult times versus allowing the difficult times to pass through me. When we hold on to either good or bad experiences, they become our identity and create a world of problems. When we become an open instrument of life to pass through us and are able to welcome and let go good, bad and ugly, we are able to pass through life with calm and peace. Just like the tree that does not take changes personally and allows the seasons to pass through it and becomes strong, so must we. Someone sage once noted that we cannot stop the birds of dark days from flying over our heads, but we can certainly stop them from allowing them to build nests over our head!

> *"When feeling is divested of the feeler and the felt, it shines as love; when seeing is divested of the seer and the seen, it shines as beauty."*
>
> *Rupert Spira*

There was once a contest in my neighborhood where ten women were given the same recipe and identical ingredients and were told to create a dish. When they did, the ten dishes tasted very differently. Though ingredients were the same, why did they taste different? You may have had this experience yourself. When you cook from a family recipe, it might not taste the way you remember, because the recipe has an irreplaceable part that cannot be added: the part of Mom making the dish. Life is comparable. It might look the same externally, but each individual might go through an experience in a way that is different and unique. Just as two snowflakes are not the same, so are our life journeys. Life loves to create new experiences. The ability to stay in those experiences, enjoy those experiences and be transformed by those is a gift that all do not have.

It has been said that you can never step in the same river twice. So it is with human experience. Life expresses itself anew every day. Stick your toe in and feel the flow!

We humans are taught to consume life, but what we really need to learn is to consummate life. Our deep and erotic intimacy with daily life experiences, with an open mind, will create new life for us and others. Life will then be a continuous experience of bliss. Just like the two young lovers written of in the Book of Song of Songs, we need to engage our senses in an intoxicating union with our everyday experiences. This is easier said than done, because it takes time and practice. It takes time to grow in a love relationship, and it takes time to grow in intimacy with our own life experiences, but the reward is awesome. Life gushes forth fresh and new at every moment.

If life loves to create new experiences and transform us constantly, why are we resistant toward change and newness? Fear of the unknown and comfort of the known hold us hostage. It is much easier to get up in the morning, follow the same routine as the day before, and know what my evenings would look like. Humans are addicted to that which is known, comfortable and easy. We are less adventurous to navigate through life's unexplored shores. Only the brave can chart their way through the new, unnavigated territories.

There are several predominant wisdom traditions around the world. The Bible, the Talmud, the Koran, the Code of Hammurabi, and others. People spend years and entire lives to studying and writing commentaries on them. What if each one of us was a wisdom tradition? How much time and energy do we spend to learn and understand this wisdom tradition? This does not mean I have to throw away all the old wisdom traditions that have provided needed knowledge and tools to get through life. The wisdom traditions keep renewing and completing themselves through every person who dares to contribute fresh material to the path—often in the face of great resistance. But perhaps I could stand strong on the strength of old traditions and enhance it with the unique wisdom tradition that I am. Jesus said in Matthew 5:17, "Do not think that I have come to abolish the law or the prophets. I have come not to abolish but to fulfill." Jesus is a good example of someone who understood the laws, followed them, questioned them and broke them when necessary. With every breaking of the law, he created a new one, a more loving one, a kinder one, a more just one. An evolution to something higher and better.

It would be foolish to reinvent the wheel, but new uses of the wheel would benefit everyone. Like Jesus, if we are able to enhance the old wisdom, we have lived a worthwhile life.

There is a delicate balance between using definitions and concepts as long as they work and breaking free when they don't. In and through the experience of breaking free, you venture into an unknown journey—the journey of an abundant new life. No matter how intense and tough such a journey may be, there will also be an experience of bliss, where life has the freedom to express itself anew. This process is not unlike being born. Physical birth is our most basic understanding of birth, but we need to be born every day. As we grow with newer knowledge, skills, wisdom and insight, we are being reborn daily. Rebirthing is at work in us even when we are unconscious.

There's a beautiful encounter in the Bible between Jesus and Nicodemus in John 3:1-8. "Now there was a Pharisee named Nicodemus, a ruler of the Jews.[b] [2] He came to Jesus at night and said to him, "Rabbi, we know that you are a teacher who has come from God, for no one can do these signs that you are doing unless God is with him."

[3] Jesus answered and said to him, "Amen, amen, I say to you, no one can see the kingdom of God without being born[c] from above."

[4] Nicodemus said to him, "How can a person once grown old be born again? Surely, he cannot reenter his mother's womb and be born again, can he?"

[5] Jesus answered, "Amen, amen, I say to you, no one can enter the kingdom of God without being born of water and Spirit. [6] What is born of flesh is flesh and what is born of spirit is spirit. [7] Do not be amazed that I told you, 'You must be born from above.' [8] The wind[d] blows where it wills, and you can hear the sound it makes, but you do not know where it comes from or where it goes; so it is with everyone who is born of the Spirit."

Jesus was telling Nicodemus that physical birth might be a onetime event, but we are being born anew in our spirit. The spirit needs to be born of the spirit, as indicated by Jesus.

A few years ago, I was fascinated by the Jesus and Nicodemus story. I wanted to give myself a new birth. I decided to accompany my own "infant self" in the womb of the spirit for nine months. I developed some simple rituals and even ate a healthy diet to have a healthy spirit baby. Six years after this experience, I intentionally accompanied myself as a nurturing parent. I provided myself with all the opportunities needed to grow in the experience of love and freedom. This mindset truly helped me to come out as a mature adult and set myself free from my past emotional baggage. The whole process helped me to work through some of the limiting self-beliefs and conditioning I had been weighed down with all my life. This exercise and experience helped me to feel that I am the fresh revelation of life.

Some Thoughts on Self Identity

All the concepts, ideas and beliefs we learn in earlier life are tools to get through life successfully. These tools hold value in that they help us organize how we view the world and ourselves. But gradually those very tools become self-identity. We identify ourselves by our concepts and as we move along in life, our identity gets energy of its own. It furthers itself and gets invested in more concepts like threads that are woven through the fabric of our lives. We deeply identify with what we think and know. Our thoughts, emotions, likes and dislikes become our identity. We filter all our life through this self-identity. Money, job, religion, family, spouse, children, political party affiliation—everything is viewed from how they make us look and feel. Even difficulties and tough times, too, can become sources of self-identity. In the process, we forget to see things and people for who they are. We see them from the judgment of how they make me feel and look. Once we are caught in seeing life through the filter of self-identity, everything in life loses its original, fresh, unique and creative identity. In an effort to polish our created identity, we forget that we are whole.

Self-identity is also dependent on one's level of consciousness. Family, culture, personal interests, and friends help to shape our earlier identity. Eventually this identity acquires complex form. Our ideas, speech, social activities, work and personal tastes of different genre get added on to the identity. If one is not aware, then things, relationships, and experiences will all be viewed through the lens of self-identity. Life then becomes mundane, consumerist and dry. We deprive ourselves from the beauty and fullness that life provides in and through daily events. It requires baring our wrappings, so that we can see and accept life as it is. Baring our wrappings…what does that sound like? Opening a present! Stripping away the trappings of self-identity and joyfully finding the gift inside. As we realize our own wholeness, we will be able to accept others as whole and learn to enjoy life and relationships. Otherwise life can turn into a self-improvement project.

Personal identity is dependent on the contents of our psychological mind and so it keeps changing as circumstances change in our lives. Of course, personal identity is different for each person depending upon their experiences, their learnings and the content of their minds. Personal or self-identity often vanishes in persons with dementia or Alzheimer's due to their inability to analyze concepts. Self-identity also changes with each experience we go through. Something gets shifted and changed. Changes like these are subtle and often go unnoticed. I am not the same person that went to bed last night.

In the last few years, I have become aware of the complex interdependency between self-identity and consciousness. As we move through life, we begin to see and observe life—and death— differently. Death that was once viewed as a great human tragedy has now become a way the universe renews itself. Consciousness of death as part of life has changed self-identity. This change affects how I see people and life events. If self-identity is the sum of my conceptual thoughts, so is my approach to everything else. Understood in such a context, it is a daily effort to come to terms with changes within and out, to redefine my concepts and learn to see life as it is. A spiritual exercise of this sort is a meditation and prayer.

> *"There are three possibilities in life: to be something, nothing or everything. In the first there is suffering; in the second there is peace; and in the third there is happiness and love."*
>
> Rupert Spira

When you feel weak, vulnerable and incomplete from within, life can become a scary and difficult experience. You will then put every ounce of your energy in building up an image you think the world wants of and from you. This only leads you into more fear and disconnection from the wholeness you already are. The more you come to accept and live your wholeness, you will connect with your deepest self and become a shining light vibrating greater life force to everyone around. You are the message of wholeness and as the old saying goes, we are the wholeness we are seeking.

> *"Living the Life That You Are weaves together psychology, ancient wisdom, and honest personal reflections into a coherent and inspiring whole. If loneliness is the great disease of the modern age, then Nic's heartfelt plea for self-love is much-needed medicine."*

—*Jeff Foster, author of Falling in Love with Where You Are*

Relationships Channel Wholeness

I have had a good friend for over thirty years. We have regular phone conversations and share almost everything with one another. Having been friends for such a long time, we have weathered many seasons and lived through various life challenges, and we have grown together from these experiences. But through the years, I noticed that my friend was not truly "present" to our phone conversations. She would call me or accept my call, and when we would be deep in conversation, she always seemed to find the first opportunity to end the call. We do have wonderful, in-depth conversations where we both seem to be one hundred percent present, but these are rare occurrences. Although aware of this situation, I have tried to overlook it, thinking my friend may be busy or perhaps has something else to attend to. There are times when I have brought this issue to her attention, and we have been able to speak about it openly. We have made promises to one another to do better, but our efforts often fail. I am certain that her behavior has less to do with me and more to do with her life and experiences.

After years of this pattern and maintaining the status quo, I decided to once more look into the matter and perhaps try to improve the situation. Since I had made similar efforts in the past, to no avail, I asked myself why I would want to attempt to do so one more time. Instead of once again pointing out to my friend how she was not present or listening, I decided to look in the mirror and ask myself some questions. Why do I have the compulsion to tell my stories, and what do I feel when I am not listened to? After some soul searching, I realized two things about myself. First, I am a storyteller, and I feel rejected if people do not pay attention to my stories. This realization was not new but was the first time I had acknowledged that I needed to take care of my own behavioral patterns, needs and feelings. I did not need another conversation with my friend about what I felt was a lack of presence or listening.

Prior to this discovery, I had focused on my friend and expected her to pay full attention to my stories, as I did to hers. I thought I was rightfully justified to expect such a return in a mutually dependent friendship. Now I am grateful that after more than thirty years, it had finally dawned on me that I needed to take care of my own needs, rather than teaching others how to relate with me. I spent almost two weeks chewing on this realization, journaling and reflecting upon the deeper dynamics within. The following journal excerpt sums up my inner journey followed by the mentioned episode:

> *Friend, I do not need you for my happiness.*
> *I do need you to share the love I have within.*
> *If you do not enjoy the love I am sharing,*
> *I will move on to those who need it more than*
> *you do.*
> *Hey, wait. Am I going to go friend shopping?*
> *Will I ever find a perfect friend? No.*
> *Let me turn within and gratefully accept...*
> *every person and relationship I have, because...*
> > *I need the other not only to share love but also*
> > *for my wholeness.*
> > *Every family member, friend, colleague, and*
> > *neighbor...*
> > *are all thoughtfully placed in my life by God*
> > *to help me become aware of the inner gunk I*
> > *need to work through.*
> *So, each time I blame others for the way I feel and am*
> *tempted to move on,*
> *I am going to stop in gratitude and say... thank you, friend.*
> *You provided me the needed trigger for my wholeness*
> *Please relax as I do the growing up!*

I am deeply grateful for the opportunity and the grace that helped me turn inward to realize that every relationship channels my wholeness. What a comforting thought! I do not need to run hither and yon looking for people with special abilities to channel God's mind for me. What I seek is right here in my own backyard, staring me in the face. My family and friends are doing it constantly and consistently. The challenge or question for me and for you is, can we summon the courage to use the experiences generated from our relationships to clean up our inner selves? This experience with my friend prompted me to cultivate some inner space and provided me with needed fertile ground to grow spiritually. Every experience in a relationship is a precious mustard seed that has the potential to grow from the fertile ground into a huge, luscious tree providing shelter to the weary soul.

Many people turn to isolation, solitary retreat, or even lifetime cloistering to traverse their spiritual journey. We all know the stereotype of the solitary hermit or spiritual wise man living in a cave high up on a mountain. In my own experience, it is not on the meditation cushion or self-awareness retreat that I get to know myself and become a better person. It is in and through every relationship— and how I conduct myself moment to moment to respond to the other person in the relationship—that helps me gain deeper insight

> Every relationship channels wholeness.

and ultimately to work out my salvation. People with whom I have relationships become mirrors to my inner self and reflect areas where I need inner work. From the spiritual perspective, this effect is reciprocal. We all share in one humanity. We are all bits and parts of one human race. By interacting and rubbing shoulders with one another, so to speak, we then help to polish the other to help them become a diamond.

Relationship Mindfulness

The experience with my friend helped me realize how important it is to become mindful in relationships. To illustrate this point, let me share a few snippets of heated conversations I have had with family members, friends and colleagues.

Colleague:	You were so creative when you first started work.
Me:	What? Are you saying that I am not creative anymore? Do you think I am not working hard enough?
Colleague:	I never said you don't work hard. Now you are making a mountain out of a molehill!
Me:	How dare you say that! You're so ungrateful! I pick up so many of your tasks and let you take care of your family matters at work!
Colleague:	That's because you have no one to think about. You are jealous that I have a family.
Me:	You are the most stupid person I have ever known!
Colleague:	Just shut up! I have had enough!

Is this an example of a conversation, an argument, or a fight? We are all familiar with interactions like this. Why do we react so strongly to simple remarks or statements? A simple passing comment can blow up and become a relationship-threatening event. There may be triggers that can reopen hidden wounds from the past and spark a defensive or irrational response. Based on our emotional points of view, we tend to magnify the comment (and injury) and at the same time deflect/attack back toward the other. Such reactive responses are usually unconscious, and they come out of an unhealed past. If we work to become self-aware enough to recognize these triggers and interior wounds, we can move on and grow spiritually.

What happens if we do not do the spiritual work to recognize our weakness? In a conversation, angry and accusatory responses tend to have a snowball effect. They get repeated in our being for days and even for weeks and months. We keep replaying the tape in our heads and processing who was right or wrong. What should I have said? What should I not have said? Did I win or lose? Inner conversations such as this one can consume a great deal of interior energy and occupy valuable mental space. You have heard the expression "living in your head rent free." You let the conflict live in your head completely rent free. If there is an opportunity, some people may try to talk about these struggles with someone who has a listening ear—a trusted friend, a counselor, or a family member. However, if we are honest and reflect inwardly and honestly upon what is really going on, we might notice that we tend to tell these listeners only what suits our own perspective. These stories thus have an underlying attached version of which we are totally unconscious. We discuss the conflict from our own perspective, we set ourselves up to look good, or we may not convey the other person's point of view. As a result, we may waste a lot of good energy and time in justifying ourselves with no positive results.

When two people relate to one another from their unconscious past wounds, they key off each other when they are triggered. In that state, past resentments begin to spill out, and they operate under the illusion that the conflict is all because of what the other is doing. This is a normal human reaction: it is easier to blame "the other" than to look within and own one's part. Looking within is difficult, and we do not always like what we see. In the absence of awareness of a personal lens that is the product of our past experiences, our brain functions tend to retreat, and our out-of-control emotional centers take the wheel. We may unconsciously draw from our emotional lexicon and hurl strong, exaggerated, and hostile words or statements. Only relationship mindfulness can prevent such destructive episodes and save our life-giving relationships.

Mindfulness is a well-known spiritual practice from the Buddhist tradition. Mindfulness in relationships can become a spiritual practice to help us create our best possible selves. Relationship mindfulness helps us to discern and become aware of the childhood wounds that we bring to adult relationships. When we pay attention to our own reactions and look within for solutions—instead of blaming others—we will be able to trace the source of our reactions and ultimately to heal ourselves.

Relationship mindfulness is the ability to pay attention to feelings, thoughts, and responses when someone does or says something that triggers an emotional reaction. Our immediate reactions are automatic and mostly rooted in past painful experiences. The practice of questioning our automatic responses and reactions is immensely helpful in revealing an important part of our inner lives. If we blame "the other one" for our feelings and try to make them behave in a way that will not produce those feelings, we are caught up in very frigid relationship dynamics. There will be no spontaneity if we hold the other hostage to our past.

In relationships, you never know what will hurt someone. You may be afraid of hurting the other one even when you do not intend to. People often get hurt where no offense was intended. But relationship mindfulness helps us to own our part and undertake inner healing so that we can enjoy the relationship and not hold other people responsible for our feelings.

Relationship mindfulness is a useful tool in confronting the challenges of relationships. For most people, family relationships represent the primary area where we need to practice relationship mindfulness. In intimate relationships, emotional pain from earlier experiences can be a huge trigger. In my own life, I have often wondered why I behave unkindly toward the person I love the most, and have discovered that emotional pain from the past is usually the trigger. Mindfulness helps us to stay calm and centered and to maintain loving, peaceful relationships with our loved ones rather than engaging in fights and arguments. Growing this inner awareness helps us to shoulder responsibility for what we experience and allows us the space and time to decide how we want to act and react to the other person. Mindfulness in relationship does *not* mean analyzing why the other one behaves in a particular manner. Instead, it is for each individual to do their own personal work. Relationships always test us and invite us to redefine how we see self and others.

How does relationship mindfulness work? Becoming mindful in a relationship means turning inward to reflect upon one's motivations, feelings, and reactions. In doing this, some questions that might be helpful include: What am I experiencing? What has triggered these strong emotions? What are my emotions asking or telling me? What is the story hidden in my emotions? Here is an anecdote to illustrate this process. When I was five years old, my mother became angry with me for singing. I had begun to sing, and my mother said, irritably, "Keep quiet! Your singing is irritating me." As a little child, I did not know what to do with my mother's anger, and her statement found a secret, long-term dwelling within my child's soul. I interpreted her angry statement to be a criticism of my voice. Later, as an adult, I often liked to spontaneously sing in the shower. My fellow dorm students had noticed this and organized a surprise karaoke night to celebrate my birthday. The whole event turned into a nightmare and was the worst birthday party I could ever have had. I had a terrible evening and was angry with everyone, which puzzled my friends. They did not understand why I had flown off the handle and had become upset by this well-intended event. I almost did not know why myself. When

I turned inward and became mindful, I examined my own inner motivation and past wounds, and I realized that I had been holding onto the pain of that one past statement—that my singing irritated my mother. As an adult, I realized that my mother's reaction had nothing to do with my voice or my singing. She was probably having a bad day and needed a little space, and I forgave her and let it go. It took twenty years to grow enough to reflect in a mindful way upon my motivations and triggers and to heal the painful wound.

Relationship mindfulness allows us to stop and question our own behavior and emotions. When everyone involved in the relationship is able to find some satisfactory answers to their questions, they become more mindful of their responses. To grow in relationship mindfulness, it is important that each party provide the other needed time and space to undertake some soul searching. Time spent in reflection helps us notice our interior dynamics and develop ways to deal with them. Only then can we act in ways that do not hurt other people or ourselves. Relationship mindfulness does not take away our strong emotions, but rather helps us to be centered in our heart and communicate from there. It helps us to acknowledge the strong emotions, accept them and take their control away. Otherwise we let our past run the show. Acknowledging past feelings is appropriate, but we should refrain from judging our past emotions. These past feelings may have been appropriate at a particular stage in life, but they need not be carried forward to the present when we are in different situations and relationships.

The more mindful we become, the stronger our relationships. Mindfulness is the key that helps us to stay grounded in the present and not turn to past emotions, wounds, or triggers. When we are rooted in the present, we are less likely to judge or build a case against another. Relationship mindfulness helps us to take each moment as it comes and to share empathy, compassion, and love with those we care for. As we grow in relationship mindfulness, we experience a greater sense of inner peace. Everyone can benefit from the inner peace one person experiences. In the process we are exercising our attention muscles that help us to gain more power over our thoughts and actions.

There are no perfect relationships, but every relationship is worth working on. Relationship mindfulness not only helps you strengthen relationships, it helps you to become the person you want to be. Mindfulness clears the space and provides greater space to live and relate from the heart. Relationship mindfulness is all about shifting our consciousness and making reflected responses.

Relationships are Living and Sacred Spaces

Relationships are living, breathing organisms. When two people talk about a marriage not working, they are really saying that their relationship is not working. Relationships also have an identity of their own. The ground formed by relationship is holy ground, like a sacred temple where God and human beings meet. We often go about our daily tasks and activities to maintain the relationship and fail to delve into the deeper dimension of relationship that is full of life and new possibilities. Relationships change and grow from moment to moment and this calls us to learn to relate from moment to moment. We cannot use yesterday's responses or those of our parents to grow in a current relationship, even if we acknowledge that most of our behaviors in relationships come from our past emotional and cultural conditioning. Recognizing that such interactions carry the energy field of the past, to experience freshness and newness, we must examine our relationship patterns daily and develop new ways of living and maintaining them.

Let me return to the situation with my friend whom I felt did not listen to me. In the early stages of our friendship, I acted, talked, and agreed with everything that my friend believed and shared. Upon reflection, this behavior indicated to me that having a friend was more important than being true to myself. Perhaps underneath there was fear of losing a good friend. Maybe the fear of displeasing her made me act like a social chameleon. I didn't know who I was and what I wanted. I held tight to this friendship as it provided me some inner safety. However, over the years, we have gone through a lot of changes and have persisted with the friendship. In the last ten years, life has changed us both a great deal, and I have grown by leaps and bounds. I am sure this has taken a toll on our relationship, and my friend has adjusted considerably. I have become more confident and centered within myself and am able to communicate my truth without fear. Over the past few years, I have brought to her notice that I do not feel listened to, and she shared her viewpoint, observing that I dominate the conversation. As a result, I have carefully considered her feedback and have become more mindful about giving her the space to talk about herself. I now make a more conscious effort to inquire about her so that she can share about things going on in her life. Also, I check her availability and intuitively sense if she is in a good space for me to share personal stories. Since I value our friendship and her feedback, I have made changes to the way I share my stories. After all these efforts, I still have not felt satisfied that she has responded in kind. I have felt our conversations happen without the awareness of this mutually considerate sacred space. Still, I am grateful for the opportunity for spiritual growth and am learning through observation and reflection how the other person in a relationship becomes part of me. I need to get to know who she is becoming and vice versa. This knowing happens in the sacred space where time, commitment and depth need to be invested. I am committed to my friend and our relationship and hope to bring more depth to our long-term friendship.

Marriage and love relationships provide an even more important and unique opportunity to reflect on that sacred space to grow and deepen the relationship. When two people hold each other in total openness and dedicate themselves to learning who they are becoming in and through the relationship, they are continually creating the sacred space that nurtures their relationship and provides the energy to become more deeply part of one another's lives. While it is human nature to retreat into or recreate toxic patterns learned from childhood experiences or cultural norms, two people in a mutual relationship can create sacred space that becomes fertile ground for new growth and new possibilities. Without these efforts, relationships remain stagnant, with one or both parties begging for attention and care from the other while experiencing ongoing lack within. In the absence of mindfully cultivated sacred ground, people in relationship are often fearful and constantly seeking for what the other one can and will provide.

Love, care, and attention shared in a relationship also create safety, intimacy, and an experience of inner freedom—an experience where one can venture out in the world and explore new avenues. The mindful, sacred space of relationships thus becomes a launching ground from which we can take risks, have new adventures, and grow. Consciously nurtured sacred space in a relationship gives us the power to return and relive our adventures and to experience needed relaxation for life's next adventure.

Relationships Are an Opportunity for Inner Work

To create sacred space in a relationship and reap its fruits, we must take responsibility for our inner work and give ourselves generously to the relationship. If two people use a relationship to take what they need and keep drawing without replenishing its reserves, then the sacred space becomes empty space. But generous giving of self and presence creates the transmission of energy needed to undertake creative projects and activities. This mutual energy field fortifies us to grow and to return to the well and enjoy that growth. It becomes a haven where people in relationship relax and rebalance their systems. Relationship energy fields can likewise come from negative emotions. If there is fear, worry and anxiety in a relationship, then we are likely to live and move from that negative energy field. While no relationship is totally free of low energy fields, these emotions in general do not help individuals become their best selves. We need to become mindful of these low energy fields and to mutually undertake inner work to heal and recreate a more vibrant, life-giving energy field. Relationships thus become a source of healing and wholeness.

Blaming others for the way one feels is normal. It is natural and easy to blame the other one for the way I feel. This is simply human nature. We make the quick and easy assumption that our own feelings were caused or created by the other person. If you become aware of your own inner voice, you may hear yourself say, "If only the other person had been kinder, I would not feel hurt," or "I am angry because she was so mean to me," or "I said things to him because he did not keep his promise." Every day, we encounter thousands of such instances where we may automatically jump to blame the other. We may think we need to change others to solve our problems. But growth and transformation can only come about when we take responsibility for our own selves, our own thoughts, and our own emotions. As Mahatma Gandhi said, "Be the change you wish to see in the world."

Most of our reactions in relationships are unconscious, automatic, and rooted either in our upbringing or in unhealed past wounds. Awareness helps us to consider the source of these unhealthy reactions in relationships and to heal from within, and then to make conscious, intentional responses that are characteristic of whole, renewed human beings. How does this process work? When you notice a strong emotional response, it is time to stop and do some soul searching. It is helpful to ask: Where is this stuff coming from? What is happening (inside)? Is there a past story attached to my present emotion? Once you name your feelings and their source, you can deal with them from your present and not your past. You can ask yourself: Who am I right now? What is my situation right now? How can I approach these feelings from who I am today? When you reflect upon these self-questions, you will be better able to control your situation and not remain a victim to your past.

In all types of relationships, we have the gift of meeting our unhealed inner selves and can work toward healing and growing stronger. This is not unlike going to the gym to work out. Every time we take an opportunity to use our emotional triggers to our advantage and to do inner work, we strengthen our relationship muscles. But one needs to be centered from within to undertake the workout regime. Our journey in wholeness is not a journey outside. *It is a journey within.* Through relationship interactions our deep-seated fears, anger or need for control gets triggered. When we become centered from within and approach the event from the present moment, we will be able to do our interior work more efficiently.

I have often observed that no two people are in the same place within their lives and hearts. My friend might be coming from a very positive place and telling me something for my good. If I am not in the same place as my friend, I can take this as a criticism and waste an opportunity for growth and damage the relationship. We need a very fine-tuned inner sense of self to know and understand the inner ground of the other. Even if the other one is not coming from a good place, I can always be in a good place and use the triggers for good, but this requires a high level of self-awareness of my attachments and expectations from the other. Unconscious motivations and goals can also trigger unnecessary reactions and struggles in relationships. It might be helpful to turn inward to ask: Am I in this relationship to meet the other person's needs or my own? Or am I here to share myself with the other person and create a conductive and pure biosphere to help us each reach our full potential? To be able to create a clean and pure "relationship biosphere," each person in a relationship must do the necessary inner work.

When we do inner work and heal our wounds, we create good energy within ourselves—a positive energy essential to maintaining and enjoying relationships. If we keep taking energy from the other and do not regenerate and return the energy, then our relationship wells will run dry. Our interior energy may be low because we unconsciously hold a negative image of ourselves and view our relationships from that negative image. For example, I might think that I am putting up with another person who is not making an effort to grow, but this view may have more to do with my negative image of myself than with the other person's faults or lack of growth. Self-awareness is thus critical for inner work in relationships and is heightened in and through relationship conflicts and triggers. This can be painful, but it helps us to accept and own our own mess. It is up to me to acknowledge or deny that my friend, family member or spouse is a gift sent by God to help me become a whole human being—and this wholeness will never happen if I continually blame "the other" instead of focusing my attention on my inner work.

Relationships Help Us Share Love

Wholeness comes from the ability to love and be loved. There are as many definitions of love as there are people on the earth, so it may be difficult to arrive at an objective definition of the ability to love. Ideally, we will grow in our ability to love throughout our lives, but we may never arrive at the point where we can confidently say we are done learning. We may never arrive at the fullness of our ability to love. The heart is ever expanding, and the more we sharpen our ability to love, the more we become aware of the need to do so regularly. In all close relationships, we may observe that we keep going between harmony and disharmony, closeness and disruption. Through all such episodes, we work towards wholeness by inner repair.

A friend of mine confided in me about her recently ended relationship. Although it was her decision to end the relationship, she felt it was inevitable as she had not experienced any warmth from her partner. She was devastated and had almost concluded that she was not lovable. This was not the first time she had experienced a relationship such as this, and she had become tired of repeating this painful cycle. My friend wondered if the experience was repeating because of her choice of people or perhaps owing to her own flawed perception of relationship. She was ready to shower love and affection on the persons she dated, but she always felt her partners were not responsive or ready. Many issues and questions tormented her. Was this a reflection of an unmet inner need for affection or was it due to her ability to give and receive love? Was she not able to feel or experience love she was receiving because she was so focused on the love she wanted to share?

Most human beings are born in love and develop an ability to love. Love is our purpose and destiny. It is our fulfillment and our seeking. Some of us are natural at loving while others face challenges and find it very difficult to love. Why? Why is loving others easier than being loved? Though we speak of love, there is no formal training in how to do it. We all discover it through our own trial and error. Is the ability to love innate, or is it learned? Experiences of love differ from person to person. There are no all-purpose answers to all the questions about love and the ability to love. We just must seek for our own answers as we go along. It does take some discipline and hard work to love. It is like a two-edged sword. On one side, you need to work on the inner blocks to share and receive love and on the other side you need to develop skills to love. It is worth investing our time and energy in learning to love and be loved. It makes us feel satisfied in all other aspects of life. How many of us have it as our life goal to become the most loving person I can be? Relationships are the only place where we can grow in our lovability—and love ability. Loving others without loving one's self is a compulsion to please others and loving self without loving others is narcissism. We need a good balance of self-love and love of others. Forgiveness is also an important dimension to loving. The more we heal from within and can forgive—others and ourselves—the more we grow in our ability to love.

The ability to love means offering unconditional support, understanding and acceptance to other people and to ourselves. The ability to love—love ability if you will—means interacting with others with absolute compassion. It means letting go of expecting others to always behave in ways that make us happy. Instead, love ability is letting everyone be their true selves. Love ability means surrendering self-importance and seeing the personal stories as they are. Love ability is not an experience of falling in love. Rather, it is an ability to see an individual's potential beyond behavior we may not like. It is making efforts to introduce activities and avenues where persons will discover their new selves. It is constantly focusing your energy on the good and positive.

Relationship as a Spiritual Practice for Wholeness

No one teaches us how to "do" relationships. Sometimes we imitate the examples of our family traditions and at other times, we follow cultural or societal trends. We may seldom be aware that in and through every relationship there is a seeking taking place. In relationships, I am seeking an extended part of me, the part that is of the Divine, the part that understands what it means to love. When I touch that core in me and approach relationships from the point of view of seeking the Divine, life moves into a transcendent realm.

Just as with spiritual practices we may seek peace, calm, discernment, or the security of God's protection, similarly in relationships we seek acceptance, belonging and meaning. It would be a good exercise to become aware of what we seek in each relationship and what we hope to give. Relationships are not random happenings. They are intentional, and we invest a lot of time, energy, and money in them. As part of a spiritual reflection or journaling process, it would be enlightening to list our relationships and ask questions that help us to become aware of what we seek in each of them. Once we grow in such awareness, we can develop tools and rituals to achieve them.

As part of a spiritual practice, we may go to church, attend services regularly, pay tithes and invest some time in keeping ourselves scripturally and theologically updated and informed. We may not stop to consider that experiencing the Divine occurs through relationships, too. Relationships invite us to grow in our practice of belonging and help us to develop meaningful activities and rituals through which we will grow open to one another and come to understand and accept the other person unconditionally. It is in open and loving relationships that we discover who we are and who we could potentially become. In relationships, we learn the art of connecting deeply with another human being which later becomes the blueprint for our connection with the Divine.

> *In relationships, we learn the art of connecting deeply with another human being which later becomes the blueprint for our connection with the Divine.*

Most of us have friends with whom we pursue activities of common interest. We may meet over coffee or dinner or attend common activities together. When friendship becomes a spiritual practice, then friends together decide to move beyond these common activities to commitment. They mutually commit to seek and speak the truth. This commitment is not always verbal, it is simply an understanding that with a certain friend, you can tell—and will hear—the truth. The friendship may move from common interests to giving and integrity, and from basic maintenance of friendship to growing together. In such openness, God, The Divine, The Universe, sends people who are needed to help us move to the next step in our personal spiritual evolution. Friends like these help one another to become aware of their hidden fears and desires and to grow through them. They challenge the behavior that is coming from our lower selves and support our inner healing. From my own perspective, the total openness where I do not have to pretend to put on a mask or worry about choice of words for the fear of being misunderstood leads us to an experience of inner expansion.

In any relationship, we are naturally invited to think of the other, an invitation that connects us to someone outside of ourselves. Sacrifices become a joyful event. We learn by degrees to let go of our *need* to be loved and accepted, because we come to know that we *are* loved and accepted. The easiness and joy that we experience in the presence of a friend is related to the level of trust and acceptance we have with them. Our superficial, "false" selves become smaller, and we can share our vulnerabilities and speak transparently.

Relationship as Spiritual Practice

Any spiritual practice is aimed at self-transformation, and relationship is no different. Sharing love in relationships helps us grow in our capacity to love. The true and deep connection that we share with another person melts down the boundaries that we create around self. Loving then becomes the doorway into the vastness of life. We learn to accept the other unconditionally and in doing so, we can honor the creativity of God who creates everyone uniquely. We learn how to manage and communicate our emotions. We are able to give up the need to be right or to win. The more we grow in relationship, the more our impulses toward defensiveness, manipulation and control slip away. That's how relationship becomes spiritual practice. And the more we practice, the greater the benefits.

In true friendships, we learn to own our dark parts. Relationships are not always about the good and the positive and they can lead us into some dark and tough places. With the support of the other and with their love, we can bring healing and wholeness to those areas of our lives. In a supportive and non-judgmental relationship, we can work through our failures, betrayals, fears, distrust, and inadequacy. We experience true freedom in a relationship where we know that the other person sees the very worst about us and still loves us.

It is not uncommon to hear someone rail against God when challenges come their way. They may ask, "Why me? I am a faithful person. I go to church, give freely to charity of my time and treasure, and have done everything required by my faith community." These are the people who try to show their best side to God, and they expect reward in return. They follow the rules and regulations, they abide by the dogma and doctrine. They check all the boxes. Practicing virtues and good works is upheld as spiritual practice. Shadow work is not seen as a spiritual practice. In authentic relationships, however, one cannot escape the challenge of finding the lost part of ourselves. For this we need to do the inner work of befriending those parts of ourselves that we feel ashamed of. We are called and supported to take care of our crazy thoughts, deep desires, fears and failures. In accepting the rejected parts of ourselves, we become healed and whole.

Relationships as a spiritual practice are thus valuable tools for experiencing the fullness of life. The incredible power of relationship offers us the possibility to accept the rejected or shadowy parts of ourselves, and to move on, whole and healthy. We can free ourselves from the fear that I am not good enough. The power of relationship transforms us and gives us needed courage to embrace our shadows. It empowers us to bring our whole selves, to hold nothing back, and to be open to giving and receiving all.

Human relationships thus are a true portal into wholeness and serve as a doorway into the Divine. Relationships lead us beyond our individual selves to shared selves and put the ego into a back seat. In the shared sacred space, the holy ground of relationships, we learn to truly connect with the other. The shared presence in relationships is healing, transformative and creative. In a true relationship, something greater than "me" is born. In such a moment, there is an experience of belonging to one heart and one soul, and this is none other than the Divine. Relationships as spiritual practice thus not only provide us with a sense of wholeness in our own lives, they help give birth to great visions that benefit the whole of humanity.

Relationship with Self

While this chapter explores relationships in the context of two or more human beings, it is important to note that relationships go beyond humans. Our relationships with food, money, material goods, and all of creation are areas that offer a glimpse into our inner journey toward wholeness. While our relationships with all these areas reveal something about us, there is one essential relationship that is most important of all: our relationships with ourselves. How I relate to myself serves as the crux and mirror of all my other human and extra-human relationships.

Through the years, I have come to realize that it was I who abused myself more than anyone else. I did so through mindless eating, a secondary lifestyle, harboring negative thoughts, making judgments, having false expectations of others, blaming others, and avoiding taking responsibility for myself in a myriad of other ways. As we noted previously, it is easier to blame "the other," or other factors than to take a raw, honest, naked look into the soul and view the shadow self and shadow behaviors that hold us back. In my own case, the more I became aware of my self-abusive ways, the more I began to heal and to relate positively with myself. And consequently, I began to relate well with others. Once I began to understand my own inner demons and to embrace them, I began to accept others with their vulnerabilities. This process—which is ongoing—helps me to grow in accepting, understanding, showing compassion and sensitivity to myself and others. It felt as if a miracle had occurred: When I stopped judging myself, I stopped judging others. This transformation spurred the revelation that my relationship with self is the mirror of every other relationship in life.

We must love ourselves enough to repair and heal our relationship with ourselves. This is different from narcissism or selfishness. As we learn to love and accept ourselves, we find space in our hearts to love others. Therefore, my best counsel to all those who are reading this book and considering its thoughts is simply this.

> Relationship with self is the mirror of every other relationship in life.

Love yourself, my friend, so that you can love others.

> "A good relationship is when two people accept each other's past, support each other's present, and love each other enough to encourage each other's future."
> *Heartfeltquotes.co*

Liberating Self from
Other People's Shit

You and I are whole right at this moment, just the way we are. On the surface, the title of this section may sound contradictory—as if the title of this chapter indicates that I am whole, but others are not. That's not what is meant here. Though we are whole just as we are, we are all at a different point along our life journey. Our personal history and the conditioning of our minds form the way each person thinks, and this is unique and different from one individual to the next. Consider that a thousand people decide to travel to Chicago on a given day, but each is at a different point in their journey because they have chosen different modes of transport or times of travel. Recognizing that we are all at different points along our journey, each person needs to pause and reflect and simply ask, "Where am I at this moment?"

It is not helpful to keep a log of where everyone else is along their path. Instead, I have learned that I need to turn my attention inward to determine where I am at this moment. This approach helps to prevent the natural human tendency to get caught up in other people's dramas and baggage and moves individuals from being merely reactive to becoming more deliberate. It does take some effort and attention to unhook our attention from other people's drama and to focus energies on our own journey. As social beings it does not take long to get locked into the complexities of the human web, but when we decide to carry others' baggage, we lose our own ground of being. It's essential to remain established and well-grounded and to conduct ourselves from that place. Again, this is no small task: it is an ongoing process and requires continual mindfulness. One constantly needs to be aware and bring their attention to the present moment.

The human mind can be such a complex tool. We might consider the example of a young girl who had been abandoned by her father.

She grew up watching her mother work very hard, and as a result, has difficulty trusting men or developing healthy relationships with them. Her brain and body have stored all the memories of her past life and she filters life from those experiences and has developed a pattern of behavior—of reacting—to deal with life. Somehow her filter of perception, influenced by her history, has become her reality. Her stored experiences determine how she goes through life.

It is the same with us. The stored experiences, if we have not consciously moved past them, become our baggage, and we use them to judge every situation and everyone else. It's not our intention to judge someone else or to give them a hard time, but our minds have come to believe past experiences and filter every present experience through this lens. If we are not continually vigilant and self-reflective, we will not only get caught in one another's shit, we will likely get caught in—and draw others into—our own past shit. This is the very thing that prevents us from experiencing the bliss of wholeness. As we journey in wholeness, we must consciously work through this baggage. We are whole, but our conditioned minds act as a veil that prevents us from living in wholeness.

> *Every time you feel yourself getting pulled into other people's shit, repeat this Polish proverb to yourself...* "Not my circus. Not my monkeys."

There is a biblical teaching from the Book of Matthew (5:38-42) that helped me liberate myself from others' dramas. Jesus told his followers:

> "You have heard that it was said, 'Eye for eye, and tooth for tooth.'[a] 39 But I tell you, do not resist an evil person. If anyone slaps you on the right cheek,

turn to them the other cheek also. [40] And if anyone
wants to sue you and take your shirt, hand over your
coat as well. [41] If anyone forces you to go one mile,
go with them two miles. [42] Give to the one who asks
you, and do not turn away from the one who wants
to borrow from you."

Reflecting on this teaching of Jesus, I thought to myself, Well,
Jesus was, indeed, a smart guy! He had studied the Old Testament,
observed its impact in his life and came up with new, more evolved
teachings. That's a good example of the journey in wholeness. Jesus
did not get caught in someone else's narrow perspective of life. He
studied his religious tradition's dogma and doctrine and used it as a
foundation to create, change and grow. He had taken time to read,
reflect and watch its results in everyday life. He recognized that,
when you react or retaliate with the attitude of an eye for an eye
and a tooth for a tooth, you are already in the grip of someone else's
shit. And you are totally unaware of it! When you choose your own
actions and respond from your own ground, then you are in control
of yourself. The journey in wholeness calls us to remain deliberately,
reflectively grounded and to act from our inner frequency, or else the
two personalities—the reflective, grounded one and the reactive,
unaware one—will become entangled in the drama while our souls,
withering, wait patiently for attention and life.

The world teaches us to react, to pay back, to resist—a message
prevalent in our culture and lifestyle. Survival of the fittest. Every man
for himself. The reactor must be stronger than the attacker. That's the
only way you are going to get even and survive in this world. Fight
back! If hit, hit back much harder! Repay! Don't allow others to take
advantage of you! But Jesus clearly does not teach us resistance. He
knows well that when someone is behaving in an evil manner, they are
doing so because they are acting out of their own pain and suffering.
If I react, I become the victim of their suffering. Why would I like to

be part of such a lower field of energy? Why is there even a need to react? Because that is what the world teaches us. Remaining silent is seen as a sign of weakness. But Jesus' teaching is totally different. He asks us to offer the other cheek if struck on one. He encourages allowing the other one to act out of their will, while calling us to hold onto our inner ground.

It is also human nature to defend one's stand and think, "The other person acted out of his will, and I took the higher ground." But one needs to become honestly aware and reflect deeply upon the question: "Am I defending from being hurt by reacting to past wounds?" Every moment is an opportunity for introspection and self-examination. I need to question my stance, scrutinize my intentions and question my thoughts and behavior.

Jesus teaches: "Allow the other one to go to court and give him not only your tunic but also your cloak." That sounds impossible! Someone takes me to court through no fault of my own, trying to claim my tunic, and Jesus says to offer my cloak, too. What an insane teaching! On the other hand, isn't it wise? If the other one is living from an identity of the material world, let him have the material things. In fighting for life's basic survival needs, we can easily forget our spiritual needs, and our spirits lose their identity and become caught up in others' views and values of life. The truth is, only wounded and suffering people strike someone else and cause them harm. Anger is a cry for help. Violence is a cry for help. Attack is a cry for help. These come from deeply rooted fear and pain. No person grounded in peace and love will ever cause harm to someone else. When I am in peace with myself, why would I hurt someone or carry their wounds?

Jesus also says, "If anyone asks you to go one mile, go with them two miles." Doesn't that sound strange? The world is full of people who want you to walk their walk. They are so overcome by their own needs that they fail to see others. Instead, they try to use them for their own needs. When we are caught up in our survival needs, we tend to use others for our own needs, too. This is the universe's default system. When I am in need, I look at everyone and everything as an opportunity to meet my needs, and when we lose our ground of awareness, we can indirectly or subconsciously invite other people to use us. Being used by others can be an exhausting and depleting experience, but on the other hand, being needed and used gives some people a form of self-identity. Babies use parents. Bosses use employees. Many pray, "Jesus, use me as you will." At different moments in our lives, we need and use one another. Most relationships are based on some form of give and take. So how does one tell the difference between being used in a negative way and serving or giving freely one to another? In the absence of awareness, I could be blinded to even realizing that I am being used. This is precisely why it's important to turn inward, reflect, become aware, to know and recognize not only our inner motives and grounding, but also our interpersonal dynamics. In this way, we can take not only care of ourselves, we can respond well without hurting others. These small but essential moments of awareness and stepping back are our holy moments of meditation, prayer and Sabbath. These sacred moments present us with an opportunity to realize that the whole universe and life itself is interdependent. Accepting and aware that I am being used by the other, what do I do? Do I resist and distance myself? No! Jesus says to go the second mile. To some, this almost sounds ridiculous. Wouldn't going the second mile require a lot of inner strength? It would seem like walking on fire with open eyes. What would that achieve? In walking that extra mile, I can get in touch with my inner, spiritual strength. If my reflection and journey inward reveal that it's a harmful experience, I will learn how not to get drawn into such a situation in the future. What is important in life situations is constant awareness about my actions and reactions. As long as I act from my ground no matter what others do to me, I am free. The moment I react, I am in the grips of other's shit. This constant awareness itself is a tool to regain one's freedom and inner ground.

"A life of reaction is a life of slavery, intellectually and spiritually. One must fight for a life of action, not reaction."

Rita Mae Brown

One of Jesus' most difficult-to-follow teachings is: "Give to the one who asks you. Do not turn from the one who wants to borrow." The world teaches that what belongs to me is mine. I alone have the right to use, lend or give it away. Why would Jesus say not to turn away from the one who wants to borrow? Would I not become the victim of a lazy person? After all, I have worked hard to accumulate what I own. If I lend, I should be able to lend on my terms. I am the one who is in control. What Jesus is trying to point out is that it is easy to forget that when someone comes to borrow, I have and the other one does not. In compassion, I should recognize the other one's plight and gratefully acknowledge my gifts. I can also be grateful for being in the place of the giver rather than the borrower. This also presents an opportunity for me to examine what I want to give or not give. My reactions to the borrower are revelations about me when someone comes to borrow from me.

Jesus is not asking you or me to turn back. It is not easy to give things away that I have worked hard for. If I give away easily, then I must push myself to work harder and longer. Doing so could potentially compromise my quality of life. But is there also an opportunity—a call to grow in my capacity to think about others, notice their needs, share my gifts and be grateful for the ability to work harder and learn to live with less? We may never understand why some people have better opportunities than others. Why are some born rich? Why do some die young? Why do some suffer pain or disease or war? These are mysteries that I don't understand. But my inward reflection has taught me this: I don't deserve anything that I have. I am grateful for everything I have. I am not better than someone who does not have. My journey inward allows me that continual process of examining my spirit and going to my higher ground. For example, I realized that is possible that I don't like to turn people away because I have a compulsive need to be a do-gooder, or that I might choose to turn people away if I see my need above others. There are no readymade solutions to these life situations, and in each given moment, we need to examine our life stances and question our choices based upon our higher, holy ground.

In the Gospels, Jesus introduces us to three types of people. The first group of people are evil, because they hurt others willfully and deliberately, and seem to take pleasure in it. The second group of people will use the system for their own benefit (most of us fall into that category at times). And the third group include selfish people who use others to get their way, with no regard for whether they hurt others. Jesus' advice to us is to offer no resistance to evil. Give your tunic and cloak to those who use the system, and with the third, selfish group, go the extra mile, but don't get drawn into their evil or become like them. In these situations, it's not about who the other one is; it's about who you're becoming in relationship with others. If we continue in the ways of the world and give an eye for an eye and a tooth for a tooth, it will not take us anywhere. In fact, as we have seen through history, if we become reactive and respond out of fear, hate, anger, or payback, there will be a cycle of escalation and repetition. Instead, without getting involved or becoming like who the other one is, I use the opportunity to remain grounded in my higher self and liberate myself from others' shit.

———————————

Let me share the true-life story of a homeless woman that took place while this piece of the book was being written.

Anna was a fifty-something choir director at a small church whose membership was shrinking due to demographic changes.

While its leaders pondered ways to reach out to the growing African-American population, the church creatively continued its mission to serve the poor—growing vegetables in a garden and giving them to a local food pantry, offering free community dinners and sack lunches, and providing affordable daycare to the young children of working families. As its membership aged, the church had to cut costs such as janitorial services and so, after every Sunday service, Anna emptied her choir room's waste cans and some of the other church waste cans. As Anna was gathering a bag of trash, an African-American woman entered one of the side doors, waving and smiling, and rolling a suitcase behind her. Anna greeted the woman, who introduced herself as Betty White, and after a few minutes of conversation, realized that the woman was mentally ill and perhaps close to homeless. Pondering the message of the sermon that day, *The Beatitudes,* and the teaching, "Blessed are they who show mercy, mercy shall be shown them," Anna decided to be patient and kind to Betty and listened to the woman ramble from one topic to the next. The woman's eyes darted about as she talked uninterrupted about being abused, being afraid of various serial killers, and needing bus pass money--all while waving a battered cell phone on which she displayed pictures of serial killers and played Christian hymns at a loud volume. Betty told Anna that the church's pastor had in the past given her money for her cellphone minutes. Thinking about Jesus's teaching, "When someone asks for your cloak, give them your tunic also," Anna had already reflected inwardly and decided that she would give the woman money for the bus, if that's what was needed or requested, and she tried to find Betty something to eat. As the one-sided conversation continued, however, Anna began to feel the need to use the bathroom and get something to drink. Anna tried to interrupt the woman's monologue to excuse herself to use the bathroom, and the woman began to clutch Anna's hand and grab her arms to draw her back. Anna began to feel uncomfortable and realized she might need help in dealing with the woman.

Anna stood up with Betty still holding onto her arm, and led her into a nearby conference room, where several church members were discussing a book by Jennifer Harvey, *Whiteness and Morality: Pursuing Racial Justice.* Harvey's book makes the argument that white Americans are caught in the midst of a moral crisis because they unfairly benefit from the white supremacist infrastructure of America, and that white people of America can only atone for their "sins" (and those of their ancestors) by paying out reparations to Native- and African-Americans. As Anna and Betty entered the room, the group looked uncomfortable and fell silent, some looking down as Anna asked them if they knew where the cookies and refreshments served after church had been stored. Betty got out her phone and declared that she wanted to play "Here I Am, Lord," for the group, turning the music up loudly and waving the phone back and forth. One group member grew annoyed, saying to Betty, "And it's all about *you,* isn't it?" Anna realized she had interrupted their discussion on racism and had made her colleagues uncomfortable and, still arm in arm with Betty, removed her to the hallway.

Dan, a member of the discussion group, came out and gave Betty a $25 gift card to the grocery store across the street. Anna went to her choir room and found $13 in her purse, giving it to Betty and telling Betty it was every dollar she had. Betty sat down on a bench outside the conference room, stating that this wasn't enough to buy a weekly bus pass, and she couldn't use the $25 grocery gift card to purchase a bus pass, which was $27.50. Betty further stated that she would wait for the church members' meeting to end so that she could ask them all to pitch in more money for a weekly bus pass. Dan checked the Metrolink website on his cell phone and told Betty that she could indeed spend the grocery store gift card on a bus pass. "Why don't you call the store and ask them for me?" Betty told Dan, who replied, "I don't need to, I'm looking at their website right now and it says they will take the gift card for bus passes."

Betty continued to ramble on, talking of serial killers, music, her living situation, and anything and everything related to her needs. She never paused and Anna, growing impatient and unsure what to do, interrupted Betty mid-sentence and told Betty that she needed to leave.

Anna left, feeling badly about leaving Dan to deal with the mentally ill woman, and reflecting that perhaps she hadn't, in keeping with the Beatitudes, shown enough mercy. At the same time, she also felt that she was getting drawn into another person's crazy shit and that Betty was "working them over" for more and more handouts. She also remembered hearing someone on the church staff talk about a woman who had regularly come into the church demanding money for her cell phone and realized that the church might have a history with Betty.

After the meeting, Anna went home and got herself busy with her household chores. Even when she retired for the day, Betty kept occupying her mental space. Anna was unable to sleep peacefully. She got up to journal her experience and penned a few reflective questions as follows.

- If Jesus asks us to give not just our coat, but also our tunic, was our response enough? Should they have given the woman more—more time, listening, money?
- Should I have let the woman hold my hand, or should I have set boundaries and refused to let the woman touch me?
- Was I getting drawn into "other people's shit"?
- In light of the fact that the book club members were discussing a book on racism and reparations, was their silent, uncomfortable response to Betty appropriate?

Life situations have the power to transform us and make us whole, if we are willing to welcome and come into direct contact with them. Embracing daily situations and making them a practice to journey in wholeness, is both fulfilling and liberating.

Looking back at my own life, I have moved in and out of different stages of consciousness. Culturally, as a female growing up in India, I had assimilated the notion that I was one step lower than men. I accepted without question that my language was inferior to the language of the Brahmin caste and that Sanskrit was superior to Kanarese. Before the age of twelve, I took pride in my identity as an Indian Catholic female. Belonging to the Catholic Church was one of the proudest experiences of life then. I firmly believed that it was the only religion that owned the full truth about life, about death, about anything and everything. I was taught that, as a Catholic, only I was entitled to heaven and all the institutional service the Catholic Church had to offer. For a young child from a lesser caste, studying in a parochial school in a Hindu country was nothing less than a privilege.

Joining the convent out of high school further reinforced my religious identity. As I studied theology in the convent, the doctrines, dogma, beliefs and morality became more entrenched within me. Service was held up as the highest calling, but as with the social structure of India, there were grades or castes among the types of service. For example, a sister who served as a school principal was higher on the ladder than the sister who cooked food in the kitchen and served it in the refectory. Under the vow of obedience, I could not dare ask questions. Not only was I taught to never ask questions, I was also taught that something was wrong with me if I had any. Blind obedience, complete submission and unquestioning acceptance was expected and revered. So, for the major portion of convent life, I suppressed all the questions that fluttered through my brain. But by my late thirties, I could no longer continue to act incurious, especially when I saw discrepancies between daily, lived experience and teachings. I began to ask questions, and, as a result, I was labeled a "rebel." While I experienced power in working with people in the community, I experienced a loss of power in my personal life at the convent. Remaining within the confines of Catholic beliefs, traditions and teachings began to suffocate my spirit. The religion that I once took so much pride in now felt small. I came to feel that it did not contain the whole truth. I came to believe that every religion shared part of the truth and that everyone, in seeking and naming that which is Divine, was striving toward higher ground. I came to believe that, just as there is diversity and variety across all aspects of life, there is diversity and variety among religions for people to choose, to grow into and to find a home in.

After leaving the convent, I shed my identity as a religious sister, yet I remain a truly practicing Catholic. I am proud to be Catholic and to share deep affection with the person of Jesus, my friend, master and my hero. With its focus on Jesus' teachings, its meaningful and beautiful rituals, and its many wonderful people, Catholicism will always be a wonderful gift, and I will always cherish the gift of Catholicism in my life. I love going to the local church regularly to join the worshipping community. It's wonderful to belong to the church and have a community to celebrate life's transitions.

Departing the convent, however, gave me a fresh breath of air. I came to see everything differently. For the first time I could see my identity as a human being. Away from the walls of the convent, there were different roles and needs, and I saw that people out in the world have the opportunity to do exactly what they feel called to do, rather than what they were ordered to do. All services were worthy of dignity. There was no high or low job, persons, or position.

Once out of the convent, my view of God expanded as well. God was one. He was life giving force and energy. He became much bigger than I had ever been taught. For me, God became someone or something—a creative force if you will—who moved in and through the whole of the universe, beyond what my limited brain could fathom. This new, expanded experience of God brought a sense of deep gratitude for the gift of being a human. From the inner experience of freedom and spaciousness, I was able to give my best to everyone and everything. I was able to see life's process and dynamics beyond the boundaries of my individual body. Life is at work in everything. There's an experience of vastness within. God is alive in the universe—in you and in me! I view life as one and eternal, and there is only the eternal now. It's only you and me that come and go. Past and future exist only in our minds. There's a growing sense of oneness with all human beings, nature and the world.

> *"We examine everything in existence and we come to see that everything is transitory and temporal, that which is left over is God, is eternity, is the Self."*
>
> Frederick Lenz

Because of this change in my views about God, my views, perceptions, feelings and reactions have changed a great deal. Transformation seems to take place more from within than outside. I notice my ideas about things have changed drastically, and my opinions and affiliation to political parties have loosened up. I have also taken full responsibility for my own personal growth and happiness. I notice, too, that I am now able to make better daily choices and to manage my gifts and potential in a much better way. Life seems to be less stressful and more peaceful. Events and experiences happen, and they pass through time and through me as I calmly observe them. This has transformed my relationship with myself, things and others. There's a deeper sense of presence. The change from within gives me an illusion that things have changed externally, but I know that it's really my inner expansion that has changed everything. As Dr. Wayne Dyer once noted, "If you change the way you look at things, the things you look at change."

———

Having traced my own journey of growing into awareness, I am certain that people live from their own levels of awareness and consciousness. Our attitudes and values depend upon where we are along the path of our lives. We act and react from that stance. So, if we encounter someone operating at a lower level of consciousness, taking people's actions and reactions personally may draw us into this reactive level. One must be continually vigilant and aware of the dynamics within and around one's self to avoid becoming entangled in a "lower frequency."

Reflecting inward will usually reveal what "frequency" or level of consciousness we are operating from. For example, a few months ago, a friend of mine lost her father. He was 96 and had lived a fulfilled personal, family and social life. My friend was fortunate to be able to spend quality time in the last few years with him to support him and the rest of the family through this loss and transition. Life could not have been any more gracious to her than it had. Everyone in the family had been available and had reached out to offer support in caregiving. Being close friends, I also made myself available to my friend in this journey of life. I was happy for all the good times and opportunities they had to express loving care and that they were able to say a heartfelt goodbye to the man of the house. The whole journey had lasted a couple of years.

I know that people grieve differently and take their time to heal. However, after a period of time and grieving, I began to lose patience with my friend. I felt I could no longer take her emotional outbursts and listen to how much she missed her beloved father. It had become too much for me to calmly listen to the good old stories of her dad and their intimate connection. Enough was enough! Upon self-introspection, I found that my discomfort came from my perspective on life and death. Since I felt I could take it no more, I was truthful with my friend and asked her to call me only after she had come to terms with the loss of her loved one. I kept ruminating about this conversation, however, asking myself if I had been rude and insensitive. I had to admit that I did not feel that I was. I had patiently accompanied my friend for years. When everything came to a beautiful end, I thought my friend would move on. I had lost my patience to listen to the same stuff again and again. Why? My truth is that I am in a different place than my friend. I view life, death and the world very differently. In my role as a full-time caregiver, I have touched and felt death more often. I know deep in my heart that life is one continuous cycle. So, for me, death is just one side of the coin and we are all united in the process of the renewal of creation—and new life is on the other side of the coin. This was a moment of epiphany for me.

This is not to minimize my friend's grief. Everyone grieves differently and for differing periods of time. But the point is, each one of us is at a very different level of consciousness based upon our history and perception of reality. We grow up differently and not all of us complete the developmental stages in keeping with our biological age. Our values and self-perception are dependent on our experiences as we go through the years and on our level of consciousness. In the absence of this awareness, we can remain "stuck" and perhaps underdeveloped in our relationships, communication and conduct. We can get overwhelmed and resent other people's emotional stuff, yet carry ourselves politely under the pressure of other people's pain. We may call it compassionate accompaniment or playing into someone's drama. One has to respond from one's inner status and there is no clear-cut standard set of behavior to adhere to. It is said that the world is not out there but we each inhabit the world we create through our perceptions.

―――――――――

Our level of consciousness—along with our views, beliefs, and perspectives—prompts our brains to act and react in a certain way. Since we are all at different places along this spectrum of consciousness, we may sometimes have difficulties enjoying every event, interaction and experience. That is human nature. We experience conflict and call such episodes "baggage." However, this luggage is not simply garbage to be disposed of! Each suitcase, if you will, is essentially a gift. Our baggage can teach us things. If we can honestly open and peer into the luggage, we will find the gift of lessons learned, the teachings of wisdom. The more we can unpack our baggage, the more we will become wise and learn the lessons that life is trying to teach us. If we fail to learn the lesson, the baggage comes around again in one form or another, like a wayward suitcase circling the airport baggage carousel. In some ways, this is analogous to what is called the "baggage trigger" in the field of psychology. An emotional charge or reaction, your baggage or response, is triggered by an outside factor. We can get stuck in that emotional reaction and continue to operate from a lower level of consciousness, continually triggered by outside factors. Or we can choose to look inward and choose a different, more evolved response.

Let's return to the example of my friend who lost her dad. My emotional trigger was losing patience with listening to her story. I became upset and had to continually bite my tongue while listening to her stories. When I felt that I could not take it anymore, I suggested she attempt to move on from the loss, grow and heal. I was aware of the consequences. Speaking my truth could mean losing a long-lasting friendship, but oddly enough, this part of the situation did not bother me at all. What bothered me was facing my own truth! Had I been selfish, insensitive, abrupt? Where had this reaction come from? Had something in my schedule been weighing me down and I had displaced my emotional baggage onto my friend, just as I felt she had been doing to me?

Reflecting inwardly and asking these questions at the deepest spiritual level helped me to become aware of the level of consciousness from which I was operating and handling life and viewing my friend's death of her Dad. Since I had come to terms with life and death as two sides of the same coin, I found it hard to be sorrowful for an extended period about a wonderful, whole, full-fledged life that had been very well lived. But I also realized that my friend was certainly not at that place with her father's death.

By reflecting and meditating upon this experience, I began to understand the complexity of human dynamics that are mixed with one's level of consciousness, developmental stages of emotional/ spiritual growth and cultural norms. Since our lives are complex, and humans are, in effect, creatures formed by layers upon layers of experiences and conditioning, we are called to pause, reflect, and examine life in a deeper, more meaningful way. Every such moment of taking such breaks for introspection is true meditation. It's been said that we should "err on the side of caution," and as a precautionary or preventive measure, it's a good idea to meditate for twenty minutes every day to prevent the normal tendency to operate from a reactive level of consciousness. It can be a challenge to find the time and will to honestly turn inward to examine our life's experiences, but we will always emerge transformed and renewed!

———

Consider Jay's case to illustrate levels of consciousness and how we can get drawn into others' reactive levels—in other words, how we get caught up in "other people's shit."

Jay is a 48-year-old father of seven. A hard-working man, he holds three jobs to provide for his family's basic needs. He is a manual laborer at a landscaping company, holds two side jobs, and spends his days running from one job to the next. Jay is equally caring towards his extended family members and goes out of his way to get together with them, providing some fun time and food. He likes to see his family members happy and well fed. Jay also values belonging to his community and church, and the family enjoys participating in local community events—festivals and parties where they can eat more than needed.

Jay had noticed one of his colleagues acting inconsistently. Sometimes the colleague would steal an object or two from the workplace. Jay gently tried to help out his colleague by letting him know that his action was wrong. But his colleague did not believe what he was doing was wrong. He believed the rich had a lot and would not miss one little thing from their plenty. And if they did, he assumed, they could easily replace it. And if they did, he assumed, they could easily replace it. At the time of political elections, Jay feels overwhelmed and confused. He is not able to discern what type of candidate would be the right person to vote for. He talks about this confusion with his colleagues and ultimately votes for the candidate that most of his friends recommend. He is rather impulsive in his choices and actions. He can enjoy life without regrets. He will go to any extent to protect himself and his family and to see them happy. He is good hearted and always looking for any and every opportunity to ensure that his goals and wishes for his family make his goals for himself and his family come true.

Having an interactive, give-and-take conversation with Jay is not possible. His mind is not curious or open to new ideas. Shortly after beginning a conversation, he will either attack or attempt to "win," and one can easily be drawn into his "shit." But attempting to build a friendship with him—or with people in a similar state of consciousness—is a loss of good energy. He is a good man with limited consciousness.

Sheila is a social worker by profession, working in a community center and often putting in sixteen hours a day. She is very mindful and committed to the welfare of the people she serves in the community. Sheila is also very creative in organizing events and formation programs to teach people how to live a value-based life. She values peace and harmony in the community and neighborhood. The community members can count on her. Senior members in the community can call on her anytime for minor needs like getting their eye drops administered. People note that Sheila has a sweet demeanor. She has a good sense of community ethics and calls people to be responsible citizens. In her personal life, she is a good mother, a faithful wife, and a regular member of the church.

When you engage in conversation with Sheila, you might get drawn into "us versus them" types of stories. After a while, you might notice all the "shoulds" she uses in discussions. The conversation will end well if you offer Sheila compliments, but as a result, you might feel as if you are walking on eggshells in her presence.

Someone who has a strong sense of identity tied to community service can easily make you feel uncomfortable if you are not from the same background. Potentially, conversations with her could help you come out of yourself and reach out to others—or they could provide a moment of clarity and insight that you are exactly where you are meant to be.

Aaron works for UNICEF in an international position as a coordinator of services for children. He has a solid understanding of the problems of children worldwide, using his knowledge and skills to progress in the organization. Most people find Aaron very attractive: he is professional, well read, and uses rationality and technology to advance his career. He can analyze the system and initiate goal-oriented programs. Aaron is also conscientious and able to take criticism well. He is always looking for an opportunity to get ahead and enjoys personal accomplishments.

Friendship with Aaron is complex. Although he has a strong opinion about everything in life, he does pay attention to others' opinions. Aaron likes to find solutions to problems. If you share any of your problems, he immediately provides you with several potential solutions. No matter what you discuss with him, he always finds the root of all problems in the issues from his childhood.

Spending time with Aaron can be a good experience. He has an increased understanding of life's complexity. You can question assumptions and talk about interpretations. There's an experience of openness and acceptance.

All the above cases have one thing in common: we all view life from the level of consciousness that is inside of us. If we are not vigilant and mindful, we can easily get trapped in other people's consciousness and get pulled backward. Or we can choose to open the baggage and see the gift inside, using such incidents and relationships to grow in the wisdom of life.

While awareness about one's consciousness is important, it's also important to be aware of cultural currents and values and how they affect our consciousness. Sometimes friends and family can trap us under the obligations of cultural or familial expectations and keep us from our journey in wholeness. It is true that we are all whole, but we can get sidetracked or pulled away by complex social, cultural and interpersonal dynamics. Once we lose the ground within and get caught up in these dynamics, we are drawn further away from our higher level of consciousness and the feeling of being whole.

A friend of mine has a very sound, evolved consciousness. She is an ecology activist and strongly believes in the dignity and equality of all life. She's a big voice for the voiceless and on a personal level has a very healthy lifestyle. Her husband was diagnosed with a terminal illness in his fifties. Before the full diagnosis had been completed and a treatment plan put in place, he passed away. A decade later, she has yet to come to terms with his sudden demise. Her grief has given her a sort of new identity and purpose of being. She participates in every program and event for widows and those who are grieving. She dwells in her grief and seems unable to move on with new activities or new people, even ten years later. Her husband's death was untimely and unfortunate, but if she could allow herself to evolve to a higher consciousness of life and death, perhaps she might realize that she is grieving more than just her husband's loss, but the expectation that she would spend a happy old age with him. She is grieving her lost expectations and plans for her life, while she could be moving on to create a different kind of happy old age. Life has no guaranteed plan as to when it will end. The grief could come from her expectations about life. Terminal illness had shattered all of her plans and dreams. Is the grief about those dreams and plans or the loss of life? Only she will be able to accurately assess her inner stance.

It's possible that my friend's seemingly limited internal awareness could be, at least in part, due to a gap between her level of consciousness and personal growth. For me, to accompany this friend along her journey of grief is very complex, a struggle between being empathetic and supportive but also trying not to get caught up in her grief. Since I see the passing of an individual as a necessary phase of the life cycle, I have been able to more easily accept the death of beloved family members. In the space of one year, I lost three male family members between the ages of sixteen and sixty. While certainly I will miss my loved ones, I did not wallow in grief, but chose to view their deaths through the lens of life's natural cycles and to honor their lives by remembering all that was good about them.

Reflecting inwardly gave me the insight that my attitude toward death has to do with my consciousness of life in general. When my friend slips into a sorrowful mood and begins to discuss her husband as if he had died yesterday, I want to show empathy and compassion, but I also become uncomfortable and sense that I am getting drawn into a lowered level of consciousness and frequency. Healing can and does take time and involves processing memories, but if I offer even a word that it's time to move on, she resists and reminds me that I don't know how it feels. She is correct. Human personalities and experiences are unique and complicated, and no one can ever really understand where another person is coming from. We cannot get inside someone's head, and we shouldn't try. When we do, we are taking on other people's baggage and getting drawn into their "shit." When this happens, the intelligence of your body may send out signals, such as my level of discomfort and feeling of lowered energy with my friend. The journey in wholeness is a call to be continually aware, continually reflecting, and continually mindful of one's field of energy and to remain in that ground of wholeness.

Human beings need to experience all levels of consciousness. Each level is essential for us to grow to the next stage of the journey in wholeness. The challenge is not to judge where we are, but to realize where we are and then move toward a deeper and more insightful level of self-awareness. Unwittingly getting drawn into other individuals' levels of consciousness—others' shit—and reacting from these deprives us of our own unique journey in wholeness.

> *"The level of consciousness you choose to tune in to each moment of each day will determine the quality of your experience of the world."*
>
> Debbie Ford

"Life isn't always about customer service. We aren't here to enable or encourage someone else's bad behavior. We aren't here to be a doormat that collects the debris of other people's insecurities and projections. Sometimes people need to be called on their shit."

Becky Vollmer, Author,
You Are Not Stuck

"Shit gets old. You get tired of trying to work things out. You get tired of giving chances. Sometimes you just have to let people go."

Thegoodvibe.com

At War with Wholeness

It has been amazing to realize that, after years of seeking and struggle, I have come to be at peace within and to accept that I am whole just as I am. The haunting questions that I seek to answer are these: Why did I think that I was not whole? Wherever did that feeling come from? Why did I struggle for so long to be someone different than who I am? What a waste of time and energy! Perhaps I had picked up a fictitious or inauthentic sense of self from life experiences that contributed to an inauthentic sense of self and years of growing up in religious, family or social traditions that said, "You are not okay..." I always felt that I needed to be someone or to become someone, or else life itself was in vain. It's not hard to pinpoint the people and institutions that told me (along with everyone else) that I was not enough, and I internalized that message without questioning.

At the age of five, each grade in school taught the lesson that the quality of my memory to recognize and repeat lessons determined whether I was good, better or best. Getting grades such as "A" was celebrated and getting grades such as "D" meant being deprived of daily privileges—or even being punished. As a child, I came to accept that my identity of "GOOD" versus "BAD" depended upon remembering and repeating back the lessons and thinking of others. This, at the time, was my accumulated knowledge of the world. For all children, learning the tools for a meaningful life is certainly a necessary part of growing up. However, success was put before meaning, and I was taught to compete and to push myself ahead of others. The positive side of this type of education was that I excelled at school and became very competent in language, math and scientific skills needed for adult life.

But as I moved ahead in life, I felt I needed to prove my worth every step of the way. College education wasn't much different than elementary and high school. I believed there was an underlying requirement to give my best, gather all available knowledge, write superior assignments, and do better than my other classmates. During my last year of college, I finally realized that I had, indeed, developed a strong foundation of intellectual skills. It seemed I was able to understand concepts in-depth and much more quickly. I was able to produce better results with less effort. I did not have to work all that hard. Sometimes I even felt sad for those classmates who worked much harder and received lower grades. This was another positive side to the education I received at school. These years of formation awakened a great deal of dormant potential within me, and I'm deeply grateful to my teachers and mentors who contributed to this process.

As a young adult, I entered the convent to become a nun and my training and education continued in both secular and theological fields. My need and drive to excel continued unabated! I voraciously consumed a great deal of information and regurgitated it on exam papers. In the convent, questioning was not encouraged or entertained. I remember asking a theological question about the Trinity, and I was told to recite The Apostles' Creed ten times. Doubts and questions regarding God were not welcomed by a believer. A good religious believer blindly accepted whatever was told to them and that was considered to be faith. Still, I wanted to be the best, so I shut my questioning mind and allowed myself to be brainwashed with all the available knowledge and information. After all, I desired to be a good nun and bring others to bow at the name of Jesus Christ.

During this whole process, I assimilated everything that was taught to me and wholeheartedly believed that this was the true and best world. I consumed all the knowledge and information without question and considered it my duty to dish it out to others for their consumption. To the best of my ability, I faithfully and creatively repeated and reproduced those ideas in multiple programs for the people I served. As I took on a leadership role at different forms of services, I continued to promulgate what I had been taught. I was quite community centric and conservative in my beliefs. I believed in one God who was the father of us all but did not believe in the equality of all human beings. There are, as in India or in the hierarchy of the Church, ranks, grades and status—castes! A bishop was above the priests, and mother superior was higher than the rest of the nuns in the community. There are multiple grades and echelons of all types. That was simply part of my unquestioned life. It was my sincere desire that I should rise from a lower grade to a higher one.

Over time, I realized that in my heart of hearts, all my efforts to serve were camouflaged by that desire to rise. I felt that if I did not achieve the highest and the best, I would be incomplete. It was not enough for me to just be me. I needed to be that person who others too wanted me to be, and my years of conditioning led me to believe that only then would I move to a higher place in life. I somehow became caught in a cycle of drama and wanted to do only that thing which would put me on the next higher rung of the ladder of success I was climbing. This ladder is no different in the church than the one in the corporate world. The only difference is the language used to describe the ladder. One has a spiritual language and the other a secular one, but essentially, they both have similar dynamics and rules. This "cycle of drama" had two faces for me. On one side, I was determined to climb the ladder but on the other side, I was being eaten alive by the belief that I was not whole. This internalized belief that I was not whole, that I was not okay, that I would be whole if only, unless, until, kept pushing me to practice virtues, acquire new ideas, develop new programs and so on. I truly believed that the experience of the inner vacuum I experienced would vanish if I filled it with the things the world considered success.

Since leaving the convent life ten years ago, my life has been transformed. I work for myself. I do not feel the need to please

71

anyone. I enjoy giving my best to the people I serve, but I have no need to prove myself to anyone or to be any different than who I am. I have learned to be comfortable in my own skin, and as a result, there is much rest and peace within. I have come to recognize the internal war with wholeness that I had been waging within—the many-headed voices of Hydra that say, "you're not enough," "if only," "until," and "unless."

The Very Idea of Wholeness is the Beginning of War

When we seek something other than what life has given us, it can mean the beginning of an internal war. In my own experience, I've found that when I act out of an underlying belief that I need something other than what I have, I am really looking for something other than what life has served me. This can be the beginning of internal conflict. There's an assumption that I need something other than what I have because what I have and am is incomplete. There's a difference between recognizing and working toward my potential and feeling so incomplete that I feel the need to seek wholeness in what the world defines as whole.

At my women's prayer group meeting, the discussion was on the recent sex scandals in the Catholic Church. One of the women asked, "If the church once had married priests, why did they consider celibate priests were a holier option?" I commented that my insight on this practice or teaching was that it was due to changing historical ideas and concepts from the time. As life events and conditions change, we have new ideas and perceptions, and we create certain practices to live them out. While this was a simple life philosophy for me, it was not for some of the group's participants. They seemed amazed at this comment. One of them said, "I have always held the celibate priests and priesthood in a high place of honor and dignity and considered celibacy to be a gift of holiness." She continued, "It cannot be a mere idea for someone's fancy." I realized that it was very difficult for her to let years of dogmatic belief evaporate with a new idea. Isn't that the truth we face daily? The perceptions, concepts and needs of our life get turned into unwavering practices and we invest our lives and the whole of our beings into them. They become the reality, the dogma and doctrine, we live by.

In a similar way, my sense of self and wholeness came from the story I had created in my head, and this story came from what people told me or did. The school grades, the recognition or punishment, the practice of virtues, and the compliments were all components of my story and sense of self. As I moved through life, these concepts kept changing and my chase kept intensifying. At school, wholeness was getting better grades. At work, wholeness was performing better than others. In the convent, wholeness was being more virtuous than the rest of the nuns. The world kept showing me definitions of wholeness that I kept chasing without questioning.

When I look at people with more money, fame, status or material possessions, there's a sense that these individuals are more complete than me. Society teaches us that. Advertising, marketing, peer pressure teaches us that. The wants created by those things turn into a sense of self. I think that I will be whole when I have similar things or achievements—or more than what others have. To make matters worse, the idea of more keeps changing, too! The ring that we strive to grab at is dangled and then moved out of reach by some vengeful puppet master. For example, I watch the contestants who come for blind auditions on a voice reality show. Their only desire at the auditions is to be selected for the program. Once selected, they want to win the competition. As the show proceeds, they are happy each week when they are not eliminated. Their definition and perception of happiness and self keeps changing. Happiness and success are continually redefined externally, and they are forced to internalize these new milestones. After the whole show is over, they try to celebrate what they achieve or to make peace with where they ended. Some are happy that they made it to the top ten, while others are content to be part of the top five. It would be interesting to know whether they were perfectly happy and whole before they even thought of participating in the show. In the same way, many people are quite content to not participate in the race of society—what some call "the rat race." Once an idea of having more, being different, gets into our head then we start chasing those ideas. A friend notes that she has companions who like to "go shopping" as a way to spend time and as a means of recreation. My friend doesn't like to "go shopping" just to browse and look at things, because she feels it puts into her head the thoughts and ideas of things that she might want to buy—not things she needs, just things she thinks might be fun to buy. Pretty things. Interesting things. Better clothes. Nicer furniture. She would rather not have those ideas polluting her mental space and consuming her thought time.

The point is, notions of having more, doing more, or being more not only pollute our understanding of wholeness, they can create an inner conflict or war within. While these ideas or goals can provide us fuel to evolve to our next step in life, it is not these things that make us whole. We must observe and reflect on how our minds work and be cautious about driving life toward pursuing those ideas, things, achievements or goals. It is the journey along the way that is meaningful, we are whole in that journey, right now, just as we are.

> *"Wholeness is not something that 'happens' one day, it is that which is already present. Life itself – what you really are, beyond your image of yourself – is already whole."*
> *Jeff Foster*

Concepts are Mere Tools to Discover Life

It has taken me five decades of searching to realize that I am whole just as I am. For many years, I thought that I was defined by concepts: cultural and social expectations, religious doctrine, academic teachings or any other conditioning concept that forms a human being's sense of self. But these *concepts* really serve as tools to discover life. They serve as a lens through which we can journey in wholeness. Earlier in life, I believed such concepts were real and were my real life. I tried to fit my life into those impressions, rather than developing concepts from life experiences. I came to realize that beliefs don't create my real life, they only help me explore its depth.

Through the years, I had assimilated cultural concepts and ideas and developed a sense of wholeness and self from these. Those ideas became an identity to pursue. I never realized that identity of self does not come from accumulated knowledge. In fact, my sense of self and identity was the sum of my accumulated knowledge. From my perception of people's behavior and relationships with me, I had developed a fabricated sense of self and I constantly worked to enhance it. Every time I heard the world say that I had not made it, I worked harder to make it. There were times when this nagging inner voice reminded me that I hadn't made it. The way people conducted their lives was a message loud and clear that I needed looks, professional success, money, and the esteem of others in order to be whole. We pursue these things so that we can feel whole, feel happiness and enjoy the journey of life. But some have figured out that they don't need these embellishments to feel whole, happy or to enjoy their lives.

Consider the story told by a Jesuit priest from India, Anthony de Mello. Father de Mello was a psychotherapist and storyteller who offered spiritual retreats and taught "awareness prayer" principles inspired by the teachings of St. Ignatius.

A rich industrialist from North America visited the beach in Brazil and seemed disapproving to find a fisherman sprawling leisurely beside his boat in the middle of the day.

"Why aren't you fishing?" the rich man asked the fisherman.

"Because I have caught enough for the day," said the fisherman.

"Well, why don't you catch some more?" said the rich man.

"What would I do with them?" the fisherman replied.

"You could earn more money," said the wealthy man. "With that, you could fix a motor to your boat, go into deeper waters and catch more fish! Then you would make enough money to buy nylon nets. They will bring you more fish and more money! Soon you would have enough money to own two boats—maybe even an entire fleet of boats. Then you will be a rich man like me."

"What would I do then?" asked the fisherman.

"Then you'll really enjoy life," said the rich man, smiling broadly.

"What do you think I'm doing right now?" said the fisherman.

We all have different definitions of happiness, success, peace, love and joy. When we compare those ideas or push ourselves to measure against our own or others' ideas, then we get into war with wholeness.

Life is expressing itself in each of us in a very unique way. Instead of discovering life's unique manifestation in me, it is tempting to try to fit into or conform to definitions provided to me or internalized by me. The discovery process and looking inward can be more difficult, and quite frankly, more frightening, than molding one's self to fit external expectations. But it can also be a process of joy and revelation. The wisdom of life is in aligning with what "is" in the moment.

Consider Ann's journey in wholeness. Ann has always had an expectation about how her aging husband should be and how he should act during his senior years. As he aged, however, his poor physical health and dementia totally made him into another person--a person Ann almost didn't recognize. The man of Ann's expectations and the man who existed were two different people. Ann consequently suffered in her mind, fighting with her own ideas about him and the reality of his real condition. "He had never been like this before," she said. "Why is he getting violent and abusive in his language? He was always a perfect gentleman." Yes, she knows that his illness has made him so, but her heartfelt question is, *Why him? Why did he have to lose his memory and health?* He has always taken good care of himself, she asserted.

While Ann suffers from seeing her husband decline and become vulnerable, I see his current situation to be whole. The man is going through the natural stages of his life. His human body is slowly wearing out, and this is happening one day a time. He is whole. Ann may disagree, but it depends on one's definition of wholeness. Wholeness, as I see it, is whatever *is* at the moment, just as I *am* at a given moment. When I have ideas and expect life to happen according to my thoughts, then I am at war with wholeness.

> *"Wholeness does not mean perfection: it means embracing brokenness as an integral part of life."*
> *Parker J Palmer*

Freedom! Accepting the Transient Nature of Thoughts is Liberating

Life is a process, and having watched my evolving definitions of wholeness change, I have come to realize that most of my definitions about life will also change over time. Accepting that most of our definitions are passing ideas will not only bring rest to our minds and spirits, it will also bring a sense of freedom to our souls. As noted earlier, all ideas, all definitions, all concepts are simply tools to help us get through life. They become limitations when we identify ourselves too closely with them or when we want everyone else to fit into those parameters. Some of the thoughts are not even ours! They are borrowed ones—thoughts that, somewhere along our journey, we adopted, built our sense of self around, and expected everyone else to live by. We attach grades and values to people who do not think like us or live by our thoughts. There's a tendency to forget that thoughts are like waves in the ocean. They come and go. They move *through* us, but they are *not* us. Depending upon the weather and wind, they change. Life evolves at every given moment.

It is wonderful to watch our thoughts and enter into conscious relationship with them. Each thought has many underlying processes. Questioning our own thoughts can lead us to some insightful discoveries. Here's the amazing story of a woman called Byron Katie.

"Byron Kathleen Reid became severely depressed while in her thirties. Over a ten-year period, her depression deepened, and for the last two years Katie (as she is called) was seldom able to leave her bedroom. Then one morning, from the depths of despair, she experienced a life-changing realization. Katie noticed that when she believed her thoughts, she suffered, and that when she didn't believe her thoughts, she didn't suffer. What had been causing her depression was not the world around her, but *what she believed* about the world around her. In a flash of insight, she saw that our human attempt to find happiness was backward—instead of hopelessly trying to change the world to match our thoughts about how it "should" be, we can question these thoughts and, by meeting reality as it is, experience unimaginable freedom and joy. As a result, a bedridden, suicidal woman became filled with love for everything life brings."[1]

As with most people, I am sometimes able to ignore my most difficult, dire, negative or desperate thoughts, but there are times when I cannot, and I feel overwhelmed by them. Some thoughts make me feel out of control or feel that I am going to lose myself. I forget that these are mere thoughts. They are, like wind blowing through tree branches, just passing through my mind. If treating thoughts for what they are could become second nature, we could avoid much suffering caused by them. Becoming aware of our thoughts at any given moment is very helpful. When we become aware of them, we will be able to anchor ourselves in the present which is whole. Our thoughts pass through us, but they are not us. Becoming aware of your thoughts can be very helpful. You are not your thoughts. I am not my thoughts. The arise spontaneously. They will flow through and other thoughts will replace them. I am not those thoughts, but I am the one who is aware of those thoughts and the one who is able to watch and let them pass by. On the other hand, there are times when I consciously romance my ideas and have tea with them. This book is an outcome of such romantic experiences with thoughts and ideas.

Wholeness: An Idea

I do believe "Wholeness" is another passing idea. We keep chasing it in different forms and in different places. Our minds deceive us into seeking wholeness outside of ourselves, not realizing that these

---

[1] Katie, Byron. *The Work of Byron Katie*, Byron Katie International, Inc., 2018, p. 2.

ideas exist only in our heads. Underneath the chase for wholeness, wealth, success, happiness and adventure, there is a deep-seated desire for more. There's a repressed part of me that is manifesting as an incomplete self. Rather than pushing aside wholeness as a mere idea, it would be helpful to discover the repressed part of self and heal it, and get out and look at it – to reflect. Maybe there's a part of me needing acceptance and affirmation. Maybe there's part of me waiting for newer expression and manifestation.

There is certainly practical value in chasing after our ideas! However, it's important to realize that my ideas do not reflect the universe outside my mind. Each of us will have to test our ideas against our life experiences. Where did my idea of wholeness originate and where did it lead me? Of course, it has been one of the most interesting chases of my life: the pursuit of wholeness. Having sought wholeness in the world outside me, I have come to realize that wholeness is what it is at any given moment. This realization has brought a deep sense of peace, acceptance and surrender. The war within is finally over.

I have struggled over many years to understand wholeness. It has taken five decades of serious inner work to arrive at that peace. Only now do I know that my true struggle was not with wholeness itself, but with the *idea* of wholeness. My understating of wholeness as a concept had limited my pursuits, although it had at least provided some sense of direction. In the process, I have come to realize that my ideas and concepts will never be able to define wholeness accurately. Real life happens at every moment and it emerges uniquely at different moments. I cannot have one idea and try to fix the whole of my life around that idea and see life through that idea. Life is bigger than my flawed human concepts and understanding. Welcoming every moment with total awe and acceptance has given me some taste of wholeness. It is difficult to explain that experience to another person. They must personally embrace and experience it within themselves. Mere ideas and preconceived notions can blind us from seeing things as they are. To embrace and live the fullness of every moment, we do not need any explanation or idea. It simply is...

The wholeness we seek is our true self and not an idea. An idea might set us on a journey in wholeness but it ends in the experience of harmony with who we are, just as we are.

Becoming a Hostage to One's Thoughts

Franklin D. Roosevelt said, "Men are not prisoners of fate, but only prisoners of their own minds."

We could be at war with life itself when we get trapped in our own minds, by our compulsive thinking and rigid thoughts. Have you ever noticed some of the thoughts that have taken you hostage? I am more attractive when I am thinner. My friends should be respectful of my schedule. My siblings should listen to my views on family matters. Once thoughts like these become our default lens of seeing life, we have already entered a hostage situation. Our true self, spirit, soul—whatever you want to call it—has been taken into hostage by our mind. Living as a hostage to one's thoughts does not help us to live in wholeness. It is like living life in a box, boxed in ideas and thoughts about life. It brings much pain and suffering. The truth is that life is ever new and dynamic. You never know where it comes from and where it goes. Every moment and each experience are new and fresh. Ruminating repeatedly on old thoughts is like eating an already chewed fruit. It has lost its punch and zest.

There's a Buddhist saying that manifesting the process of thoughts becomes a prison for self.

"The thought manifests as the word;
The word manifests as the deed;
The deed develops into habit;
And habit hardens into character.
So, watch the thought and its ways with care,
And let it spring from love
Born out of concern for all beings."
—*Anonymous Buddhist Quote*

An unexamined thought that has not sprung from love and concern limits us from experiencing the fullness of life. The only way to free ourselves from being held hostage to our "monkey minds" is to be in the present and welcome life as it is NOW. Why the emphasis on NOW? Because now is where wholeness is. The present moment is the only thing we truly have. The past is gone and will never come back. The future is elusive and is beyond anyone's grasp. Whatever you can do now happens at this moment and is where meaning and wholeness exist.

"Protect yourself from your own thoughts," said the great poet and mystic, Rumi. If we are not mindful about the thoughts in our heads, we can easily be done in by them. Our own thoughts can create conflict, restlessness and war with one's self and others. If we carefully observe our relationships, most conflicts are rooted in our passing thoughts. We come to identify ourselves with our thoughts and we defend them with our lives. How many families suffer from such conflicts? But one simple thought that is present today might be gone tomorrow. We hold tight to thoughts created in our mind or given to us by someone else. Those thoughts become our reality and we want to fit life into that reality. In the meantime, we totally miss the reality—and this means missing the gift—as it presents itself.

Threat to Wholeness

Our thoughts create past and future, thus posing as either a gift or a threat to our wholeness. Feelings of guilt, regret and depression come from our past thoughts, and thoughts of the future may create feelings of worry, fear and anxiety. It is not possible to live in the present and experience wholeness when we are caught up in the worries of past or future. The thoughts of past or future create a war within us. When each present moment is welcomed as it is, we are able to give our best and, in that process, there is calm and creativity. That does not mean the present will manifest in a certain way. It might bring anything – good, bad or ugly, but we will be able to face its entirety with an open mind. Much of our mental and emotional energy is consumed by worrying about the future or regretting one's past. This energy is diverted from creative and positive thinking with which we can potentially handle the present in a productive way.

Thinking is one of the best tools available to help us navigate through life's situations. But uncontrolled thoughts can be compared to a group of monkeys flitting around the recesses of one's skull. They begin jumping and squawking and careening about. If the monkeys (out of control thoughts) in our mind take on a life of their own, getting caught up in compulsive thinking, then our lives become out of control. The "monkey mind" thus becomes a harmful tool and poses a threat to our very existence. This is scary, but true.

Taking time to recognize how one's thoughts can become a threat to one's sanity can be a priceless exercise. Compulsive, negative, repetitive thoughts have the capacity to eat up our mental energy and leave us depleted and incapable of doing the important tasks of life. The thoughts of past or future deprive us of our focus on the present moment and compromise our performance at whatever we are doing.

Many of our thoughts are based on cultural, religious or social ideas drilled into us at various stages of life. Freeing self from the influence of such conditioning will help the experience of wholeness emerge. There is a part of us that may try to direct our life based on these inherited thoughts and ideas, but are they a true reflection of who we are as unique individuals? No. They are interpretations of life based upon what we believe. Identification with our thoughts, beliefs, and memories are only the definition given to us by others. While I live in the imaginary world of allowing my thoughts to interpret my reality, the real ME quietly slips by. Therefore, thoughts are, in a sense, a threat to my true self which is fully present in the now. When we recognize and accept that we are not the contents in our minds—not the monkeys cavorting about—we will begin to discover who we are.

As I am writing these pages, most of the U.S. and the entire world are under a "stay at home" order due to COVID-19 and the havoc it is wreaking on almost every area of life. This virus has managed to destroy people's health, their sense of financial safety as their jobs and savings are threatened, and has even taken away, in part, our sense of community and being together. We are observing Holy Week and Easter Sunday but are not able to go to church. A good number of my friends are already bored and think they are either sad or depressed. About half of Americans report they are anxious and fearful and that their mental health has declined. Social distancing has limited our physical movements outside the house. Our mental approach to social distancing has caused enormous pain and suffering. We have become problems unto ourselves. We do not know what to do, nor do we know how to deal with our thoughts and emotions about this unique and stressful time. In the absence of distraction from external activities and engagements, we are afraid to look inside and face our real selves. Our emotions, imagination and attitudes have become a source of difficulties. While some relationships are growing stronger, others are on the verge of breaking down. While some people see threats and devastation and rush out to buy toilet paper and guns, others see the gift of time and blessings as they reach out to neighbors, check on friends, and enjoy enforced quiet time. What makes one choose an attitude of blessing over a bleak outlook? Our thoughts. The way our fellow humans are handling this difficult situation represents either a threat to sanity or an invitation to wholeness.

On a walk in my neighborhood recently, a woman stopped me and started complaining about her husband. She said that she is a caregiver to her ailing husband and that she believes he behaves oddly in order to make life difficult for her. She insisted that she was certain about his intentions. I gently suggested to her that this odd behavior could be due to his ailments, but she grew upset and noted that she knew her husband and all his ways very well. Her certainty that she knew her husband well created suffering for her and probably for her husband as well. How often do we believe we know other people's thoughts and intentions? The truth is that we do not even know our own thoughts, and it is audacious to assume or pretend to know another's thoughts. Making assumptions about others' thoughts is a threat to wholeness.

If we had the ability to choose and control our thoughts, then everyone would certainly choose thoughts of bliss, joy and happiness. But sometimes thoughts arise, unbidden, and we can choose to view them as fleeting and realize that they do not define us. We are only the container through which thoughts pass. When we wake up to this reality, we will be able to accept that whatever is happening is what we want to happen, and we begin using every bit of this insight to our benefit and happiness. We then end the war with wholeness and become at peace with what is.

Life is offering us an invitation to free ourselves from all the frozen, entrenched ideas that paralyze our minds and create a mental prison. Life is offering us an invitation to tame the crowd of monkeys frolicking about our brains that make us feel crazy. When we step back and realize the limits of our minds and thoughts, we begin to align with the true God image in which we are created. That self is immensely deep, vast and whole.

> *"A war within self is the quietest but the most destructible war you will ever face. Because either you win or lose, you are left with nothing."*
>
> *Shreyansh*

Me Without I

The first time the thought "Me without I" crossed my mind, I experienced an interior surge of unknown energy. As crazy as the phrase "Me without I" might sound, it set me on a novel journey. A new-fangled search was born! The first thing I did was to Google the phrase to see if anything similar already existed. There was nothing except a poem by Rumi, the twelfth-century Sufi mystic who is greatly appreciated for his spiritual legacy, a collection of poems. Research found no other books or articles with the "Me before I" title, and I knew deep in my heart that I was on an innovative quest.

I felt the urge to ponder these philosophical questions: Who am I? What is me and what is I? Who is talking to whom? And who is observing whom? Are these two people contained in one personality or are they two aspects of a personality merged into one person? Were both equal or did one control the other? I needed to clarify this for myself. When someone asks for my introduction, I define myself by my name, gender, nationality, race, religion, height, weight, role, occupation, qualifications, interests, and hobbies. These are the descriptions of I, given to me by the world into which I was born. Am I all these definitions? Yes, but there is more to me. There is something beyond that transcends all such descriptions—a something that has no name and observes the one (the "I") who embodies these other characteristics. The one who is watching the 'I' is Me, that primal force of life that took flesh in the physical form. I, on the other hand, is an acquired identity that equips each human with needed tools to navigate through life.

Me, is the basic identity that is one undivided liveliness in the whole universe, and I is the functional tool that helps us to efficiently manage our daily life activities. Is the tool important or is the one using the tool important? The answer is clear. What use is a tool in the absence of the tool user? Let me share a recent experience. I work with a 94-year-old man who is experiencing the later stages of Alzheimer's disease. He is a retired engineer and had built a major portion of his house including a huge workshop in his basement. I invited him to take me to visit his workshop. As we looked at his tools, I could see a sense of familiarity and connection between him and the tools he once used. However, in the absence of their regular use, most of the tools were collecting dust or rust in the basement workshop. Similarly, all our faculties are like tools that are used by you and me. That user is none other than the manifestation of Me in the small I.

> *"Knowledge is a tool, and like all tools, its impact is in the hand of the user". Dan Brown*

In the context of developing an understanding of "Me and I," it almost feels as if we human beings have set our tools on an automated function, often with devastating results. Certainly, automated systems and tools are valuable and useful. With today's advanced technologies, we can set our heating and cooling systems to comfortable and optimal function. In my home, automated pre-sets do a consistently good job. But the system does not have the capacity to regulate itself to changing weather patterns. It needs my attention and regulation. The concept of "Me and I" is like this. Me must constantly regulate the I. In the absence of such regulation, the I could prove to be a tool of destruction.

> *There's something beyond all such descriptions that has no name and observes the one who embodies these other characteristics. The one who is watching the 'I' is Me.*

To further understand the distinction between Me and I, consider an excerpt from the following interview of Eckhart Tolle by Paula Coppel for *Unity Magazine.*

Unity Magazine: In "The Power of Now," you describe having a dramatic personal awakening. What exactly do you think happened to you?

Tolle: For many years, I had been deeply identified with thinking and the painful, heavy emotions that had accumulated inside. My thought activity was mostly negative, and my sense of identity was also mostly negative, although I tried hard to prove to myself and to the world that I was good enough by working very hard academically. But even after I had achieved academic success, I was happy for two weeks or three and then the depression and anxiety came back.

On that night there was a disidentification from this unpleasant dream of thinking and the painful emotions. The nightmare became unbearable and that triggered the separation of consciousness from its identification with form. I woke up and suddenly realized myself as the I Am and that was deeply peaceful.

Unity Magazine: You wrote that a crystallizing thought preceded it: "I can't live with myself any longer." Tell us about that.

Tolle: Yes. It's interesting that stepping out of thought was actually triggered by a thought. At that moment, consciousness looked at the thought "I can't live with myself," and I realized there are two here—"I" and the "self I can't live with." And then there was another little thought: Who is this self that I can't live with? But there was no answer; that was the last question. And then it didn't matter. This peace had changed my perception of the world of form, too, of the external world. When I woke up the next morning, everything was beautiful and intensively alive and peaceful.

Without perceiving things through the old filter of past conditioning and conceptualization, one can sense the universe is intensely alive. Even so-called inanimate objects—I often pick up little objects and just look at them and sense that they are alive. Physicists actually confirm that what we perceive as dead matter is not dead at all. Everything is an intensely alive energy field. That aliveness is only an aspect of the aliveness or life that I am.

Eckhart Tolle's description is what I imagine and intend by the notion of Me and I. 'I' is the conditioned and conceptualized self, and Me is my real, God-created essence. The term "ego" is often used to describe the I, and "consciousness" is another synonym widely used to define and understand Me. But whatever we call the "I" versus "Me," becoming aware of the difference can be a life-changing and transformative experience.

The Story of Creation

In considering the potential of "Me before I," let's take a moment to rethink the Creation Story. In the Book of Genesis, God completes the creation of the universe in seven days *(Gen. 1:24-28)*. Note especially in verse 28 what God says after creating Adam and Eve on the seventh day:

> [24]Then God said: Let the earth bring forth every kind of living creature: tame animals, crawling things, and every kind of wild animal. And so it happened: [25] God made every kind of wild animal, every kind of tame animal, and every kind of thing that crawls on the ground. God saw that it was good. [26]Then God said: Let us make[a] human beings in our image, after our likeness. Let them have dominion over the fish of the sea, the birds of the air, the tame animals, all

the wild animals, and all the creatures that crawl on the earth.

²⁷ God created mankind in his image; in the image of God he created them; male and female[b] he created them.

²⁸ God blessed them and God said to them: Be fertile and multiply; fill the earth and subdue it.[c] Have dominion over the fish of the sea, the birds of the air, and all the living things that crawl on the earth.

We are all aware of what humans have done to the earth. The results of our subduing the earth and ruling over the other living creatures and resources of the earth are before us. In this time of pandemic and climate change, no one needs to remind us of our mishandling of creation. We have turned ourselves and the whole of creation into mere tools to satisfy our artificially created need and greed. But in a reimagined Creation Story, we could turn away from the needy, greedy I, and embrace the rightful tool master: the ME.

The Creative power of ME

In the beginning, God created humans in his own image, and their bodies and minds were beautiful. God created multiple organ systems to help maintain complex physical body functions. Humans were given minds and hearts with the capacity to love and attract the spiritual forces and electromagnetic fields of the universe. It was God's plan that with every new generation, humans would evolve and grow in the functional capacities of these fields. In a newly imagined creation, God says: "Let your brain with its visible and invisible capacities be as vast as this universe itself. Let it be of a kind to understand and co-create, to process information and imagine new possibilities. With

91

its complex abilities, each generation will be able to explore its new potential and promise. It will be able to self-organize at the individual and collective level. Its capacity to network in the relational field will help to process and regulate the flow of energy and information. In one lifetime, you will experience a glimpse of the emerging capacity of a brain." And pointing to the human heart, he said: "Let your heart have an immense capacity to regenerate all the beauty, goodness, peace, compassion, and love you need to experience the fullness of life. Your heart will give you the needed vision and help you to face your fears and demons. It will help you overcome the challenges that keep you from higher self-awareness and from becoming the best version of yourself." And God blessed the human beings and said to them: "Male or female, as I created you…be equal in your dignity and power. I give you the keys to your infinite potential. Explore and use your potential for co-creating so that you might forever experience fulfillment despite the challenges. For I will be on a journey in your life." Having said that, God took a back seat and placed humankind in the driver's seat.

Humans Created the I

When humans were given dominion over all of creation, what did they do? They took the powerful "Me" with infinite potential and turned it into the limited "I" with fewer possibilities that provided only safety and comfort. In pursuing these goals, humans focused more on the gifts of the brain and exceeded their own wildest expectations of what they could achieve! They created huge systems and structures but eventually became slaves to the very systems they created for their help and needs. Humanity's wants exceeded their needs and they managed to get anything—almost anything at all at a magical click of a mouse. In the excitement of co-creating, we human beings forgot our infinite potential and began to redefine ourselves by name, gender, nationality, race, religion, role, occupation, possessions, and education. Our spirits withered from these pursuits, and we forgot that God was part of us, walking with us on our life's journey.

While some did what they could, most of humanity got caught up in others' material pursuits and lost sight of life's larger purpose and meaning. People became so entangled in the conditioned pursuits of humanity that they even killed those who tried to stand up for their original Me. Life became a game of "who is better than whom." It became all about competition and proving to self and others. All world wars are a proof of I's need to control and prove the power of I. The small I created by humankind became so dominant and visible that the God-creative power that made this manifestation possible, became totally invisible. The I that was meant to be the medium of expression for the Me came to believe that it was all-powerful by itself. In its insanity, the I began to think of itself as bigger than, apart from, and independent of Me. And in this terrible autonomy of separate self, it lost its capacity to see the common good and treat the humanity as one whole entity.

In my own five-decade life, I can attest to the fact that I was taught to identify myself with my mind and was made to think that I am a separate individual operating on my own, creating my own world in competition with others. My upbringing and education made me forget that I was created with incredible gifts and energies of mind and heart. I forgot that I had an immense capacity for infinite creativity and happiness. I was limited by the conditioning of my language, family, culture, religion, and values. I was taught to fear life. In trying to protect my temporary physical appearance, I

We have forgotten who we really are.

ignored the tremendous potential and capabilities of my interior self. I focused so much on taking care of my visible body, that I overlooked the invisible and dormant capacities that lay within my heart and mind.

Sages and saints of all ages have indicated that we are asleep to our true nature and have forgotten who we really are. Social scientists and psychologists have described this phenomenon as false and true self. Jesus said in Matthew 10:39,[39] "[a]Whoever finds his life will lose it, and whoever loses his life for my sake will find it." Is it possible that Jesus meant we should lose the I in order to find the Me? Once you find the Me, the 'I' does not entirely vanish, but it does lose its power. It does not have energy of its own but instead becomes a tool in the hands of Me. A much more powerful tool than it when it is in its I mode.

As we noted earlier in the experience of Eckhart Tolle, we can be transformed when the 'I' finds it difficult to live with Me. Once we understand this difference and start living the Me, we are on the first step of the journey in wholeness. Wholeness is our true nature and nothing else will ever satisfy or fill that hole until we touch the wholeness itself from within. This is what Jesus meant in John 12:24: "[a]Amen, amen, I say to you, unless a grain of wheat falls to the ground and dies, it remains just a grain of wheat; but if it dies, it produces much fruit." 'I' is the grain of wheat and the many seeds is the Me. Jesus also indicates that this is what it means to be born from above. In his teachings, Jesus does not discuss morality, but continuously calls us to recognize and let go of the I that must die. In all four Gospels, Jesus is not teaching dogmas and doctrines. Instead, he shows us how to be present and see. The wisdom of life consists in acknowledging that humankind created the I, and our job is to free the Me from subservience to the I, using it only as a helpful tool.

I and Me can be viewed as the two sides to our being. The 'I' is the manifest side and the Me is the unmanifest side. The 'I' has form and humanness. Me is the unborn aspect of human nature. It is the eternal aspect of that which was in existence before the birth of the manifest one. The Me continues to exist during this birth and will continue to exist even after death. Me is the uncreated and undying aspect of our very essence. We can easily forget the unmanifest aspect of our existence because the manifest aspect can be seen, heard, touched, tasted and felt. Yet the unmanifest, unseen and ungraspable Me is the greatest gift we have. It is the silence and spirit that is not born and yet it is in that existence which we live and move. 'I' is constantly trying to survive and continue itself. Me is free of that struggle because it does not die. The desire of I is so intent upon ensuring its own survival that it ignores the Me. Every 'I' is very competitive and wants to be better than the other I. Me is always present despite being ignored by I. Its nature is presence. It is not an overpowering presence, but a silent one. The moment I begin to acknowledge the presence of Me, there's a great experience of transformation that results in radical living of the I. All the choices then are made not from the fear of survival but from the security of the eternal Me. This recognition of Me by I adds all the meaning and beauty to life because it then ceases to live from a small vision of the temporary body and mind. It begins to live from the eternal Me. The body and mind, the I, can be free to be what it can be once it recognizes the presence of Me.

Without the transforming acknowledgment of the Me, the 'I' is merely caught in a continual, competitive survival struggle. This is not a free life and is not a particularly desirable way to live out one's days. But when 'I' recognizes Me, it overcomes its need for survival and learns to live from its true depth. Such a living is a life of wholeness. Struggles cease and every moment, as it manifests, becomes a pure gift.

Once you learn to recognize the depth and dimension of Me and come to taste its beauty, then you touch the Me that is hidden in every I. In that experience, a miracle happens, and you will experience self as a vast Me. You will experience yourself as wholeness itself. The journey in wholeness is nothing but I living in full awareness and presence of Me. At this stage of awareness, the I will freely use all the definitions to describe itself but will be untouched by its vain grandiosity. At this time, 'I' becomes the servant of the Me who is the essence or life force of which we are all a part—the Divine, the One, what we call God.

I at the service of Me

What does it mean to have I at the service of Me? As I said earlier, I is not totally useless—it can be a powerful and useful tool. However, 'I' flowers into its fullness, when it is at the service of Me. Serving itself, it can dissuade and delude itself. When I identify my existence with physical body alone, I live in fear for its worldly needs. Safety, survival, and security become life's goals. Much of my energy and time are invested in achieving these goals. But that's not who I really am. This mask is acquired to help meet my physical and material needs. It provides a sense of identity in relation to others and helps me to live in the social context. As Jesus said in John 17:16 (Bible version) "They do not belong to the world any more than I belong to the world." The 'I' is in the world, but the Me is not of this world.

The Me belongs to the other world. It is that pure part as created by God. I am that image in which God created me…a God image. I am not I—it is a mere external expression of me. Me is the nature of God, in which all of us share and appear as I. Me is that part of me that does not die. In the I category, Agnes is different than Ellen. In the Me field, we are one. Totally one. No separation. In the I world we are different in terms of our personality, possessions and achievements. Once we get this straight, we will be able to use the individualized I, to serve the greater Me. I is that in-between stage about which Jesus says (Bible verse & version) "I come from the Father and I will return to the Father." We all will do so. The I must serve that Me, which will continue to live after the I is gone.

It's possible to view the difference and clarity between I and Me, especially while our world copes with the COVID-19 pandemic. During this time, everyone ran out to the grocery stores and hoarded as much as they could, so that some supply purchases had to be limited or rationed out. Gradually, however, there was a change when neighbors started sharing their goods with the other, more needy neighbors. "I" was fearful about its safety and security, so it ran to collect things for itself. When that veil falls and the "I" is able to notice the Me, the miracle of sharing then begins. The experience of dissolving I into Me is immensely fulfilling. From that experience, we can handle life in a much different way than we would otherwise. All inspirational stories of caring and sharing during the COVID-19 period are testimonies to such an experience. When you experience meaning in life, know that you are living from the sense of ME and using your I at the service of Me. Such experiences are deeply fulfilling and they create a sense of expansion of self from within. Living from the sense of Me helps connect with others at a deeper level and allows me to use my gifts and energies to contribute to making a difference in the world. The fears of I prevent us from living the Me. "I" wants to live up to the needs and expectations of social and cultural identity, whereas Me will always seeks to live in such a way that it is able to create more goodness and beauty.

There is a story that illustrates my beliefs about how I and Me are different:

> *A high government official in Japan went to see a Zen Master and asked him, "Can you explain to me, what is the difference between Me and I?"*

> The Zen Master said, "What a stupid question that is! Why are you asking me such stupid questions?"
>
> Immediately the government official responded, "How dare you talk to me like that? Don't you know who I am?
>
> And the Master said, "That's the I. Me is beyond the identity of concepts and forms. It does not get easily hurt."

"I" has clearly defined boundaries of self. Me is vast and contains everything. One is a conditional lover and the other one an unconditional lover. As we noted, I can be a very useful tool, and it would be foolish to discard the I completely, but it's important to learn the art of using the tool of I in the service of Me. How can we do this, and how do we tell the difference when discerning whether we are acting out of I versus Me? We must turn inward, reflect and examine our motivations. Just remember, 'I' is fear based, and Me is rooted in love. 'I' helps us to develop survival skills and Me helps us to move beyond these.

Recognize that you are not merely an I that operates externally, while the Me remains in an underlying state of peace and bliss. The 'I' has great functional value in helping us to develop dormant abilities and skills and in assisting us to grow as individuals who can contribute to the well-being of self and others. At this "I" stage, we use our gifts to develop our own selves and promote our own interests. When we live from the sense of Me, we are able to connect with others in an unconditional loving relationship and use our gifts and energies to make a difference by contributing to the well-being of future generations, humanity and the planet. The 'I' helps us learn to survive and keep the body alive and also has a need to feel safe and protected, admired and recognized, so it undertakes activities that make it feel secure and accomplished. When you live from the sense of I, your pursuit is worldly achievements, success, and fame. When you live from the sense of Me, the pursuit is to fully embrace the heart's character and purpose by accessing your inborn gifts and talents. You give your life meaning; purpose and meaning become more important than security and name.

Our culture and society are geared toward teaching us to develop the I, but we must initiate the journey toward Me, all on our own. Using the gifts from the 'I' dimension, we can move forward and grow. We can connect with others in unconditional loving relationships, and use our resources and talents to make a difference in the world. The challenge is to develop social intelligence and empathy skills to connect and collaborate with others and thereby use your gifts and talents to make a difference in people's lives. If, in your developmental years, you were not able to master your ego's safety needs, the fears you developed about forming relationships, will make it difficult to manifest your soul's desire for connection. But once having learned how to connect, your mission then is to contribute to the common good. Service is the nature of Me. Living from the sense of Me involves living a life of selfless service focused on future generations and the good of humanity. The challenge at this stage is to develop compassion skills, to embrace the deepest aspects of your soul's intelligence and wisdom, and to help those who are suffering, disadvantaged or are less well off than yourself. If you did not master your ego's security needs, it will be rather difficult to become a valuable member of the community and pursue Me's desire to find meaning. It is therefore essential to develop a healthy sense of I, so that we can successfully evolve to become Me. Those who fail to make this journey of transition, can make life and relationships difficult for others. On the other side, they provide fuel for those who are serious about this journey.

Let's explore the role of "I" in a bit more depth. It is important to recognize the role and value of I and to understand what it has helped us achieve thus far in life so that we will be able to use it again as needed. Seeing the benefits of I helps us to accept and use it as an important tool, and why would we throw a tool away if it works well in its owner's hands? We will find further joy in saying to the I: "You were great for me once, but now I have a new skill to make use of you for the greater good."

Living from Me Versus Living from I

How can we tell which frame of reference we are generally operating from—the I or the Me? Who is in the driver's seat of our general orientation toward life? While we know that I is a necessary tool, it is not a redundant device. It is therefore important to know and differentiate between the healthy and unhealthy I.

Following is a list of unhealthy traits indicating that we are operating from an I frame of reference, and this list is certainly not exhaustive. Individuals operating from an I orientation:

- Always need to be right
- Are never satisfied and always want more
- Desire to always win
- Need more recognition
- Hold one-sided conversations
- Lack empathy
- Exhibit unbalanced thinking patterns

A person with an unhealthy I orientation lacks resiliency. These individuals stick mostly to what "feels" comfortable and avoid what does not. They have unrealistic expectations which are held rigidly in place by emotionally charged core beliefs. They live highly stressed lives and are in constant fear and anxiety.

Conversely, a healthy ego manifests as a loving sense of self, rock solid resiliency, the ability to solve problems creatively, the capacity to develop meaningful relationships, and a sense of meaning. This type of I integrates the Me effectively and features the ability to learn to face challenging people in our live and to grow from our interaction with them. Challenges and difficulties are embraced to strengthen the relationship with self and others, thus enhancing the opportunity to find meaning. Individuals with a healthy I orientation exhibit the following traits:

- They are always ready to learn from life and to grow in strength and confidence in handling triggering situations.
- They can tolerate discomfort and regulate emotions without getting overwhelmed by them.
- They are curious to explore and to master what strengthens them, thus increasing their chances of finding new ways to cope with challenges.
- They are confident in self and others to handle challenges with inner resources.
- They do not personalize what others say or do, and they accept every human being as fallible.
- They do not take over others' problems (they don't get caught up in other people's "shit"). Instead, they offer others tools to take ownership of and to solve their problems.

Some people, perhaps because of their upbringing, are not able to develop a healthy sense of I. This may be because they bear unhealed wounds from the past—wounds that restrict their capacity to face life with openness and courage. Such people have limiting beliefs and toxic thinking patterns. They view life from a sense of lack and feel vulnerable from within to handle conflict or any other emotionally triggered situation. These wounded individuals may also have a tendency to use extreme anger and rage to get or teach others to recognize, appreciate or love them in the way they expect. People with this weak, unhealthy sense of I hold unrealistic expectations that others or life should take their pain away. They might depend on substances to provide them relief and comfort. They are not able to live with "not okay" episodes of life. Such people are not able to reflect deeply on life and consider the opportunities and new possibilities that life's challenges may hold for them. They get caught in their own repeating problematic behavior patterns. People in this stage might not be able to move to recognize the presence of Me and so they choose to stay where it seems safe—in the survival and comfort zone of I. To evolve, change and grow, it is therefore essential to heal past wounds and to develop a healthy sense of I that can be used in the service of Me.

If you suspect you are operating from an unhealthy "I Zone," here are some tips for self-introspection:

- I waste a lot of energy fighting and/or hating reality and wishing it would go away.
- I reject or deny the necessity of facing my fears and challenges.
- I mostly depend on defensive strategies like angry outbursts, avoidance, denial, wishful thinking, and the like.
- I refuse to accept or deal with what is happening in my life right now or what happened in the past and think escaping is a viable solution.
- I do not invest myself in the pain of growing, developing, or maturing from daily experiences.
- I have unrealistic expectations for what 'should' or 'must' happen.
- I believe happy relationships should be free of emotional pain, fear, and anger.

If your answer to most of these questions is yes, then know that your driver is probably I. It would be helpful to undertake the process to heal inner wounds by paying attention to painful feelings and beliefs, and then to move to live from the vastness of me.

Here is another set of statements that characterize someone who is learning to view life and operate from the Me frame of reference:

- I have a learning approach to life that helps me grow in strength and confidence in handling life's triggering situations.
- I have an ability to tolerate discomfort, enough to regulate my emotions, and I seldom get overwhelmed by them.
- I approach life with a curiosity and readiness to explore, thus increasing my chances of finding new ways to cope with challenges.
- I treat self and others as capable people who have inner resources to deal with challenges.
- I do not personalize what others say or do and regard myself and others as fallible human beings.
- I give others ownership for solving their own problems as necessary.
- I exude confidence in self and others to use our resources to handle and resolve life issues.

If you identify with these statements, then it is likely that you are living from the greater sense of self that is described as Me. Living from Me clearly provides a stronger sense of self that is capable of handling life's most extreme challenges, including death. In this state of living, you feel more comfortable taking ownership of your own problems and giving ownership to others for theirs. Living from the sense of Me and using I as a tool to get to Me is essential for happiness and meaning in life.

The experience of living from the Me, is not a mere spiritual belief or an idea. It does not work as a result in positive thinking. It is an everyday flow of life experience, that gives you an ability to be adaptive, flexible, and resilient in how you respond to challenging circumstances in your personal life and relationships.

Are you operating more from I than Me? You can measure your driver by evaluating your:

- Personal power to make great choices at any given moment.
- Capacity to regulate difficult emotions in order to remain in a healthy emotional state.
- Ability to accept what is, past or present, and to tolerate discomfort, stress, and frustration without getting triggered.

It would also be helpful to check core beliefs and expectations. These core beliefs provide us with invisible energy that moves us to make certain choices in difficult moments. Are they serving you or are you serving them? Living from the greater sense of Me helps to relate to self and others in ways that promote mutual cooperation and positive regard and connects us with the rest of humanity and creation.

God creates unique individuals in each one of us. That's the only way God gets to know the immensity of his creative power.

In order to make more space for ME in the driver's seat:

Learn to live in the now. All sages and spiritual leaders have emphasized the power of living in the here and now. Living in the present provides a greater and continued sense of awareness of every moment and allows for better choices.

Allow for a flow of insights. Become aware of what is happening inside and learn to solve your problem with greater ease.

Use intuition and inspiration. Released from the fears and insecurities of the I, you will be able to use newly freed interior creative space to get in touch with your intuition and inspiration.

Know yourself. True to what Socrates said, it is relevant even today to know and stay rooted in the true Me. Knowing one's self helps to maintain a stable sense of life amidst changing circumstances. A person who knows themself doesn't suffer from identity crises. They never lack anything nor have too much of anything.

Be happy, no matter what. The weather is what it is, people are who they are, things are how they are. Be tolerant towards that which is unchangeable. Remember the Serenity Prayer? "Lord, help me to accept the things I cannot change…"

Be successful. Be the master of your own life. Work on being successful in relationships, and in ensuring your own health and wellbeing. Direct your life by using the awareness of "I in the service of Me" as your powerful tool.

Enjoy the gifts this world has to offer. Finding Me and living from that state of consciousness is like finding life within life. Such a discovery helps to welcome all experiences of life and to use them for the joy of self and others. In spiritual terms, this can be called living in communion and collaboration with God. The changes are no more to be feared but enjoyed.

"I" Is the Foundation Upon Which Me Explores Itself

> *"Someday, after mastering the winds, the waves, the tides and gravity, we shall harness for God the energies of love, and then, for a second time in the history of the world, man will have discovered fire." Pierre Teilhard de Chardin*

As we discussed earlier, God is on a journey in our lives. He explores himself in and through us, and we through Him. For that journey to take place, we need to experience a healthy I so that we may move toward our Me/God essence. It is said that grace builds on nature. It has also been said that to let go of ego, you must have an ego to begin with. Only a strong and healthy I can pave the way to experiencing Me. Developing a healthy sense of I helps developing humans to make it through the first stages of life, find a place in society, etc. But over time, the very things that once provided a sense of accomplishment, eventually start to cause discomfort. We feel dissatisfied and begin to suspect that there's more to life than what we have. That is the I nagging you to move towards Me. One can easily misinterpret this voice and move towards achieving more and inflate the I further. Ideally, when the outward flow towards accomplishment turns inward toward transcendence, then one experiences the call for radical inner transformation. This radical transformation is nothing but I meeting Me, and recognizing its presence and value.

It has been said that the rules of the first half of life do not apply to the second half. Psychologists and social scientist have explored and defined the characteristics of the second half of life. Theoretically, at least, this part of life is supposed to be about depth, meaning, beauty and integrity. It all boils down to moving from I to Me.

It should be noted that, in the case of individuals who have not completed their growth process and established a healthy I, they are not—and never will be—able to move to Me. The unfulfilled tasks of I, will prevent them from undertaking the journey to Me. Some may misinterpret the call for radical transformation as amassing more—more possessions, more money, more degrees, or more worldly achievements. Some may even harbor the conceit that they are living from the Me. For example, when someone without a healthy 'I' pretends to be in the state of Me, it is merely a facade, and sooner or later they will become entangled in some negative experiences. They are the ones that get entangled in scandalous behavior. Hopefully, some will learn lessons that will enable them to move forward. Once an individual learns these lessons and completes the tasks of the "I" stage, then there will be a natural progression to move toward Me, toward true self, toward wholeness, toward God.

Sometimes people can be mistaken about their status. Because of their ability to speak or interpret religious concepts, they may think that they have made the journey to Me. That sense of having mastered these concepts, in and of itself, indicates that the person is still in an unhealthy I state. A feeling of enlightenment can create that impression. The 'I' has a great need to prove itself, to continually accomplish and to take pride in knowledge. It is always going somewhere to attain something. On the other hand, Me is completely at peace, because it is not driven to accomplish anything or go anywhere. Me has no potential to become more of itself, because it is whole just as it is. It does have the capacity to help the I to become embodied and express itself totally, and that expression is endless. Each time I becomes aware of Me, there is some degree of an awakening experience. Over time, ideally, I will become more comfortable with the unlimited, unending Me.

I have experienced the empowering movement from I to Me over the course of my own life, but it has taken many years and has been a journey and process. I joined the convent soon out of high school at the age of 15. My goal was to preach Jesus Christ to everyone and to exhort them to bend their knee and confess his name with their tongue. My zeal came not only from a traditional Catholic upbringing, but also from a spiritual spark that has always dwelt within me. However, after forty years, of which thirty were spent in the convent, I now enjoy a much better and more meaningful relationship with God, than when I was part of an institutional religious order. I can fully credit this change to the development of a healthy sense of I. In the convent, I was not allowed to develop I, and therefore there was no way to move toward and experience the Me. The order focused on following the rules and obeying the superiors. Achievements and roles were pre-defined and dictated. Experiencing the Me, the Divine, that part of us which is God, was only seen as possible through complete absorption of and adherence to rules, doctrine and dogma. It was a tremendous struggle to develop the I, and very difficult to move toward the Me. Outside the convent, there was still struggle, but I ultimately developed an effortless, enjoyable, and deep relationship with God. In the convent, the struggle was to satisfy needs arising from fear. Now that I have completed the tasks of the first half of life and have a satisfying sense of accomplishment, I have naturally moved to a sense of true self and Me. I have noted a similar progression in people around me who are at this stage of life. Those who have accomplished the "I" tasks of their adult life are able to move beyond them and evolve to something more.

"All the wonders you seek are within yourself." Sir Thomas Brown

Aligning I and Me

What is alignment of I and Me? Why does it really matter? Are they like the notion of Yin and Yang? How can one tell when the two are aligned? How can one tell if they are out of balance?

Being aligned is more an experience than an idea. When the I is aligned with Me, there's an inner knowledge that I am living my life according to God's plan, and am not being swayed by the fears and insecurities of the I or the world. For me, this means that I have finally grown to the point where I don't wear metaphorical masks to please people, but am fearless in expressing my true self and values. I am not easily bought by the market prices. We are open to small inner messages that tell us about our own inner alignment. We don't speak ourselves into jobs or relationships that our heart is telling us not to get into. We are able to read the alerts sent to us by God and make choices straight from the heart and not from the fear of society and other's opinions. We can easily miss these notices, if we are not aligned and simply follow the dictates of our conscious mind. These notices may appear as random coincidences, that keep occurring without any real influence from us, but there are no coincidences. I have noticed that when I am in alignment, I am close to being in bliss and feel as if I am in a state of flow. Everything feels effortless, and everything happens in such a grace-filled manner that I feel forever grateful and enamored. It is like being in a joyous state of love all the time. Everything is roses and golden. Being in alignment is such a wonderful place to live and work from.

When I is aligned with Me, I feel good and positive about myself. It feels like the power of love is living itself out of me. I experience enthusiasm and a flow of energy within and trust that life will flow without effort. I am not anxious or worried about the outcome of any project. Alignment of I with Me brings a deep sense of satisfaction from within. I experience abundance instead of lack. My physical and mental health improve. My life brims with passion and I begin to feel the true freedom from which I conduct all my daily affairs. Abraham Lincoln said, "If I had six hours to cut down a tree, I would spend four hours sharpening the axe." In other words, he was making sure his tool could do the job, making sure everything was aligned so that his larger purpose could be well accomplished. I is a tool at the service of Me. Aligning I and Me, heart and mind, lower self with higher self, are all one and the same.

When I am not in alignment, everything is just the opposite. Nothing seems to work out right and everything takes ten times longer with ten times the effort. I feel tired, cranky, unhappy, and just out of sorts with the world. I know there is something wrong, and I usually take a step back to understand what is going on—where did I misalign myself? It is not unlike a car that wobbles and steers poorly because it has hit a pothole and blown its wheel alignment. What happened there? I look for indicators or potholes that may have thrown me out of alignment.

Understand that 'I' is the temporary self, created by us to help us navigate through this life journey and Me is the permanent self, manifested in and through the I. When these are out of alignment, it is usually because of an unhealthy I. An unhealthy 'I' feeds on fear and thrives on a win/lose paradigm. It can be quite addictive and needy and likes to cling to people, places and situations. Negative emotions like envy, jealousy, guilt, anger, resentment are experienced in abundance by an unhealthy I. There are some positive feel-good emotions like excitement, elation and ecstasy, but these never last. When they go, we sink to the same disconnected, lonely feeling that existed before, which can feel devastating. The 'I' worries about what other people think and acts from an outside point of view as opposed to being self-directed, and just as it fears judgment, it also judges others, creating separation, loneliness and isolation. We can easily be tricked by a misaligned I, convincing us that revenge is justified, that our judgments of others are realistic, that our greed is just a healthy desire and that extreme vanity is an expression of beauty.

By contrast, the Me is who we really are and is connected to the All That Is. It is always in the vibration of love. It operates through the paradigm of Win/Win. When we are living as Me, we feel a sense of expansion and we know that we are significant, but not in an egotistical way. This feeling is quietly powerful, humble and connected. While we may experience negative emotions and thoughts, these take place at a more superficial level because underlying these emotions is a foundation of love and a state of awareness that we are not our emotions or our thoughts. We are something far greater.

When we are operating from Me state, we experience a state of neutrality most of the time—a feeling of inner peace and serenity—while the movie of life plays out just as it does when we operate from the I state. But we are not in the movie of life from an ego-based state, riding a roller coaster of thoughts and emotions driven by ego. The Me knows that in life, things are forever changing. People, places, and situations come and go. Sometimes we get what we want and sometimes we don't, but it makes no real difference to our sense of inner peace. This is true personal power! And it is the basis for true happiness.

Learning to Live the Me

We are all unique and have a special purpose. We must stop comparing ourselves to others and honor our own uniqueness. Healer and author Catherine Wilkinson's mention of Me as Spiritual Purity, has this to say:

> *"There is only one pure thing that you can be—and that is a pure you. When something is pure, it has a strength and an effect it could not otherwise have. Think about a laser. A laser is a very pure form of light, so pure that it consists of just one frequency. This purity gives it extraordinary power. A laser can travel for miles in a straight line. It can vaporize tissue and cut through metal. Ordinary light such as torch light cannot do these things. Ordinary light is not pure; it is many things.*
>
> *When you are "pure you," do not expect to have the same effect on others that another person might have. Your individual nature is different from theirs. How you affect people is a result of your individual nature. The important thing is to become ME. Just Me. The real me.*

> *Every time you take on the goals, attitudes, thoughts, dreams, feelings or expression of another person, you risk diluting your purity. You will no longer be 100% you. You may become 78% you, or 45%. Some people have almost entirely lost touch with their True Self. They have so overloaded themselves with the expectations and thoughts of others that only a little of them remains, perhaps only 3%. Such people live lives of quiet desperation and their bio-magnetic field (aura) is extremely weak."*

So, begin to spend quality time with yourself and listen to yourself! Become aware of how much you take on other people's energy and beliefs. Your ME Self, already knows what you want and what will make you happy. Honor those things. Steve Jobs said:

> *"Your time is limited, so don't waste it living someone else's life. Don't be trapped by dogma – which is living with the results of other people's thinking. Don't let the noise of others' opinions drown out your own inner voice. And most importantly, have the courage to follow your heart and intuition. They somehow already know what you truly want to become. Everything else is secondary."*

Let's begin taking the first step in knowing Me and enjoy the journey.

Agnes in I and ME mode – The difference

As the author of these thoughts on "I and Me," it's important to note that I am not finished with my journey. There has come a time, when I have been able to distinguish between the fearful I and the powerful Me. I can sometimes see myself teetering between the two. For example, one moment, I can abide in Me, and the next moment, my ego dominates my thoughts and actions. I experience the power of vibrations stronger in Me than in I. The Me self continually challenges how I think, see the world and live my life in the I state. I have witnessed the inner struggle between I and Me, and realized how I is fearful and resists Me from manifesting its higher expressions. Through this struggle, I have seen the Me emerge as a powerful force. There's always a temptation to go back to the familiar ways of I. Especially during difficult times, there's a very strong tendency to retreat into the known dynamics of the I. In the Me territory, not every step is charted, and I fear the uncertainty of the next step.

As we noted with alignment, I realized that much of the uncertainty and confusion comes from I and not Me. The 'I' struggles against that which it cannot control. These struggles are actually birth pangs that must be experienced in order to move from I to Me. As I grow to trust in Me, I take small steps and am kind to myself, seeking help in spiritual community, practices and prayers. The 'I' struggles to find an identity in spiritual practices and community. It can hide under Me and pretend to be Me. This is a very tricky stage and requires careful self-observation. Sometimes it seems that I am living from Me because my words are meaningful, my appearance simple, and I am able to intuit situations well. All of these offer the feeling that I am operating from Me. Under these traits, however, there are old ambitions, fears, and the quest for personal name and fame that still surface from time to time. It's important to closely monitor my need for control over life situations. Whenever I pride myself on being spiritually accomplished, this might be the I raising its ugly head. When I expect divine reward as proof of living from the Me, this might be ego and not the Me. In general, I try to be kind with myself, to not judge or overthink, and to become mindfully aware of my inner state.

Through such experiences, I have learned the difference between living from I (ego) and Me and try to purify myself through moments of awareness. There has been a good deal of inner struggle and a lot of internal anger and fear, as the 'I' works hard for its survival. When I is fighting for its survival, there's a strong tendency to highlight and strengthen the achievements of the new inner knowledge and dynamics, and it is very important to be vigilant not to let I find a new identity. Awareness and gentleness towards self at this time is a great help. Learning to live from Me feels more spiritual and over time, has enabled me to recognize how fear and worry are one expression of I, while self-glorification is another expression of the same I. In the beginning, it has been difficult to recognize the difference, but moving along, it has become possible to catch myself and begin again. In some ways, this process is like learning to ride a bike: falling and wobbling along are all part of developing the new skill. So also, is the movement from I to Me.

It should be said that I have learned to face my old or former self daily. Old situations, old attitudes, and even old friends show up to attempt to keep me rooted in the I. On the path to Me, it is possible to recognize these old ways and move on in the new direction without being pulled backward. Trust and dependence on God have been a tremendous source of strength and help along this path. The struggle to accept my personality and align it with soul has been another difficult task. The end result has been beautiful. I have gained some insights to use my personality skills of thinking, feeling and acting, to connect with the divine power. Much of our thinking, feeling and acting comes and is dependent upon our cultural conditioning. The delicate balance to recognize the conditioning and open up the inner faculties to sense the soul and spirit within, has caused the breakthrough or surge of the Divine experience. Not that I have achieved or harmonized all these traits and struggles from within.

These struggles are simply the path I have chosen, and I am determined not to settle for a lesser I. A new dawn is awaiting, a new dawn of goal and direction, a seeking far greater than anything before.

The power of that vision provides the needed strength to keep moving forward, along with the knowledge that I am not on this journey alone. God is with me. Grace and compassion have been steady companions along the way, providing needed power to take one step at a time. This journey has helped me to discover a new strength that I did not know I had, a rising strength that serves as a wind beneath Me.

> *"Truths cannot be acquired from words out of other people's mouths. Before Truths can be internalized, they must come from one's own realizations and practices. Through a lifetime of personal practice, human beings are capable of revealing all of the secrets of the cosmic essence. You are your own best judge." - Buddha*

> *"the cosmic essence. You are your own best judge." - Buddha*

It's All Relative(s): Family as Spiritual Guru

Like most people, I was not brought up to view my family setting as a spiritual place. Spirituality was something special that happened in the churches, temples, convents, and monasteries—or in Himalayan caves where mystical and solitary figures dwelled. In the convent, I was taught to believe that I was special and set apart as God's sacred vessel whose purpose was to love and serve him through vows of chastity, poverty, and obedience. Marriage vows were not held to be as sacred as the religious vows. The dignity and respect offered to priests or nuns was far superior to that offered to ordinary married couples. People who gave up family life for the sake of the Kingdom of God were special people, as opposed to the people who chose or were engaged in family life.

Once I stayed overnight at a friend's house and was given a glimpse into her family life. She had four little children and held a full-time job. She was up from early morning until late at night, giving herself to the needs and demands of growing children and her job. Her husband held a full-time job and served actively as an equal part of the family's activities. I could see that their dedication, sacrifices, hard work and trust in God through the sickness and suffering of daily life was far superior to mine in the convent. My calm institutional life offered a regular schedule and a well-placed, comfortable house to live in, with people helping with various household needs such as cooking, cleaning and repairs. My only responsibility was to follow the well-planned prayer schedule and to work in a school/parish. I was never disturbed by anyone and had few worries about my physical needs. Seeing my friend's immersive, chaotic family vocation, I began to question life itself. How could I possibly be holier than my married friend? I had it easy. And yet, oddly enough, society attached more respect to my call than to hers.

Observing my friend's family vocation led to the revelation that everyday life is holy! Gone are the days when we separated life between sacred and profane. All of life is sacred! Everything reveals the glory and magnificence of God. Spiritual life is not devoid of my everyday ordinary needs and responsibilities. In fact, the two realms are intertwined. We may have different drives and desires, different choices and paths, different activities and settings, but everything in life is good. God created the universe and looked at this magnificent creation and said, "Everything is good." Who am I to say otherwise or attach grades and values to God's creation? I am here to follow and fulfill the purpose for which I was created. The Book of Romans (8:28) says: "[28] [a]We know that all things work for good for those who love God,[b] who are called according to his purpose." I now understand that family life and relationships within the family are the most obvious path in which to practice spirituality. Everything that happens, good, bad, or ugly, works for our good and helps us to become the wholly realized—and holy—individuals we are meant to be. Unfortunately, our preconceived notions and definitions of family life and relationships color our expectations. Consequently, we suffer

> *"All of life is sacred! Everything reveals the glory and magnificence of God."*

in want of those. Life and relationships are dynamic and unpredictable, changing minute by minute, and no one teaches us how to deal with or work with the daily changes and shifting conditions in life. While defined perceptions and responses provide us with a feeling of safety and spare us from the challenge of fresh thinking in every situation, they might cause us to miss out on the quality and essence of life itself.

> *"Conditional thinking narrows and creative thinking expands. The latter should build and grow on the*

strength of the first one for holistic life experience."
Anonymous

Once a friend of mine came to me in deep sorrow. She had learned that her brother had come to town with his family, and he had never informed her or gotten in touch with her. She learned about their visit from social media and was deeply hurt. "How could my brother do this to me?" she cried. "Not even a word. I would have loved to meet up with him and share an evening with his family!" I could not wrap my brain around her suffering. He had really done nothing to her. He had just come to town with his family and done some sightseeing and had a good time. For whatever reason, he had not connected with her, nor did he think it was necessary to share an evening with her. Her pain was great, and I totally understood where she was coming from. "Look at other families!" she said. "They are so happy, and all of the siblings meet and celebrate their life events, but mine is a dysfunctional family!" was her sorrowful lament.

The idealized image of a perfect, happy family seems clear to many of us, and we keep chasing this image rather than working with what we have in hand. The perfect family picture is fed to us through the media and other cultural institutions—a picture where everyone is loving, kind, healthy, attractive, personally successful in finances and relationships, accomplished in education, and contributing to the welfare of others. But the reality is often messier. There are all sorts of deviations and situations in family life that occur due to events beyond our control. These events and situations flow like a mysterious current and can provide everyone with the impetus to grow and change, but only if we accept conditions as they are— without idealistically expecting them to be different. This is not to say that there should not be an expectation of happy family life. If that is what drives you and provides you with purpose and meaning, go for it! But it's important to realize that everything that happens in the family has the potential to become raw material for spiritual growth—the growth that helps us connect with our inner self and align with that greater power called God. The way you experience life through this connection will be different and more fulfilling than when you chase lofty expectations and pursue idealized images about how family life should be.

The principles of family life and our spiritual path are one and the same. Both have the goal or intention of helping us live our lives meaningfully and happily. The innermost core in the family is relationships, which become the fertile ground on which the seeds of holiness grow. In most families, it is easier to work with one another when everyone fulfills their roles in a responsible way. However, difficulty arises when we must negotiate those roles. For example, the brother who was visiting town was expected to connect with the sister who lives in town. When that did not happen, there was pain and tension. The perfect family picture was shattered, sending out rippling undercurrents and assumptions that will define the future of this sibling relationship.

Instead of pain and mutual tension, situations such as my friends could be addressed through relationships and communication that, when practiced with integrity, transform us from within and without. Love, a non-judgmental attitude, acceptance and letting go are supposed to be the spiritual virtues that could, ideally, be employed in this situation.

Though relationships and communication are the crux and core of family life, they are not permanent and change from day to day. We lose family members and we welcome new ones. We face the pain of separation from death, while experiencing the excitement of new family members joining by birth or marriage, and these events provide us with strength, joy, and new vision, and call us to profound inner conversion. They serve as the spiritual experiences and events that call us to grow and become renewed human beings. We don't need to fall from the horse as St. Paul did in Damascus or to leave the family like Buddha. Spirituality is right in the midst of life in its rawness. Each individual in the family is getting older one day at a time and changing inside and out.

The question we must ask ourselves as individuals is: How skillful am I in engaging my family and life situations to accelerate my personal growth and to become the best version of myself? We can float above the fray, practicing various meditation methods and techniques to feel peaceful and connected. This is certainly much easier than engaging our own difficult, messy, life situations to connect with our soul and the Divine. Life itself—the dirty diapers, the arguments, the bills to pay, the hurt feelings and complicated relationships—must become our spiritual practice.

> *"You don't choose your family. They are God's gift to you as you are to them".* Desmond Tutu

The Family: Sacred Practice for Everyday Life

Our daily lives are a unique merger of the sacred and the secular, and God is found there. As much as one finds and experiences the presence of the Divine in the practice of rituals such as attending church, chanting mantras, reciting prayers, and doing yoga and meditation, God and the Sacred can be experienced in washing the dishes, balancing the checkbook, cooking a meal, welcoming extended family members, getting the car's oil changed, or assisting the kids with school work. Living a spiritual life in the family means approaching family responsibilities with contemplation, patience, dedication, and love and giving one's self totally to the task at hand. This is never easy, and more often, is quite difficult—more difficult than the disciplined and scheduled life in the monastery.

I am reminded of a story I read some time ago. A busy mom with five kids wanted to find some quiet time to say her prayers and to spend quality time with God. She failed to find even five minutes to have that special prayer time, and she felt guilty about this, asking pardon from God. She said, "Lord, I am sorry that I have not been able to make time to be with you. My hands have been full, and I can do better." The Lord replied, "I don't need those dry prayers you can recite from a book. I am enjoying being embraced by your arms in the form of your children. Just continue doing your mom chores. They are the best prayers you can offer me." This woman, let's call her "Rita," has freely chosen to give herself in love to the vocation of marriage. In her motherhood and in all the chores her role requires, love is freely and generously shared, and thus the will of God is consummated through Rita's life as a mom. In her every act of service done with love, she has opened her whole being to let love grow and mature through her. She does not feel the need to take on any extreme paths to look for God apart from her call as a Mom. This is not to say that a life of prayer or being part of a church community are not important in the life of a Mom. They are needed and essential in our lives. Indeed, it is helpful to get a break from physical chores and spend thirty minutes of silence in prayer or inward reflection. It is life-giving to belong to a worshipping community and feel supported by a community of faith-filled people. But spiritual life is not contained in those practices alone. God's presence can be experienced when one is able to become still and connect with every experience of life in a deep way. In this way, life's chores become a source of contemplation and the division between sacred and secular is merged within.

Teresa of Avila said, "God is on a journey in our lives. The Holy Spirit moves in and through us along its journey when we hold all aspects of our lives as sacred. Everything that is created by God has the touch of His hand. So how can it not but be sacred?" None of us can create our children. It is in the submission of two people to total love that the power of God comes alive in the form of a new baby. In helping raise that little life, we are fulfilling the most sacred duty of human life and God's creation. How could anything concerned with raising that life be considered less than holy? In taking care of one another, we learn to acknowledge the expansion of life in other persons and in basic human needs. When we can put aside our personal projects and plans to reach out to those needing our attention and help, when we understand one another's needs and pains, we automatically grow in virtues like compassion, service and caring.

Spiritual practice is that place where we learn to share love, care, accept, and respect, and to work for one another's welfare. In the convent, I came to understand that in addition to the three vows, the fourth vow of "community life" was the most important spiritual practice in religious life. If community life is thought to be the spiritual practice in religious life, certainly family life has an even greater spiritual possibility. Parents who provide for children and build up their God-given potential by engaging them in meaningful activities are performing their most sacred duty. No matter what they do, their children are on their minds, even when they have grown up to become adults with their own families.

Let me describe two families. The Smith family members experience unconditional love between the members. Even when things don't go well, they are able to feel valued and loved despite their weaknesses. They are supported to work on their weak areas and don't feel ashamed because of them. Everyone feels safe in one another's presence and they feel free to share their innermost secrets. They have clearly spelled out and understood rules and roles. Everyone knows what is expected of them and they have mutually agreed to be faithful to a common vision. There is enough love, trust, openness, and support to pull them through good and bad times.

On the other hand, the Heitz family members live from their past wounds and hurt. They are always walking on eggshells around each other. They never know what will make the other one melt down or create a scene. They do make efforts to gather as a family around important festivals and experience behavior rooted in unforgiveness and bitterness. They work hard to meet their physical needs and have very little laughter to go around.

On the surface, these two families could be described respectively as healthy and dysfunctional. From a spiritual perspective, we can easily recognize the sacredness in the first family. Their practices have added to the spiritual value of the family. There are many families, and every family is different. They cannot be put in strictly definable categories, but we can recognize sacred traits in families. When we approach family as a spiritual practice, there is an intentional investment to live a meaningful life. Family members in such environments have a greater possibility of becoming the best version of themselves. Not everyone is fortunate enough to grow up in such a family, but everyone has the potential to create such a setting to make up for the losses of the past.

> *"From sacred practices in religious families, we need to practice family as a religious ritual to become truly spiritual."*

Transformed by Family Practice

Recently I asked a close friend of mine, "How has family life changed you?" She told me to give her some time to put her thoughts together. A week later, this is what she wrote: "I am definitely a different person today and family life has done that to me. Until I got married, I was trying to be someone I was not. I was always trying to impress people, I was fashion obsessed, a party lover and sort of a tomboy. Since being married, the love and commitment to another person triggered a sense of responsibility in me. For the first time in my life, I felt safe in the cocoon of committed love. Before I had even realized that the honeymoon was over, I was a mom. As a mother, I had no time to be someone else. I was so awestruck by the purity of my baby that all my energies got directed toward her care and in efforts to become her mom and a friend. I got so lost in loving my little angel and husband, that I simply started living. Without much effort or intention, I had started to love these new beings in my life. Today as a mother of four children, I am amazed at my expanding capacity to love. At the birth of each child, I wondered if I would be able to love the new baby as I had loved the older one. I am amazed at the abundance of love released in my heart. From a person who had been self-obsessed, now I am taking care of six of us. It is simply amazing to see how family life has turned me into a loving, caring, patient, understanding and self-giving person. I am truly transformed."

Every human being will have similar accounts to relate. Sometimes by choice and at other times just by the inherent force of life, we are transformed by life experiences. Just as we undertake practice in other fields of our lives like sports, hobbies, and meditation, marriage and family life can also be practiced. What I mean by "practice" is an intentional discipline of life's activities and energies for the purpose of happiness and meaningfulness. The end product of all that you have engaged yourself in should bring peace and contentment. We cannot plan all the events in our lives. But while much is random or unexpected about life, we can plan our attitude, choices, and response, and that is what ultimately causes transformation.

Consider the story of Jim and Sharon. After 14 years of marriage, Jim woke up one morning. Looking at his sleeping wife, he asked himself, "Who is this woman I am sleeping next to?" He had been feeling deep pain and dissatisfaction in his life. He had no feelings for her and had been feeling disconnected and lonely for a couple of years. He did not know how to acknowledge these feelings or to figure out a way to talk with his wife, a friend, a family member, or a professional counselor about his feelings. Sharon was totally unaware of his inner turmoil. Jim plodded on for another year, and on their fifteenth wedding anniversary, he decided to write a card to let his wife know that he was not happy in the marriage. Upon receiving this shocking note, Sharon grew angry and approached Jim crying. "No! You can't do this to me!" She had been happy being his wife and could not imagine life without him. It took them a few weeks to realize that their marriage was in trouble, but once they came to accept the reality of their situation, they decided to seek help. Jim thought he was done. He had no more desire to continue with the marriage, but he wanted to do one last favor for his wife, and so he decided to go for the marriage counselling. The therapy proved helpful to both as they learned to face their own wounds and acknowledge what each had been doing wrong. Sharon had never realized that the problem had existed for some years, but she was ready to work hard to make the marriage work. When Jim saw her sincere desire to work, he decided to give his best effort, too. Both had to come up with small and big plans to improve their relationship and reorient their common life. They created small six-week plans to make a conscious effort to support one another in this venture. Their first task was to practice mutual respect by speaking politely and respectfully without accusing the other. The weeks that followed featured different goals, and their list went like this:

- Maintain emotional connection by engaging in mutually enjoyable activities.
- Practice honesty and openness in communication.
- Handle conflict by sharing thoughts without judgment or assertion that "I am right."
- Share chores at home.

In about six months, they were both beginning to feel happier and noticed that they had become different persons. They had been transformed.

This is what practicing family life is. When there is a practice, there is transformation. The practice must be adapted to the situations, happenings and needs in the family. Each person must give one hundred percent. Despite our best efforts, things will happen, and we all will experience pain and difficulties. In moments like these, it makes more sense from a spiritual standpoint to ask not, "Why did you do this to me?" but rather, "Why did this experience come my way?" As we discussed in the chapter on relationships, people come into one another's lives by the mysterious force of the universe that wants to help us become the best version of ourselves. How beautiful life would become if we could turn life's tough times into opportunities for spiritual practice instead of blaming others in our lives for not meeting our expectations. Blame and judgement are easy because they push the responsibility on "the other." Instead, we should take the responsibility—the practice—to look in the mirror, to examine our motivations, and to work towards desired goals. Undertaking this practice will produce positive results instead of fault finding.

This transformative process continues throughout our lives. No matter what size or shape the family is in, it can become fertile ground for personal transformation. Life has a default system to cause changes and these occur despite ourselves, but *intentional* changes use our energy without making us feel exhausted. Resisting change is a waste of energy that can instead be used to grow and evolve. We all have gone through these experiences one time or the other. We have an image of how our family should look or should be. We want the family members to make that picture come true. When they behave differently, the picture in our head becomes distorted. We desperately try to correct the distortion, sometimes in the form of trying to get those members to behave the way we want them to, because only that will correct the picture we have painted. Our desperate attempts to keep that picture intact make us work harder and push life in our direction, but quite often, such efforts are a losing battle. How can a small individual fight against the forces of life itself? Paying attention to life's direction and moving in that direction is much easier than struggling against life's currents. That means I must be open and ready each day to become a new and transformed person. It is said that a man never steps in the same river twice. It is also true that we never meet the same person again. If we are open to meeting this new individual both inside of ourselves and in others, then life will become an ecstatic experience.

"Transformation occurs when we open our hearts to love and make it not a demand or compulsion but a sea that moves between the shores of our souls." Anonymous

Family as an Experience of Wholeness

One Thanksgiving I travelled from St. Louis to Cincinnati with a friend and colleague. My friend was exceedingly kind and had invited me to join his family for the celebrations. On the way, he wanted to talk about his family members to help me interact with them meaningfully. He talked about each family member's personality, professions, interests, and sensitivities. That sharing opened my eyes like never before! The diverse personalities he described were like different pieces of the same puzzle. I saw in my mind's eye that each one was wonderfully crafted to be exactly who they are so that they could make the family picture whole. For the first time, I saw how people and personalities needed to be different to be part of one whole unit. Imagine how boring life and families would be if everyone did the same thing and had similar gifts and personalities.

When it comes to real life, we want everyone to be and think exactly as we do. This is the driving force behind teams, groups, tribes, and religions. We have difficulty living and working with differences. Differences challenge us. By grading and attaching values to differences, we create a ladder forcing people to climb.

Differences are meant to help us create one whole unit by letting everyone be who they are and contribute from their being, but instead we use these differences to feel superior and "get one up" on the others.

I am reminded of a family that had six children. Each of them was uniquely blessed. When it came time to take care of their elderly parents, each of them chipped in what they could. Some of them supported financially, some emotionally and some physically. It was wonderful that they all had different gifts to contribute. However, I also noticed that those who offered financial support felt superior to those who provided emotional support. I could clearly see that the parents valued emotional support as much as they valued financial support. In fact, it would not be wrong to suggest that they appreciated emotional support over financial support. Their body language revealed that very clearly. That does not mean that the financial support was not needed or was not important. Yes, it was! I could not help but reflect that the way society is set up today, we value economic factors over all other systems. People with money have more power and say in every other aspect of life. The same often goes in families, too. Thank goodness that all six of the children had different gifts and blessings to contribute to their parents to make their aging meaningful. If all of them had plenty of money, then the parents would have been deprived of the emotional and physical support they got. Of course, the family members would have hired competent caregivers, but nothing can replace the presence of children in aging parents' lives.

There are similar trends in my own biological family. All of us have gifts quite different one from the other. While one is good at social communication, the other one has shrewd business skills. One of them is very oriented toward social service and another focused-on family and the welfare of family members. Each one is doing well in their own personal and family life. However, if everyone would pool their gifts, we could potentially become a large and successful family of entrepreneurs. When we do not view the family as one whole unit but think only of our small enterprises and nuclear families, we might have to do things that we are not good at. I personally think that God wisely places us in our family so that we all need each other for growth and transformation.

> *"Even if a man has everything – money, power and the key to eternal life – he still is nothing if he is without a family to love him and for him to love". Latricia S Nelson*

Some of the most well-known and successful business families in India belong to the joint family system, a system where the support of family members and trust in their gifts and hard work can go a long way to benefit individuals and the extended family members. The family provides the fertile ground for every individual to mature and develop to their fullest potential. In Indian culture, family is always greater than an individual. In a culture that values individual independence, however, it is often difficult to work together as a family. It can be a challenge to merge individual gifts for the collective welfare, while still allowing for space and freedom for individuals to be their true selves. No perfect image or idealistic picture can hold together all aspects of such a life, but each family can discern how they could become that container where everyone has the support and opportunities to become their best selves. It is enough to know that one individual does not have everything to make it through life. We need one another and while we are many parts, we are all one body. In the Bible, the Book of Corinthians talks about this (1 Corinthians 12:12, 14-26):

> "As a body is one though it has many parts, and all the parts of the body, though many, are one body, so also Christ. [14] Now the body is not a single part, but many. [15] If a foot should say, "Because I am not

a hand I do not belong to the body," it does not for this reason belong any less to the body. [16] Or if an ear should say, "Because I am not an eye I do not belong to the body," it does not for this reason belong any less to the body. [17] If the whole body were an eye, where would the hearing be? If the whole body were hearing, where would the sense of smell be? [18] But as it is, God placed the parts, each one of them, in the body as he intended. [19] If they were all one part, where would the body be? [20] But as it is, there are many parts, yet one body. [21] The eye cannot say to the hand, "I do not need you," nor again the head to the feet, "I do not need you." [22] Indeed, the parts of the body that seem to be weaker are all the more necessary, [23] and those parts of the body that we consider less honorable we surround with greater honor, and our less presentable parts are treated with greater propriety, [24] whereas our more presentable parts do not need this. But God has so constructed the body as to give greater honor to a part that is without it, [25] so that there may be no division in the body, but that the parts may have the same concern for one another. [26] If [one] part suffers, all the parts suffer with it; if one part is honored, all the parts share its joy."

This oneness can be experienced at various levels. The ultimate truth is that we are all one human family, and we are all part of one creation and universe. Differences exist to enhance the oneness. When cells in the body detach themselves and start growing on their own, they become cancerous. Doing our best as part of the whole body is much more useful than trying to see ourselves apart from the rest and using everyone and everything just to develop that one small individual self and identity.

Family as Spiritual Guru

We all know the role of a guru in the life of a spiritual seeker. In Christian tradition, we call them spiritual directors or companions. In world religions, every religion has a form of spiritual teacher or guru whom people seek to gain spiritual wisdom or enlightenment. Some say that we are almost out of the age of gurus. We have all seen scandals and abuse among spiritual gurus of all religious traditions and genres. Now it is said that we are moving into the "age of community," an age when spiritual wisdom is sought and resides not within individuals, but within a community. To some extent, this is happening. We see people coming together in small groups and communities to unite their energies and resources towards a common cause. In a supportive community, seeking is easier and helpful.

In my own case, I have for four decades sought guidance from spiritual directors, retreats, spiritual studies, and prayer gatherings. These have all been helpful in one way or another, and I needed these experiences to help take the next step in growth as a spiritual seeker. Now I seek spiritual growth through daily life events and have come to accept every person and event as my spiritual guru. Family life is—or can be—an intense impetus for spiritual growth. Family obligations and commitments are the deepest in life and can be carried out with or without devotion and love. Through relationship struggles and family events, it is possible to learn, mature, and grow spiritually.

I am reminded of a famous story entitled "He Ain't Heavy, Father…He's My Brother." This story is said to have taken place in 1918 and can be found at www.boystown.org.

A boy named Howard Loomis had been abandoned by his mother at Father Flanagan's Home for Boys, which had opened just a year earlier. Howard had polio and wore heavy leg braces. Walking was difficult for him, especially when he had to go up or down steps. Soon, several of the home's older boys were carrying Howard up and down the stairs. One day, Father Flanagan asked Reuben Granger, one of the older boys, if carrying Howard was hard. Reuben replied, "He ain't heavy, Father... he's my brother."

In my years of caregiving, I have closely observed how families rally around their elderly loved ones and go to all lengths to take good care of them. They are very attentive and available to the needs of their aging parents. I often wondered about the friends and acquaintances of these elderly persons who leave the scene mostly because of their own life situations and concerns. This is not to dismiss the place and importance of friends in life. We need friends and they can serve as a lifeline. However, there are self-imposed obligations that only occur within family relationships. In normal life, these kinds of obligations seldom occur outside the family circle (although there are always exceptions to the rule!). But in general, families are the focus of the sacred bonds that we experience in life. While there is usually plenty of love and care to be experienced, there are no perfect families, and so it is also in families that we suffer our lives' deepest wounds and conflict.

"When we heal, we heal the next generation that follows. The pain is passed through the family line until somebody is ready to feel it, heal it and let it go". Anonymous

"Families are the compass that guide us. They are the inspiration to reach great heights, and our comfort when we falter". Brad Henry

Many people go around the world looking for spiritual enlightenment. They may seek remote gurus with magical powers or self-help experts who can provide us with a glimpse of the divine that we seek. But I view family as my spiritual guru. Every family is unique, and through the unique dynamics within each family, we grow, evolve, and ultimately become our better selves. Relationship dynamics and events within the family can be challenging, but also provide us with an opportunity to become better people. What we often fail to see is that the answers and enlightenment we seek are hidden in the messiness of our family life. For example, a family member whom we have for many years taken for granted may have the greatest insight about us and could potentially support and promote the growth we are seeking. We do not usually grow up magically upon finding the right guru. Growth is a process and a journey, and we grow along the way by learning to handle relationships and life situations. Family is the place where we least expect to find these growth opportunities—a familiar place where it is easy to fail to find the extraordinary in the ordinary. The Vietnamese Buddhist monk Thich Nhat Hanh said, "Without the mud, there can be no lotus." The lovely lotus flower needs the mud, the fungus and nutrients in the soil, and the moisture. Our souls need the family experiences that help us grow up. It is necessary to get "down and dirty" in the muddy messiness of our lives to nurture the beautiful Me growing like a lotus flower.

Once upon a time, I renounced family life, took vows of celibacy, and sought God in religious life. At the time, I did not realize that true growth happens in the experiences of love. This is not about celibacy versus sex or sex with love. In the convent, showing any human affection or attachment was considered a taboo. A celibate is supposed to express all love solely to the Divine One, and that posed a dilemma. How

> *"Without the mud,
> there can be no lotus."*

could I express love to the Divine without expressing or experiencing it from the human? Since I was born in human form, I felt I needed to experience life from human aspects. I could not imagine love in my thoughts and could not build loving relationships solely with my thoughts. As a nun, I travelled the world to visit various retreat centers and spiritual directors, but it was all in vain. While all of this was probably helpful in preparing my heart as fertile ground for the "lotus," the flower fully bloomed when I started loving and giving my all to life's daily chores and relationships. These daily chores and interactions have now acquired a new quality and meaning not only for me, but also for many people around me. I have learned numerous important lessons from my family, friends and people who have come into my life. I have learned from difficult experiences in relationships, and from sharing the good moments. I considered myself initially to be a selfless and thoughtful person who did many kind deeds for my family members, and at times, it seemed they were very cold and only wanted to be on the receiving end. After blaming them for years, I came to see that they were being very patient and allowed me to do things for them because it made me feel important and needed. I examined my motives and realized that what I had really wanted was some control of their lives, and I could exercise some degree of control by showering favors on them. It took me a long time to recognize that it was not my family members who needed to change, it was me! Since that epiphany, whenever I have a difficult experience with any of my family members, I have the grace to turn inside and reflect upon what is really going on. Slowly but surely, I have come to accept my woundedness and need for healing. Fifty-two years of consistent relationships have served as an important foundation, a spiritual guru, upon which I can stand and have the courage to look at myself.

Spirituality is not confined to rituals or religious practices alone. It is the byproduct of learning from our life experiences. Spirituality can be cultivated through the snapping, irritated response from a family member who tells us to stay out of things; it can be found in a humble or loving gesture, such as the gift extension of unexpected forgiveness. These experiences—not so much the expert spiritual gurus—transform and shape us into new human beings.

While some spiritual transformations are gradual, I have witnessed nearly overnight, radical transformation among my friends who have become first-time parents. They become new persons. Their values, priorities, and choices change, and they can focus their energies and attention upon the new human being in their lives. It is a magical transformation, and why would it not be considered a spiritual transformation? Dr. Shefali Tsabray in her book, The Awakened Family: A Revolution in Parenting, shares the story of her own transformation while she was raising her daughter. She advocates in her book for full family transformation through open conversations and a willingness on the part of parents to flip the script and learn from their children. She shows how the parent-child relationship can be a transforming one by allowing the parent to learn about their own childhoods and how they might be living in a constant state of fear that now gets projected onto their children. It gives parents tools to transform their fear into a portal of higher consciousness and connection. She writes, "We are here to evolve from our children. They are here to teach us how we need to grow up." That is a beautiful example of someone treating family as spiritual guru.

As I was writing this passage, I took a break and went for a walk. On the way I met a middle-aged couple from my neighborhood. The wife was almost hanging on to her husband and leaning on him. I inquired whether she was tired or perhaps feeling unwell. She smiled and replied, "Oh, no. I'm alright. I just like hanging on to him."

The man smiled and said, "She's trying to attract some extra love and attention!"

His wife turned right back to him and asserted, "I am trying to teach you how to love and care."

Isn't that the truth? We are, or should be, constantly teaching one another how to give their best. I have noticed this in families who have children with disabilities and within myself while working with the elderly that most compassion comes forth when faced with vulnerable people and vulnerability in people, unless we use blame to hide our own guilt. Each time someone asks for our love, attention, care or time, we are called forth to grow in our capacity to share those gifts. There we are surrounded by plenty of spiritual gurus right there in our surroundings, right there in our own backyards. I guess, it's all relative and relatives...

> "Everything is relative except relatives. They are absolute". Alfred Stieglitz

Boxed-In Versus Fresh Perspectives

In my role as a spiritual counselor, I once found myself in conversation with a couple who had been in a live-in relationship for five years. They seemed comfortable with their relationship as it stood and were reluctant to make any changes or move forward. I was curious about that length of time and asked them how their living together was helping them. They said they were content in getting to know each other and needed some more time before they decided to say, "I do." I was not kind to them and taunted them, sarcastically joking about whether they felt they would know each other in the next two years. They replied that maybe they would. "What happens," I asked them, "if you think you know a partner well enough after several years and decide to get married, and your partner changes the day after the marriage?" They both looked at each other as if that had not occurred to them, and they told me that they would think about it.

After meeting with them, I questioned myself. What *would* happen if one—or both—individuals changed the day after their wedding? These two individuals would probably not know how to handle the changes, and their world would collapse. They might wonder what had happened to the partner they thought they knew. The truth is that human beings change every day, and as we noted before, we never meet the same person twice. Our commitment in relationships is to the changing person and not a static person with whom we know how to behave. Life is explored daily through loving, healthy relationships that offer a committed companion with whom we can walk the journey. We humans often find it easy to see the other person from a fixed perspective based on our past experiences. But it takes ongoing courage to wake up every day and see a partner anew. I have been trying to do this over the last couple of years. Life has become more exciting by doing away with fixed ideas about how people should behave in relationships. In doing so, I have experienced the blessing of meeting a new person each time, and every day is an adventure.

Many families are simply unable to experience one another as spiritual gurus or sources of growth. Some of the episodes on Dr. Phil's show are quite painful to watch. There's so much filth and dirt in relationships. I often wonder what some individuals must be going through in their hearts to be so hurtful to members of their own family. Why are some people so much under the bondage of the past that they cannot see past it? Why is it easier to see others through the filters of the past rather than seeing them as they are in the present? Why do humans find safety in holding on to that which is gone? Why do many seem fearful to welcome the fresh and the new?

Sometimes the family setting can become a place of excess emotional baggage if members are not willing to develop new perspectives. In my experience, it is easier to employ fresh perspectives with friends while the family becomes a laundry place to wash our dirty linen. For example, once I became friendly with an older woman. I admired her for her seeming openness to learn new things, to embrace new perspectives, and to question without rigidity. However, some of her children had a hard time seeing this woman the way I did, and I realized that was because they were viewing their mother through years of emotional baggage. They were boxed in. We humans often carry so much baggage, and eventually it boxes us in.

We need family and friends because they can offer us new perspectives or even a place to embrace our demons. Slowly but surely, I am also coming to accept that when family members cannot let go of the past and are unable to develop fresh perspectives in relationships, it can harm every member. By allowing fresh opinions, we bring new life into our family. If we are not able to get out of the boxes, we have locked ourselves in and support others who are doing so, our family setting can become a breeding ground for contempt and unnecessary suffering.

It has been said that when one member in the family changes, the whole family changes. This is true in general but often becomes more visible in a time of crisis. A friend of mine once shared how her 16-year-old brother's car accident affected the whole family. They never met again at the table or undertook any family vacation. Following the accident, each family member would get their food, take it to their room, and lock the door. Each of them was trying to deal with the pain in their own way and none dared to touch or engage the other members. Each of the three children continued that pattern until the day they left home for good. One large, negative incident can affect everyone in a substantial and life-changing way. It has been my observation, however, that positive change does not always happen in the other direction. When one family member changes and experiences renewal, others may become cautious around them. It may take a long time to accept that the change is for real. When one person changes in a positive way, others are affected, but the renewed person will not enjoy their support until and unless the other family members go through similar experiences. Over the last few years, I have changed radically in all areas of my life, and I have often noticed that my family members find it difficult to deal with the "new me."

They notice a change but do not know how to respond or articulate their new or changed view or perspective of me. They seem unable to develop a new perspective. They are stuck in the past ways of behaving and reacting. It is much easier to conduct family relationships based on past knowledge. There is some safety in relating that way. Approaching everyone from where the person is today or 'now' can be rather difficult and stressful. Known actions and reactions don't take much energy. Thinking anew means pausing to observe the present moment. Not everyone is skilled at this—they may not have the time or interest and feel that it would be better to take the beaten path. But the truth is, when we take the time to be open at every given moment, the ecstasy of such openness is tremendous. It is an experience of birthing new life and expands hearts and minds. Human beings love risks and new adventures. Relating to another human being in and from the 'now' provides the same thrill and even joy that can come from adventures and risks. This new energy within us creates an experience of interior expansion that in religious language is known as a spiritual experience.

On the other hand, boxed-in views are mostly based upon the wounds and hurts of our past experiences. Relating from a place of such woundedness and "pain energy" only multiplies it and creates more pain and injuries. When we become aware of our boxed-in views and perspectives, heal ourselves and approach every given moment, person, and event from a fresh perspective, we create a powerful experience. We can raise our "spiritual frequency" by freeing ourselves from the baggage of old hurts and inner wounds. When I hold onto past wounds, I operate at a low frequency and disconnect myself from the possibility of letting higher energies flow through me. The more we clean up these wounds, the more we let the God Spirit dwell in and work through us and the greater and deeper life becomes. We must cultivate an openness to living every moment as it appears. This releases powerful creativity, contentment, and calmness, like lifting weights with the muscles of the soul. With strong muscles, our spirit connects deeply with the power of the new life that wants to move through us. Imagine how exciting life would be with newness flowing in and through us at every moment!

> *"The heart is a muscle, and you strengthen muscles by using them. The more I lead with my heart, the stronger it gets". Mark Miller.*

The Bucket of Crabs

There is a story about a crab bucket that goes like this (www. guidezone.e-guiding.com):

Once a man was walking along the beach and saw another man fishing in the surf with a bait bucket beside him. As he drew closer, he saw that the bait bucket had no lid and had live crabs inside.

"Why don't you cover your bait bucket, so the crabs won't escape?" he asked.

"You don't understand," the fisherman replied. "If there is one crab in the bucket it would surely crawl out very quickly. However, when there are many crabs in the bucket, if one tries to crawl up the side, the others grab hold of it and pull it back down so that it will share the same fate as the rest of them."

Sometimes unconsciously, we can make this story our way of family life. The bucket becomes our family unit where, through our perspectives and attitudes, we keep the others from becoming the best version of themselves. When one member wants to live life differently than the rest of us, do the family members accept, support, and encourage them, or find ways to pull them down by showing them the negatives? Our boxed-in ideas and approaches are somewhat like the crabs in the bucket. They keep others down with them. In such circumstances, we become life suckers rather than life givers. Each member in the family is going through their own struggles to get through life. Instead of seeing and appreciating their efforts, we can sometimes see them as challenges and prevent them from moving on to their next steps in life. We have not chosen our family members. They are a gift from above. God in his wisdom has put us together to help one another and to serve as stimulus for mutual growth. Each of us, by our very being, becomes a stimulus for another to grow up, to evolve, to mature spiritually. If we are together along the same path, why not support one another through life? As the 17th-century poet and novelist George Eliot (who by the way, was a woman named Mary Ann Evans!) said, "What do we live for, if not to make life less difficult for each other?"

Why do we fail to provide support that will benefit everyone? Human beings are flawed. We tend to see life and others from where *we* are and not where the other one is. Here is an example. A man calls his wife to inform her that he would be late coming home from the office. One woman says to herself, "He's called again…this is three days in a row that he has been delayed in coming home. What is happening? Is he having an affair with someone?" She is so upset that she goes to bed and pretends to be asleep when he returns home. There is another woman who feels compassion for the husband who has been delayed three days in a row. She says, "Oh honey, you are working so hard for our family. You give of yourself beyond my expectations!" As she waits for her husband's return, she cooks his favorite dish. When he arrives home, she welcomes him and listens to his stories as he freshens up and then takes him straight to

> "What do we live for, if not to make life less difficult for each other?"

the table where his favorite dish awaits. She tells him, "You must be tired! Let's relax over this meal." They enjoy a beautiful evening together, appreciating one another's company. One situation and two different responses! What's the difference? If we had interviewed multiple women, we might have several different kinds of responses. What makes each respond so differently? In the first case, the woman responded from her own perspective and could not put herself in her husband's shoes. This happens when we fail to notice our flawed human tendency to blame "the other one" and to put the blame and responsibility for our feelings on them. The first woman in the above case came from a broken home and the second one from a home where she enjoyed the security of a loving father. Those kinds of experiences have a lot to do with how each person will deal with challenges. Becoming aware of our past wounds and freeing ourselves from "the crab mentality" will ultimately help everyone in the family.

Low-energy attitudes and perspectives present among various family members are, like an undertow in a river, hidden beneath the surface, difficult to see, but capable of dragging everyone down. These negative forces can keep everyone from moving forward and becoming their best selves. In the name of family, love, and commitment, some members hold others captive, a sometimes-subtle occurrence that takes an extra sense to recognize and break free from. Whether we accept it or not, the views and opinions of family members do matter. In families where there is no direct communication, a member may hear of a conversation through a third party or hearsay, and this can cause damage, distrust, doubt, and fear. To become aware of these undercurrents, you must summon the courage and energy to name them and free yourself from them! You will be able to reclaim your inner strength and true nature.

Almost every family has a crab or two, and they can drag every other person down to remain in the low frequency created within the family. It only takes one person who is insecure from within to set this dynamic in motion. If members do not take notice of such behavior, the crab bucket mentality will begin to weaken the health and inner life of the family. It takes grace to become aware, distance oneself from any toxic engagement, and bring it to the attention of the family members. Each family member may not want to disturb the waters and may try to play it safe. They may also fear becoming the outcast by making the first move. In the final run, remaining in such an environment is not helpful nor healthy for anyone. Since families are the basic units of our lives and relationships within the family are important, it takes a lifetime of work to move from one step to the next, but it is worth the effort.

> *"The greatest gift one can bring to their family is creating a healthy container for everyone to be happy and explore their true selves." Anonymous*

Seeing Every Day and Every Person as New is a Meditation par excellence

Most of my heartaches within my biological family have come from my expectations of family members and unhealed wounds from negative experiences. I was emotionally dependent on my family members, and many favors I did for them came from this neediness to feel their love and gratitude. While I worked hard to do things for them, I also expected some form of emotional reciprocation in return, and when I did not get it, I experienced a great deal of pain. It took a long time to realize that I had bound myself with my need for their acceptance and had inflicted chains upon myself to do favors for them. This process decreased my good energy and deprived me of the better self I could have become and the positive things I could have done. In recent years, I have become aware of my inner self and how I conduct myself and my relationships in general and specifically with my family members. I have freed myself from the self-inflicted obligation to take care of adult members and this has, in turn, freed them to live their lives according to their dreams. This has decreased my heartache and brought me tremendous inner freedom and has helped my family members to grow and move along with their lives.

Growing spiritually within my family setting has not always been pretty or neat but it has been lifegiving. In fact, I noticed that my need to caretake, rescue and do favors had created a need in my family members to expect all of this from me. When I started withdrawing, I was told that I did not care for them anymore, but I saw this as a natural and human response and did not engage in a guilt trip. Instead, I honestly recognized my own goodness and weaknesses Most people will agree that family can be one's greatest strength but also one's greatest weakness. I had been operating as if family was my weakness and realized that I needed to work towards making family my strength. First, I started building up my emotional strength by doing acts of kindness towards self. I was 45 years old when I bought my first birthday gift for myself. I took swimming lessons, a process which helped me not only overcome my fear of water, but also helped me realize that fear was not in the water out there but in my mind. I applied that to the rest of the areas of my life where fear ruled, and ultimately was able to overcome all fears about life, relationships, and the future—including death. I was able to let go of a lot of baggage. I set goals and made specific plans to take care of myself. In my race to take care of others, I had abandoned my own self. This abandoned self, needed more attention from *me* than from others. I became a nurturing parent to my new self and held many conversations with the child within. That child needed lots of assurance and comfort. I learned some good parenting skills and provided that to my fearful child within. It took a few years, but I noticed some growth in that child. Having turned attention within to take care of myself taught me to stop rushing to rescue others, which in turn helped free them to solve their own problems.

When one person changes in the family, it can upset the rest of the members and the relationship dynamics. The reality is that every member must work on themselves to adjust to such changes and learn to connect in a new way. Since we are not particularly good at articulating or communicating nuanced inner dynamics, each one must deal with it in their own way. Relationship dynamics can run like a wildfire, and sometimes the only strategy you can employ is to take care of yourself and to remain calm while working on yourself. Sending prayers and good vibrations to the rest of my family members is often all I can do.

As I started changing from within, I became aware of my expectations of the family members that were causing me pain. Some of these expectations came from the picture-perfect family image acquired from society and some came from past wounds. I wrote down a list of my expectations for my picture-perfect family members, and then I let them go one by one. I examined and noted that my lens was colored by past wounds from which I was conducting my relationships. One at a time, with the help of God, I was able to heal those wounds and free myself from all expectations whatsoever. I practiced what I call "newness meditation." I wore a wrist band as a reminder that every person, moment, and situation is new, and I need to respond from the freshness of that experience. This practice has taken years and I am not fully there yet. It has helped me tremendously. I am new, the other person is new, and I am going to look at every event totally from the present. It took a great deal of awareness, energy, and attention to let go of the past and deal in the now. From a few years of practicing newness meditation, I have grown to treat everyone and everything as it is in the 'now'. This spiritual practice has expanded my heart and mind like nothing before and has helped me to experience a new surge of energy and feel connected to God and the higher spirit in a new way. I am able to use my gifts and energy for productive and creative things. I feel empowered and good from within. I am able to speak my mind as it is, without fear or blame. At the same time, I can listen to others without bias or judgment. There's a sixth sense that has become my filter which I call the Holy Spirit. I quietly ask the Holy Spirit to become my filter in every situation, so that I can act from a bigger and larger perspective.

Seeing everyone within and outside the family in a fresh way has brought me inner freedom, and I am now able to channel love in a much better way. There is an increased sense of quality in overall life events. There is less feeling of hurt and more understanding of the human condition. Instead of blaming everything and everyone else outside of myself, I have learned to turn inward and notice the folly of mind gimmicks and how the mind can succeed in keeping me operating in a constant low-energy frequency. I enjoy doing favors and thank God that I am granted the gift and opportunity to be able to do favors for others, but now there are no expectations for returns. The pure act itself has become my reward. These changes, generated from family relationship dynamics, have percolated to other areas of my life, and I am able bring this higher frequency or quality to everything I do. Life feels much better from within and without. Newness meditation has helped me tremendously and in my opinion is more advanced than any cushion meditation. It has helped me to overcome the secret conditioned dynamics operating within and to live a life of inner freedom—a much larger life than the one conditioned by past wounds and fixed ideas. The mystery and ecstasy of such living cannot be fully explained in words. It must be experienced and to experience such a transformation, one must make those efforts by one's self.

> *"I prefer wrinkled families, with wounds, with scars. These wrinkles are the fruit of fidelity in a love that was not always easy. Love isn't easy. It isn't easy. No. But the most beautiful thing that the family members can give one another is true love for a lifetime". Pope Francis*

There Is No Wound That Cannot Be Healed

As the title of this chapter states "It's All Relative(s): Family as Spiritual Guru." The dynamics present within the immediate and extended family are potentially impetus for our growth and lessons for our self-evolution. Self—which is the creative power through which we continually become new—depends on the family for its mysteriously organized raw material. The family comes into being through forces beyond our control. We cannot predict who our family members will be, nor how they will turn out to be. We have no power of choice here. God in his goodness arranges these forces and brings them together, and I believe they are in our best interests. Some of my friends believe that God does not cause things but uses them for our good. Whatever might be the truth, we do experience life that aids our becoming.

How many times do we experience conflict, misunderstanding and difficulties within our family circle and feel this is finally going to be the end, only to notice that in due time we are able to let go and come together to celebrate or support one another through crisis? I am the one who thinks that there is nothing so big that it cannot be healed. In the five decades of my life, I have seen many small and big events, and we have lived through all of them. When they happen, they seem monstrous, but as time passes, we heal. What a gift! Each time a relationship crisis strikes in the family, I become aware of my own mental chatter and internal feelings and wounds. The contents of the chatter and feelings reveal a lot to me about where I am. I pick up my worries and concerns for others and for myself in that crisis. Most of the time I find it beyond my capacity to handle even a part of these problems. Instead, I have learned to surrender them and ask the guardian angels to take the matter over and visit family members who require healing in each heart. Once I have surrendered the matter to God's grace, then I work on myself, letting the mental chatter go. Each time I catch myself preoccupied with the contents of the episode or crisis, I turn it into a prayer and surrender it to God. For me, the greatest challenge is not to react, but to wait for healing to happen. I cannot have any deadlines or time limits for this healing to occur. It happens in its own time, and I take responsibility to open myself to that healing and use any resources available to aid its speed and quality.

Sometimes I talk to a trusted friend to process my feelings and thoughts. I have learned through the years that my venting or sharing is not to collect sympathy or support for myself, but to gain an objective insight into the matter and collect multiple perspectives. That expands my mind, and I begin to see the problem beyond my personal hurts, opinions, or judgments. Venting or talking also helps me to see the fears, wounds and conditioning that are at play in specific individual behaviors. It is such a freeing experience to realize that any reaction is not directed towards me but is a result of what the person is experiencing in their own individual lives. To let healing occur, I need to hold on to the higher ground of love. Reacting happens from the other person's ground, but I can respond from an inner ground of love. From that holy ground, I can gain greater insight into the human dynamics active in individual family members and do not take anything personally. This approach holds my loved ones in compassion for what they might be going through. Acting and responding from that foundation of love allows me to maintain an inner, healing peace. We have years of trauma and wounds that need healing, and difficulties and crises hold the key to the possibility of healing. They are not to be avoided but welcomed as gifts.

> *"There are wounds that never show on the body that are deeper and more hurtful than anything that bleeds".*
> *Anonymous*

From experience I can claim that there is no emotional wound that cannot be healed. The power of healing is far superior to the power of emotional hurts or wounds. It is all too easy to get caught up in an impulsive reaction and get dragged into the lower power, but can we channel a greater power? By distancing oneself from the actual event and persons and giving needed emotional/mental space to everyone, we allow the healing to occur. Love is the highest power we have. It is difficult to remain and act from love especially when facing challenges. We get pulled away from love but must bring ourselves back into the energy of love to release the flow of healing power. By clinging to negativity and past hurts, we block these higher energies. In letting go of injuries, we must forget what wounded us, but remember the lesson we learned. As someone wise once said, "Forget what hurt you, but never forget what taught you." We can use whatever helps us to return to the inner ground of love. Prayer, religious rituals, inspirational cards, talking to a friend, journaling, music, physical exercise, watching a movie or whatever helps to change the frequency of our mind. To allow true healing to happen, we simply need to open to the possibility.

The foundations of our family life and spiritual path are the same. We seek to become enlightened on the spiritual path. The messiness of family life provides the needed raw material to enhance that enlightenment. Rather than seeking enlightenment through a one-time event or through extraordinary physical experiences or visions, we need to turn to the daily experiences and ordinariness of life in which the enlightenment is wisely wrapped. And just to be clear, enlightenment does not come in those events as a byproduct, it comes from how I embrace and respond to them. We have already discussed the importance of mindfulness in every aspect of our lives, and that applies to family life too. Mindfulness transforms family life into

> *"Forget what hurt you, but never forget what taught you."*

spiritual practice. Family then becomes our spiritual guru and teaches some of the finest lessons we can find in our lives.

Family as my spiritual guru has provided me some important teachings:

1. Every family member is unique with his or her own set of strengths, shadows, and personalities. When they act, it has less to do with me and more to do with who they are and how they are experiencing life in that given moment. My expectations of them come from who I am. This creates frustrations because asking someone to behave other than their nature is an effort in vain. We cannot harvest apples from an orange tree. I must know who my family members are and have only realistic expectations in keeping with that knowledge.

2. Whatever I do for family members is an expression of my love and duty towards them. I need to remain detached from the outcome or reciprocal expectations after completing my love duties.

3. I need not compete for love and approval from them by comparing their actions and activities. I have the capacity to draw love from its highest and fullest source, the source we call God. Human beings have only limited love to share. In seeking love from its source, I need to undertake a personal spiritual practice that is most helpful for that purpose.

4. Embodying spirituality in my being is powerful enough rather than making any efforts to teach or indoctrinate adult family members in any spiritual path.

5. I hurt others only when I am hurt. I must recognize my own woundedness and that of others in the event of a painful episode.

6. I am only a channel of love, care, forgiveness, and any other help. In as much as I allow these to flow through me, it will

make me a better person. When I hold hurts and anger and block the flow, it will prevent my growth and becoming.

7. Love is the foundation of all healthy relationships and has the power to change and transform hearts and lives. Living family life with love helps us to accept our role and responsibility as part of our duty for the growth of others and self.

8. Family is the most practical and satisfying way of practicing spiritual life. It is in the family where we learn and grow to love, care, and share.

We come into a family, we go on to create our own family, and eventually, we end up teaching our young children to create their families. All the rest is to support this endeavor. Let family be the soil where I grow and bloom to my full potential.

> *"Family is where life begins and love never ends".*
> *Anonymous*

Heart to Mouth

"[18]But the things that come out of the mouth come from the heart, and they defile. [19][a]For from the heart come evil thoughts, murder, adultery, unchastity, theft, false witness, blasphemy." –*Matthew 15:18-19*

Just when I was learning the English language in primary school, we were given an assignment. Write ten sentences on the autobiography of a pencil. I still remember to this day what I had written then. It goes somewhat like this. *I'm a pencil. I was born in a big factory. I have names like Atlas, Mango and Nataraj. I'm made of wood and graphite. I'm thin and long. They wrap my body in colored paper. After that, they pack me into a truck, and the driver takes me to many book shops. I met many friends like rulers, erasers, pens, and color pencils. Some children love me, but some children don't. Some children get angry with me when the graphite point breaks. When I'm short, some children throw me out. Some children keep me in a box. Doctors, singers, and engineers came to their current positions with my help. I'm proud to be a pencil. I love to help children.*

The memory of writing this autobiography is still alive in me because I was quite enchanted by the idea of a pencil having the ability to communicate just as I did. In my imagination, I could see pencils having a little conversation amongst themselves. My fascination with this notion continues to this day.

Recently I posted the following piece of conversation on my Facebook page. The source comes from *www.Filmsforaction.org*, a website with free internet circulation.

An imagined letter from Covid-19 to humans:

Stop. Just stop.

It is no longer a request. It is a mandate.

We will help you.

We will bring the supersonic, high-speed merry-go-round to a halt.

We will stop

the planes

the trains

the schools

the malls

the meetings

the frenetic, furied rush of illusions and "obligations"

that keep you from hearing our single and shared beating heart,

the way we breathe together, in unison.

Our obligation is to each other

As it has always been, even if, even though, you have forgotten.

We will interrupt this broadcast, the endless cacophonous broadcast of divisions and distractions, to bring you this long-breaking news:

We are not well.

None of us; all of us are suffering.

Last year, the firestorms that scorched the lungs of the earth

did not give you pause.

Nor the typhoons in Africa, China, Japan.

Nor the fevered climates in Japan and India.

You have not been listening.

It is hard to listen when you are so busy all the time, hustling to uphold the comforts and conveniences that scaffold your lives.

But the foundation is giving way

buckling under the weight of your needs and desires.

We will help you.

We will bring the firestorms to your body

We will bring the fever to your body

We will bring the burning, searing, and flooding to your lungs

that you might hear:

We are not well.

Despite what you might think or feel, we are not the enemy.

We are Messenger. We are Ally. We are a balancing force.

We are asking you:

To stop, to be still, to listen.

To move beyond your individual concerns and consider the concerns of all.

To be with your ignorance, to find your humility, to relinquish your thinking minds and travel deep into the mind of the heart.

To look up into the sky, streaked with fewer planes, and see it, to notice its condition: clear, smoky, smoggy, rainy?

How much do you need it to be healthy so that you may also be healthy?

To look at a tree, and see it, to notice its condition: how does its health contribute to the health of the sky, to the air you need to be healthy?

To visit a river, and see it, to notice its condition: clear, clean, murky, polluted? How much do you need it to be healthy so that you may also be healthy? How does its health contribute to the health of the tree, who contributes to the health of the sky, so that you may also be healthy?

Many are afraid now.

Do not demonize your fear, and also, do not let it rule you. Instead, let it speak to you—in your stillness, listen for its wisdom.

What might it be telling you about what is at work, at issue, at risk, beyond the threats of personal inconvenience and illness?

As the health of a tree, a river, the sky tells you about quality of your own health, what might the quality of your health tell you about the health of the rivers, the trees, the sky, and all of us who share this planet with you?

Stop.

Notice if you are resisting.

Notice what you are resisting.

Ask why.

Stop. Just stop.

Be still.

Listen.

Ask us what we might teach you about illness and healing, about what might be required so that all may be well.

We will help you if you listen.

Isn't it true that not only a pencil or a virus but the whole universe communicates? The grass, the flowers, the sun, the table, the bed, the water, and everything in the universe is self-communicating. Only human beings use words for the major portion of communication. It's not difficult to accept that the cosmos is constantly communicating with us in a myriad of ways. We might even argue that the words used for coronavirus derived from the imagination of human brains. While that is true, we just can't ignore the fact that the whole of life communicates constantly. Even before the dawn of human language, communication happened. Then it was all inclusive. The silence and the sounds were all part of communication. After the birth of language, we became confined to the prison of words. Restricting communication to language alone is rather very confining. Life communicates in an untold number of ways.

Let me share an incident that happened almost 20 years ago. My brother was seeking a job in a foreign country. He was sending applications directly to employers and was also working through agents. One day, one of the agents called him and told him that everything was coming together for a wonderful job and that he immediately needed to pay thirty thousand rupees for the visa and other fees. The agent specified that the fee had to be paid before the end of the office hours. Everyone in the family was excited for him! They all pooled together whatever cash they had and handed over the amount to my brother. He rushed to catch the local train to reach the agent and submit the fee. He missed the train by a just a few seconds. He hurriedly went to the bus station to take a bus instead, but the last bus had already left the station. Undeterred, my brother returned home and borrowed a motorbike from my older brother. He made it to the office barely on time and came home happily reporting that he had done his part. Nothing happened in the coming weeks, and we found out that the agent was a fraud and had vanished with the money and passport. I always remember this incident because we had not paid attention to the messages from the universe.

The universe had allowed him to miss the train and the bus, but he pushed forward and arranged for a private mode of transport to pay the fee. When we have goals and push ourselves in a given direction, we sometimes fail to see the other messages that the universe may be signaling. We often ignore such signs and communication from God, the universe, the Divine—whatever you may call it. We simply don't see it because we aren't listening. We don't have eyes to see or ears to hear, even if the message is right in front of our faces.

Life is communicating via countless ways and means. It communicates through dreams, through a feather you find on your walk, through a book that falls in front of you, and in so many other ways. Do I know how to connect, listen, and read the messages? In this section of the book, I want to explore the possibility of the human heart as the source and core of communication. Words are only a means through which to express the activity of the heart. Communication always originates in the heart and ends up in the words pronounced by our mouth. All human communication is meant to share ourselves, our love, and our ideas about life. When communication happens from the depth of the heart, it contains an untold energy that turns into a powerful means to heal and be whole. Such communication is creative and generates delight and peace.

The earlier biblical quote clearly confirms that all communication proceeds from the heart. Communication from the fragmented self is not only harmful to others, but also for self, and it loses its power to create and transform. None of us create our ideas or thoughts. They come from an unknown source. Let's give it a name: God. We are only instruments of letting those thoughts flow through us. The purer and freer we are within, the purer the thoughts and ideas that emerge and flow through us. Heart, which is the seat of love, can only carry thoughts of love, compassion, empathy, caring and sharing. Heart, in this section is also the synonym for ME. Any communication from the true me/heart, with God as the source, will have a positive effect on the people involved in that piece of communication. Communication is a complex tool that human beings use to create or destroy. Heart to mouth is simply an image or metaphor to help understand that all our communication starts from the core of our being only to express beauty and uniqueness boldly. Communicating from the heart is like providing oxygen to relationships and life events. We need to use this tool and gift wisely, lest it not become a tool of destruction, taking away the life force from within a person while he or she is still breathing.

Communication is the fabric of all relationships. It is the most important tool for daily life needs and helps us enhance our quality of life. Communication is not less than any art form, rather it is a very powerful and subtle form of art. The literary world is filled with proofs of beautiful art pieces. In the world of words, we have created and recreated our lives with every passing generation. Words that come out of us carry feelings and intentions. Intentional communication helps us to develop an increased awareness of personal energy, emotions, and thoughts. We grow every day in the skill of communication and get to experience life and relationships at a deeper level. Words, something that we so easily use in our day-to-day life, have the potential to raise our lives to another level and help us release spiritual energy. Conserving the power of words and using them to connect with the highest energy, called God energy or the Holy Spirit is no less than an art form.

"The quality of a person's life is dictated by the quality of their communication."—Ken Dyers

Why do I communicate?

Do I communicate because I was given the skill of language or do I have intention and purpose in communicating with people? Am I doing it out of a learned habit or am I mindful about why I speak and what I say? It took me some reflective time to grasp the purpose of my communication. In the past, I have communicated out of my default internal system without much reflection. The training in language helped me to learn to organize my thoughts and communicate ideas. The family and social culture in which I grew up shaped my thinking patterns and created hidden communication biases. They became filters of my perception and communication style. I subconsciously absorbed cultural knowledge, rules, beliefs, values, phobias, and anxieties, and these were interwoven in the fabric of my communication. Of course, no two people belonging to the same culture communicate in exactly the same way. Though my siblings grew up in the same culture, they communicate very differently than I do. Life experiences teach us how to modify or manipulate words to get what we want or need. As we move through life, every added experience fine tunes our ability to use thoughts and words to our advantage. Very seldom do we stop to reflect or evaluate our communication style and explore its hidden and subtle dynamics. In the past, I have spent hours in meditation and have used the gift of words to recite multiple prayers, but I never really made serious efforts to connect my daily communication as a spiritual practice. If I had done that, it would have added quality to not only my daily communication, but to life in general and to everything I ever did.

In recent years, I have started paying closer attention to life and the way I communicate. I realize that I do have the gift of speech. In layman's terms, we would call it the gift of the throat chakra. People with throat chakra are gifted orators and others like to listen to them. They carry special energy that emanates through their spoken words and these bring peace, delight, inspiration, and comfort to the listener. In addition to the gift of providing people with comfort through speech, I also enjoy people's positive feedback. This is not a bad thing in itself, however, I notice that I have developed a sixth sense as to what would make the other one happy and have grown to say exactly what I think people want to hear. There's a subtle dynamism at play. When speech comes from an expectation for approval, then it is somewhat manipulative, like a salesperson who "tells you want you want to hear." In such a situation, the listening happens not purely to hear people but to provide an accurate response in order to gain their approval. Though outwardly my communication style was fine, inwardly it was done to gain acceptance and sanction. I definitely had developed a sense about what would make people feel better, and I was pretty much able to say the exact comforting words that others wanted to hear. "Telling people want they want to hear" is not a bad trait *per se*, but it does limit your ability to communicate. The energy such communication carries is very different from the energy of pure communication that is free of psychological baggage. It has a natural flow from within and is a creative, life-giving experience. When the communication is doctored, the life within those words is not as energizing as those coming from a true heart. I realized that, in my desire to be helpful and considerate, I had developed a personality that travelled to great lengths to ensure someone else's satisfaction at the expense of finding my own voice. Communication that helps to find one's inner voice is the communication that transforms hearts. In my case, I had become a people pleaser and all my actions and words were directed by that intention. The sad thing is that I was not even aware of it. Life went on and I felt great about myself because I was socially accepted and approved. I never considered that communication was not happening from the core of my heart but rather than from my personality. This people-pleasing trait influenced my communication patterns and my life in general. I did not know who I was at the core of my being, because I was constantly looking for what made others happy. What a compromised way of living life!

In the role of a nun, this personality was veiled by holy intentions and definitions. I thought I was a selfless person, always thinking about others and their good. If someone asked me for help, it would weigh on my mind night and day. I would constantly search for ways to reach out to the person who had asked for a favor or expressed a need. Often, I found that the person who had asked for help had forgotten, and I was carrying their needs and looking for solutions that went way beyond their requirements. This communication pattern did strike me as a bit odd, but I never questioned the trait nor knew anything better. After all, I was supposed to serve the world and bring the love of Christ to all. Lately, I realize that my trait had less to do with actual problems of people and more to do with my relentless efforts to enhance good will from others. I had put my own needs, priorities, and desires on hold and spent most of my energy to further someone else's cause. It would be more accurate to say that I was not even aware of my own priorities and desires, let alone who I was. I was willingly living the life of others and giving it all away with nothing left for me, not even my own life. I was totally out of touch with who I was and what my needs or wants were, and all of my communication came from this perspective for several years.

In more recent years, I have taken time to look within, identify my wounds, heal them, and claim my true self. The purpose of my communication now is two-fold:

- To create peace and happiness
- To gain greater self-knowledge and knowledge of life

Life here is a synonym for God and ME, the higher self. Communication from this stance and intention feels totally different. I am present and open in every communication. I enjoy and learn something new every day. It energizes me and the others involved. It's free of any effort to manipulate, influence, convince, or prove. Communication has become an act and means of pleasure and creativity. It is an art form, because I enjoy the way words effortlessly take shape into ideas, phrases, emotions, and actions. I am totally in delight when engaged in a conversation. I am fully enchanted by the process of communication and mentally less focused on the words and intentions of the other. I neither want to judge, nor take responsibility for, scrutinizing others' words or intentions. As long as I am totally present from my heart, I respond from there. It has transformed the way I perceive and conduct life and relationships. There's an added sense of quality to life and everything I do. It is life-giving and transforming. It flows spontaneously and becomes a source of enjoyment both to the speaker and listener.

Learning to communicate from the heart is an ongoing process. Whenever my communication is charged with emotions or reactions, I find it a good idea to take time to address the hidden issue. Most often, these are opportunities for continued inner healing. I am also able to pick up whether the other person in communication is speaking from their personality or from their heart. This might sound a bit judgmental; however, it does not take much effort to realize the quality of communication by the peace and delight it generates.

Communication from the heart is free of arguments and debates. There's increased sharing and openness. At the end of the day, I am able to evaluate my communication by asking myself:

- Did my verbal communication flow from inner peace and happiness?
- Did it create and add more peace/happiness to others in communication with me?
- What did I learn about myself from my communication content and style?
- Is there something that I need to work on?

Ultimately, knowing self and living in peace and happiness is the end goal of human life. Therefore, the more I become aware of myself and engage in authentic communication by deeply listening to the other, the more I experience happiness emerging and manifesting in that moment. Every such experience is beautiful and mystical. I love experiences like these and want to create space for self and others to have more of such magical experiences.

How do I communicate?

Do I communicate with my head or heart? Do I communicate with a thinking mind or a loving heart? What's the difference between these two ways of communicating and what's the outcome? Should I communicate with both heart, head, and does it differ depending upon the situation? Looking back, I recognize many stages of communication that I have passed through in my life so far. I have seen the nature and function of communication change throughout life. I have noticed that these changes have redirected my energy and attention so deeply that it has given new direction and produced a positive impact on my overall mental health and quality of life.

Reflecting upon my skills and stages of communication, I would like to share some of my regress and progress of experiences. Once I had gained mastery over language, I noticed as a young adult that I wanted to use super complicated words and flowery language to impress people. The more sophisticated the words and language were, the better I felt about myself. Whether I wrote cards, made written comments in the role of a teacher, or gave speeches, it was all about sounding great, complex, brilliant, and impressive! I have no idea what I was trying to get at. My communication had nothing to do with me, but the use of words, words, and words...empty words, compound words. Most of them did not hold much meaning for me, and I am sure they had even less meaning for listeners. Yet I was elated to be noted as someone who had great language skills. What a vain way to use the gift of language!

> *"Wise men speak because they have something to say;*
> *Fools because they have to say something."—Plato*

In a position of public authority, my use of big words was an effort to impress the people I served. On the other hand, in private life as a member of a religious community where relationships were power based due to a rigid hierarchy, my communication took place out of fear and extreme caution. Communication during those years in the religious community was an experience of wasted energy. There were many hidden undercurrents that affected my use and choice of words with the nuns. How I communicated and the words I chose depended upon which caste I came from, how much money I brought in, the positions of power I held, and the person who was my community superior. And in the same way, she communicated from her caste, her affiliation with the higher-ranking superiors, her goals, and her perspective. At the back of my mind, I always weighed the pros and cons of every sentence I used. Ultimately, the goal was to get what I needed and to be spared from being misunderstood, misinterpreted, or worst of all, punished. I constantly searched for the right word, waited for the right mood of the people in authority, and presented myself from a humble place solely to get my daily needs met. While in some circumstances of my life, I used super complex words to impress people, in others I played the role of underdog and portrayed myself as humble in choice of words, tone, and communication. What a paradox! Thank goodness for the opportunity to write a book that has not only brought my own wounds to the forefront, but that has also been deeply healing within.

I never realized that my communication patterns had less to do with the listener and more to do with the speaker. The inner movements between the speaker and listener in a conversation are complex. Responsibility for the communication does not depend on the speaker alone. It is deeply connected with the listener and the dynamics in the surrounding environment. Up until that point in life, I was totally unaware of the language I was using and its impact on me as a person, as well as the quality of life it created. I guess that, as we all do, I had unconsciously developed communication patterns just to get through daily life. Communication had very little to do with my soul expression, integrity, and spirituality. These were all separate and disconnected pieces in my life. I have no intention of blaming any individual or organization from my past, but the experiences from then have helped me evolve to a new level. I needed to find my voice and myself. Every person and experience I have encountered have helped me find and share that voice. Communication from this new place is totally different. It is free of all fear, anxiety, the need to impress or manipulate, or fear of being punished. The quality of such communication is peace filled and energy generating. There's a sense of lightness and joy in my heart when I am able to communicate from the integrity of mind, heart and life. That does not mean that life is free of misunderstanding and misinterpretation, but communication is the artwork through which I express the person I am and the person I am becoming.

Probably every person goes through similar phases of change in the nature and function of communication. Sometimes we are conscious of these changes, and at other times, we are not. The changes in communication as we age have a significant impact on our overall well-being. At my current age, it does matter to me that I speak from the integrity of my being. My communication aligns words, energy, values, actions, and perspectives. It is open, nonjudgmental, and has the filter of five decades of life experience. It also finds expression in the strength and baggage of language ever since language itself has existed. Communication that is rooted in the integrity of being has unknown strength and power that affects positively all other areas of my life. Once we have healed in our being the wounds of the past generation that we carried in our communication patterns, there's total acceptance of life and others. We are at peace with where individuals are and what they are going through. Communication from such a place of healing and integrity has deep influence on those engaged in it. It generates trust in others and joy in self. You can count on your own ability to follow through on the ideas flowing through you.

Thirty years ago, I was working in a certain parish as a pastoral coordinator. One of my jobs was to ensure that the area leaders planned ongoing activities to keep their local neighborhood communities active. Each area had a leadership team made up of three to four individuals. In one of the neighborhood communities, I noticed higher participation and collaboration when the area leader, Daphne, was at the forefront. People did not respond to Raphael as much they did to Daphne. When Raphael wanted to get something done in the community, he would request Daphne to do it because people responded to her better than they did to him. Why? At one of our meetings, we questioned why people responded better to Daphne than Raphael. The answer was simple. People knew that Daphne walks her talk. She is sincerely available to the community in their time of need and not just when the activities are organized. People could count on her even outside of those activities. People are more likely to follow and support a leader whose actions are consistent with their words. That's what I mean by communicating from the heart. I don't need to be perfect with words, but wherever I am, I can match my words and actions. Living life in this way helps you play a bigger game in life and pursue extraordinary things. On the other hand, we have many instances especially in the field of politics where leaders say one thing and do exactly the opposite. It is very disheartening while at the same time presents us with a challenge and opportunity to do our part to change the situation. How does one develop the art of communicating from the heart? Having gone through my own communication evolution, the question that haunts me is: Where in the world did, I learn to communicate the way I did?

> *"Good communication is just as stimulating as black coffee, and just as hard to sleep after."*—Anne Morrow Lindbergh

Culture and Communication

Culture does condition and greatly impact communication patterns. Each culture is different, yet it has its own traits of shared language, definition of proper and improper behavior, notion of social relationship, hierarchy, and decision-making process. Assimilated cultural values color communication, and communication behavior defines culture in turn. Within a culture, there's even a subculture that each community and family develop. Having grown up in India, I inherited my communication patterns from that culture as well as from my family that hailed from the southern part of India. These patterns further got appropriated to suit my personality, gifts, and woundedness.

When I immigrated to America in my early forties, I brought with me the communication patterns I had learned and acquired in the country of my birth. Through great and painful experiences, I assimilated the cultural differences in communication. I realized that I had brought a direct communication style from my earlier culture and had to change this to effectively communicate with people in my new surroundings, where polite speech was more a standard practice than direct speech. I needed to relearn the use of language all over again! Here I am reminded of an experience. I celebrated my first Christmas in the U.S. with several colleagues. At present-opening time, I unwrapped an Indian painting and I did not particularly like it. My response was, "Oh, thanks a lot for this thoughtful gift. I do not have any taste for this kind of painting." One of my other colleagues got a pair of exercise tools. She spent 15 minutes trying to explore the exercise tools and offered tons of words of appreciation. The next day, I saw the exercise gifts dropped off at the Goodwill store. That party exemplified my initial culture shock in experiencing differences in communication. I had been quite direct, and I needed to learn to be more polite. To this very day, I keep that painting with me, not because I like it, but because it serves as a reminder of my moment of social awkwardness. I wanted to find a home in my new culture.

It's important to note that being direct has a value, and that politeness sometimes is nothing but congenial lies. The other day, one of my friends said, "Yes, we are in a culture of polite lies. Before pressing the seat button of a man on death row, the switch operator will put on the seat belt and ask the man if he is comfortable in the seat. What a mockery! The next moment the man would be turned to ashes!" The point here is not to criticize the cultural aspect of communication, but just to become aware of its inner dynamics. Every culture's communication style has its own pros and cons. As long as we are in the grip of cultural conditioning and communicate from that perspective, we will fail to experience true self and never find our authentic voice. Identifying with cultural patterns of communication can drown our true voice as well as the power of that voice. In a culturally conditioned communication, we are limited to thinking and speaking in a manner deemed culturally appropriate. True self and authentic communication can easily remain hidden under the mask of an acquired style of communication. From time to time, we should examine and become aware of the borrowed cultural filters through which we communicate and free ourselves from those filters. It is easy to get caught up in the restrictive boxes of taught language and values and to depend on them for our communication. We need to constantly learn from our own experiences and surroundings. In retrospect, I can see how culture impacts communication style and how communication impacts the person. Catching myself from time to time and seeking my true self hidden behind the words is an enriching experience—an experience worth living for! A great deal of self-awareness and growing up is possible upon examination of our spoken words and their sources.

Communication for Self-Knowledge and Awareness

As I noted before, I often catch myself communicating not from my heart but from my personality and its problems. Recently, a friend of mine offered to let me pick vegetables from her garden. My kitchen was under renovation, and I did not want to take care of the vegetables because I had other things on my agenda. However, I was not willing to state this truthfully because I did not want to offend her. So, I accepted her offer to pick the veggies with her. On the way home, I asked myself why I did this. I knew that I did not need or want the vegetables. Why didn't I say so? Why did I feel compelled to accept her kindness without stating my situation? Each time I catch discrepancies' in my communication, I ask several questions: Did I do this to connect, relate, or grow in relationship with the other person? What was I trying to prove or why was I trying to prove something? At other times, I have to ask deeper questions: Why did I feel anxious to speak my mind? Why was I getting emotionally charged? Why did I respond the way I did? Why did I not want to say something? When I sincerely look within with the help of these questions, I find underlying wounds or unresolved emotions. Moments like these become opportunities for self-awareness and inner healing. I am grateful for the grace of such transforming moments and experiences.

The personal conversations reveal more about my inner dynamics and emotional life than any self-help course or program. My daily functional communication is an eye opener about how I handle power, control, work relationships, and work pressure. No matter what type or where the communication is done, it has the potential for greater self-awareness. I consider inquiring into one's communication as a helpful means to gain deeper insight into the heart—and to heal from within. This interior inquiry changes my understanding of self and others and is non-judgmental and open. It serves more to understand the positions we are coming from than to arrive at conclusions or final judgements. Inquiry in science is a powerful tool for research and we have all gained a great deal from it. Using inquiry in personal life not only brings greater self-knowledge and awareness, it also provides fertile ground for transformation and enlightenment. In self-inquiry, the most important thing is to ask the right questions. The right questions hold the right energy to lead us to the next step in our evolution.

While writing this book, I have used inquiry extensively. Whenever a thought struck me that was worthy of writing upon, I would write the main topic and go on writing a list of questions to explore the topic. For example, when I wanted to write on the topic of communication, here are the questions I wrote down:

- What is communication?
- Why do I want to write about communication?
- What aspect of communication do I want to write about?
- Why do I communicate?

- How do I communicate?
- What does my communication style tell about me?
- How can I use that revelation to transform myself into the person I want to become?
- How will I handle inner wounds that color my communication and undertake the healing process?
- To reach that goal, what changes are required in my communication style and content?
- How can I make those needed changes possible?
- What is the end goal of this effort and exploration?
- How do I turn my everyday communication into a spiritual practice?

After writing down these questions, I carried a small notepad with me, and no matter when and where I found time, I would write down my answers and insights into these questions. I questioned myself as if I were speaking with someone else. Later, I used the answers to create the content of the chapter I was working on. The whole process has been extremely self-transforming, and I hope the same for every reader. The exercise of inquiry helped me to dig deeper and get acquainted with my unexplored self. It helped determine my level of self-knowledge and dig further to tap into the hidden knowledge of self. This helped to understand how much I knew and also to tap into the intelligence beyond my knowing. Sometimes I hit a wall, and nothing came to mind, and at other times, new information just flowed effortlessly—a flow of information providing a deep sense of knowing and completion. That's the power of inquiry. The heart of inquiry is asking questions and gaining insight. Different kinds of questions prompt different kinds of insight, but question and insight remain.

> *"Unlike seeking, which is result-oriented and rooted in a sense of dissatisfaction and incompleteness, this kind of meditative inquiry is rooted in curiosity, interest and love. Much as a lover explores the beloved, this nondual,*

nonconceptual inquiry is an act of love and devotion. Much as a child explores the world with open curiosity and wonder, this kind of inquiry is a form of play and self-discovery." —Joan Tollifson

All through history, we have heard about mystical figures retreating into quiet places and returning renewed and with newfound knowledge. Buddha sat under a tree for years, Jesus went into the desert for forty days, Henry Thoreau stayed at Walden Pond, and many others have similarly retreated to places of quiet reflection. Of the modern-day mystics, there are accounts of Sadhguru from India and Thomas Hübl from Germany who went into years of retreat and returned totally transformed. They are now world-renowned transformational leaders who have ventured to initiate unique projects to create a better world. This is the power of self-inquiry—a communication with self that enables a connection with the greater intelligence in the universe and allows that intelligence to creatively flow through. Communicating with self is a powerful act. Miracles happen in that interaction. There are vast riches hidden in the depth of our beings to be explored and shared. We are taught to learn others' theories, reproduce them in our thesis, and ensure a well-paid job at the end of it. However, every theory is the outcome of someone's audacity to inquire. Each of us have the capacity to connect with that vast field of knowledge where a new piece of knowledge is waiting to be born—if we only dare to inquire.

Let me share an extract from "Self-Inquiry for Social Change Leaders," published by *Stanford Social Innovation Review* in April 2020. Over an eighteen-month period, they conducted in-depth interviews with more than two dozen social change leaders to identify what they discovered about themselves through self-inquiry. Here's an interview by *Alker & Katherine Milligan* with Peggy Dulany, Founder and Chair of Synergos, a global organization dedicated to solving complex problems by advancing bridging leadership which builds trust and collective action.

WHAT WERE THE INITIAL REASONS YOU STARTED SELF-INQUIRY?

I have been interested in it all my life. My mother was fascinated with psychology and neuroses, and she talked about it at the dining room table. I was predisposed to be interested. I had a fair amount of therapy in my 20s and 30s, which helped me overcome some insecurities and behaviors that didn't help me along in life or made me less joyful.

In the late 1990s, I was burned out. Activists and social entrepreneurs are always pushing themselves, and I did too. I wasn't doing things to nourish myself and renew my energy and passion. So I moved to the wilderness in Montana, which allowed me to connect to a larger whole and a larger purpose. That connectedness helps me hold my hope and compassion and commitment in the midst of so many awful things happening in the world.

In the early 2000s, I did a big dive into meditation workshops with Jon Kabat-Zinn and became familiar with Otto Scharmer's U Theory. I started talking with Michael Rennie about "getting to the bottom of the U" and using the U process to do something useful in the world. We led a vision quest experience at the Montana ranch, and I found the combination of meditation, self-inquiry questions, and fasting in isolation in the wildness for 3 days to be very, very powerful. I could see how much impact it had on me and on the participants. Then we decided to do it on a regular basis and I became a guide. Many members of Synergos' network go through retreats like this that Synergos offers — and the consensus is that it is life changing. It changed my life. That's the other part that inspired me.

HOW HAS YOUR SELF-INQUIRY PRACTICE SHIFTED YOUR THINKING?

The biggest factor for me personally and for the groups we lead in retreats – to create the kinds of shifts in each of us that are needed – is to feel safe enough to be vulnerable. The tendency is to protect our wounds or to build defenses around them. That often means putting on a mask to keep ourselves safe. I had a mask. Every year, when people come to our retreats, they tell their story to protect their public self-image and omit the places where they feel scared, shame, or traumatized. When we're defensive, we go towards judgement.

If we can be curious, our imagination opens up and we become more creative. Our role is to create a safe space where people can talk about what lies underneath. And we believe that's so important because Synergos is focused on bridging leadership. To be a good bridging leader, you need to get past your inner obstacles and behaviors. Only then can we act out of our best selves in the work we do in the world, and work with others in ways that are built on trust and shared values.

WHAT DOES YOUR CURRENT SELF-INQUIRY PRACTICE LOOK LIKE?

I have not kept up with meditation as much as I should, but physical exercise is a big piece of my practice, like yoga, hiking, horseback riding, ideally in the wilderness. I have chronic anxiety and I need that endorphin release. One of my practices is to spend time with trees. The biggest thing is it forces you to slow down. Just being on the land, having my feet in the grass – that's my biggest practice.

I also really benefit from intentional group interactions like retreats. Leading these group retreats helps me learn all of the time. I try to start meetings with a short meditation or personal check-in, or sometimes recite a poem.

I am also part of a couple of different friend groups that prioritize spending meaningful time together, not just chit chat. We explore our hopes and our fears and check in with each other on where we are in our lives.

HOW HAS YOUR BEHAVIOR AND LEADERSHIP STYLE SHIFTED AS A RESULT OF SELF-INQUIRY?

I see it so clearly and I'm still working on it. I'm very driven, as most activists are. I received feedback that people thought I expected them to work as hard as I did. It really helped me step back from my expectations – first about myself, because I've burned out and I don't want to do that again – but also my colleagues. I'm more open in my life, I'm more patient.

When people feel a greater sense of wellbeing, the way they do their work is different. I make sure there is time in the workday to interact on a human level. Let's pay attention to a colleague who is facing a crisis at home. How can we be supportive? We have to be committed to being out there in the world, but we have to be human-centered.

HOW HAS YOUR PRACTICE AFFECTED YOUR WORK WITH OTHERS IN THE SOCIAL CHANGE SPACE?

Before I started doing this more personal development work, I worked in a driven way. I didn't create a safe space within which the work could happen. There's a correlation between coming to feel safe within myself, rather than scared and threatened, and the sense of security and safety that other people feel around me.

People project things onto me in terms of wealth and power. It's not necessarily true, but they project it. The more human I can be, the more difficult it is for them to maintain whatever their stereotype about what a rich person is like. So then they can interact from a place of vulnerability. That's what I mean by being a bridging leader. You're secure enough in yourself to reach out across divides to interact with all the stakeholders to create the space in which people feel comfortable saying their version of the truth. Sometimes it will be in a confrontational way. But you can listen and take in those perspectives.

It's a whole way of being based on an increased sense of agency and humility and willingness to open oneself to the other stakeholders that, as a philanthropist, I might fund rather than coming in with a fixed position. To me, philanthropy is so much more than the money applied. It's using all our assets – our personality, contacts, skill sets – and bringing those assets with us as we figure out where we put our money.

WHAT REFLECTIONS ON PERSONAL DEVELOPMENT WOULD YOU LIKE TO SHARE BASED ON ALL THAT YOU'VE SEEN AND EXPERIENCED CULTIVATING "BRIDGING LEADERS" AROUND THE WORLD?

When many people come into positions in power, that power becomes their safety. They use their power to cover up their lack of capacity. I've come to believe that ego and aggression comes out of a place of feeling wounded. Look around the world – so many countries have this type of leadership at the top.

Shifting from aggressiveness to humility is about acknowledging you don't know it all. It requires you to be curious enough to listen to what others think and understand what others have experienced, and then build a collective solution from there.

In our work with teams around the world – let's say a government ministry – their starting position is often, "We know what the solution is and what the policy should be." But what they really need is to build trust among themselves and allow themselves to be vulnerable enough to admit they don't know what the solution is. Once they begin to feel safer with each other, they can take risks and admit they don't know it all – and then together, they can come up with better answers. In our experience, that often leads to government agencies being more willing to interact with other sectors like civil society – and crucially, more willing to listen.

When people can let go of their defenses, they become humble, and that in turn attracts other people. This is bridging leadership. It's how you become an inspiring leader.

As a result of true self inquiry, we experience depth in the overall quality of life. The consistent practice of self-inquiry can help deconstruct negative habits and limiting beliefs. We grow up to cultivate more inner wisdom, self-compassion and inter-intra relationship skills. Some deep inner shifts occur spontaneously. Our life is informed with a quality of knowing that comes from deep within—the inner customized GPS. Self-inquiry is nothing less than communicating with self. Inquiry is how you do that communicating.

Communication at the Service of Life

Communication is a great gift to humanity. It helps us to organize our ideas, transform them into actions and share them to enhance the quality of our life. It makes life interesting and exciting. When communication comes to fully serve the energy of life, it gains its true power in us. Communication then is not an end, but a means to promote love, compassion, justice, peace, and unity. When I use communication to prove myself higher than the other, to control or to hurt, then my communication is nothing less than a weapon of destruction. When I used communication in my young adulthood to impress and seek approval, it was an exercise in vain. It did not bring me peace and happiness, and I am sure it did not do so to others either.

How can I use the gift of communication to create authentic power of life for self and others? It calls for conscious, consistent, and intentional effort to use this gift of voice and words. I cannot help but think of the speech of Martin Luther King: *I say to you today, my friends, so even though we face the difficulties of today and tomorrow, I still have a dream.... I have a dream that one day this nation will rise up and live out the true meaning of its creed: "We hold these truths to be self-evident; that all men are created equal."* There's no finer example of communication at the service of life. When the soul finds it true expression in words, they have deep impact not just on the day when they are spoken, but for generations into eternity. That is communication happening from heart to mouth.

Do my words carry and communicate the energy of my soul? Each time I speak from my heart and for life, words became a powerful source to create and transform life around me. When someone speaks from the authenticity of their being, you feel like listening. You are gripped not by mere words alone, but by the energy those words carry. Look at how people follow certain motivational speakers. They are hungry for something more than the words that are being dished out by these people. They are seeking an experience of the transmission of energy that heals and creates life-giving peace. I have had several such experiences of returning from a conversation that has left lingering feelings of lightness and deep joy. Life-giving communication lifts your spirits up and brings immense peace. Similarly, I have also had many experiences where I wanted to find an excuse to terminate a conversation or regretted getting caught up in others' vain communication.

Words are powered with energy and spirit. When we move beyond words and connect with the energy of the words and their origin, there's a magic of presence that creates deep connection and promotes greater life. Through experiences like these, we come to revere all of life. Through communication, we encounter the force field of our own soul. It would be helpful to turn inward and ask this question: Is my communication connected with my soul and deeper self? How do I know if the answer is yes?

In an intentional life-giving communication, there's a practice of economy of words. You use fewer but more meaningful words to say more to boost life. When we communicate while applying intention, we are able to create joy and compassion. Words have power to generate response and deep emotions. Negative emotions can destroy people's joy and kill their spirit. They can cause anxiety and stress. Just as we experience pain and hurt at others' words, we might cause the same to others through our vain or unintentional words. It is extremely important to be mindful in our communication. Communication that kills is not pro-life. It is violent. Therefore, extreme caution is necessary if we are to let our spoken words serve life.

When communication becomes a means to serve life and bring love, it becomes a virtue. The more you practice the virtue of communication, the more you will influence the quality of life. Authentic communication is one that deeply influences and transforms the people involved in it. You may measure the soul of your communication by knowing how deeply the people involved were moved and affected. It is not the quantity of our words that counts, but the quality and its impact. People are more likely to want to follow and support a person whose actions are consistent with their words. The irony is that when we are authentic, not only do others trust us, we are able to count on ourselves and bring to fruition what we have planned. This gives us inner strength to welcome more challenges. In his book, *The Four Agreements,* Michael Ruiz says: *"Your word is the power coming directly from God. Be impeccable with your word means you don't use your words to speak ill."* Speak well and speak to create life.

Communication and Underlying Problems

Problems in communication are the primary cause for most of our heartaches in relationships. Sometimes we say things we don't mean and at other times we regret saying something or wish we had said it differently. We may also misinterpret or misunderstand what the other one is saying. Such experiences cause a lot of unnecessary emotional pain to us and others. The ripple effect of such experiences compromises the quality of our daily life. Often, we communicate with the filters we already have in our default mind system. Our biases, beliefs, judgments, and sense of right and wrong are the filters through which we speak or listen. Two people can be totally on two different grounds in communication. I am sure you have had such experiences yourself. You say something and the other one understands it as totally the opposite. You try to explain your position and feel the other one just does not get you. It is because the two parties are on different grounds and each thinks theirs is the right ground. In such episodes, I used to take great pains in vain to explain my perspective in all different ways. Now I don't even attempt this anymore. When others are not on the same ground as me, I move on. I understand that the other person is on a different ground and I need to respect this and save my time or energy for something better. If and when the person gets it, they will either return or you learn to let go. This is in the context of interpersonal communication. Functional communication can be different. If the other person does not understand what you are trying to communicate, you can find ways to explain and try to learn how people understand differently.

Regarding functional communication, we have successfully developed structures and ways to find common meaning and interpretations. For example, while driving on the road, you expect people in the right turn lane to turn right. That is how everyone on the road behaves, unless someone with a lost sense of direction is on the road. Imagine how we would all be thrown out of whack without such common rules! But when it comes to interpersonal communication, though we have established words, behavior, etiquettes, and patterns to communicate, there is a lot of room for personal interpretation and emotional responses. Once I overheard a workplace conversation between two women. They were talking about their respective Valentine's Day celebrations the previous day.

"Oh, mine was a horrible one. I had expected my husband to surprise me with something special, but he simply ruined it this time," the first woman said.

"What happened?" the other woman asked.

"Well, he went very cheap," said the first woman. "Instead of getting me roses, he got me carnations. Oh boy, that set me off, and I refused to go out with him for dinner and we spent the rest of the evening each in our rooms."

'That's really very cheap of him," the other woman agreed.

The rest of the conversation followed, criticizing the guy and mudslinging at his character for ignoring the feelings and value of the lady in mention. I kept wondering about carnations and roses. What's the difference? They are both flowers. Carnations stay longer than roses. Some people even like carnations more than roses. Why should only roses represent love? Why not carnations? What a stupid way to ruin a beautiful occasion celebrating love. This example reinforces the way we communicate and projects meaning on things, causing emotional pain to ourselves. Communication that is a bridge between two hearts can become a roadblock. No one is perfect, and certainly all of us have encountered these types of barriers and problems at one time or another.

Assuming the other person's intentions or what they are trying to get at is another huge problem in communication and relationship. We've all done it. While we're listening to a friend speak, we already assume we know what is going to be said before they even finish their sentence. When we assume the other person's mind, we miss what is actually being said. That becomes a true problem in relationship. Sometimes we are in a hurry, and we try to help ourselves by assuming. At other times, we assume people will read our minds and so we refrain from expressing ourselves openly and clearly. Either situation presents problems and barriers in communicating.

It is good to be aware that there is an element of transaction underlying our communication all the time. We are either giving or receiving something. If we are aware of our hidden desires and expectations, we can be forthright in expressing them. We do not have the capacity to read someone's mind. The longer we share a relationship, the better we can read behavior accurately over time. Since we change every day, we will never be able to read someone's mind exactly at any given time. In humility, we must accept the limitation of our being and learn to be transparent and upfront in asking and stating our needs. Indirect statements and expecting the other one to take the hint are efforts in vain. This can even cause pain for everyone involved. I have a close relative who will say that she does not want any celebration on her birthday, but secretly she expects a celebration! Because of past experiences, the family members have learned to read her mind and not go by her words. After the birthday celebrations are over, she compares her birthday celebration with other birthday celebrations in the family. This is obviously a very toxic way to communicate. I am sure no one wants to have such a family member, and if we do, would like to be miles away from them. Communication that potentially can be a very intimate, enjoyable, and fulfilling act can become a source of frustration and separation.

In an effort to establish a communication connection between the heart and mouth, I want to point out the problems we face in communication and find ways to handle them. While I cannot provide an exhaustive list of communication problems here, they say that "as many mouths, so many are the problems." We should therefore attempt to become aware of the problems that can exist in personal communication. Each person will have to make the effort and move toward an authentic and integral ways of speaking and listening.

As many problems as there are in speaking, the greater are the difficulties in listening. Listening happens against the mental noise in our heads. We all have filters from which we listen. Here's an example:

> **Mark:** I'm so tired. I wish we didn't have to go to the Jones's party.

> **Martha:** You always feel tired whenever we have plans to go to a party for someone I work with.

> **Mark:** Why do you have to attack me when I share about how I feel?

> **Martha:** What's the matter with you? I'm not attacking you. I'm only commenting on what I observe and experience directly.

> **Mark:** Is that all? Give me a break. Don't I have a right to be tired?

> **Martha:** Sure, you do. Just tell me one thing. Why do you never feel tired when we're going to a party hosted by your friends?

It is easy to recognize the filters present in the above communication scenario, perhaps easier because we are not involved in the interaction ourselves. Here are a few helpful questions to become aware of personal filters in communication.

How do I rate my communication style? Why?

Do I say one thing and mean another? Why?

What difficulties do I experience in speaking my mind plainly? How can I help myself?

What do I need to heal within myself to be able to conduct transparent and authentic communication?

What are some of the best practices I need to develop in my interpersonal communication skills?

You may add more questions that might be relevant and helpful to identify your unique difficulties and filters in communication. The point is, throughout life, it is helpful to have the attitude of being a student of communication. Approaching communication from the standpoint of a student will do a great service. When we think we have mastered the language and art of communication, we may actually be stuck in a rut. Having the disposition of a student will open up new windows of learning and growth. It is always exciting to learn something new about self, life in general, and others. When we seek to learn about life and grown in wisdom, there's little room for boredom. Communication then will not be an act of mind but an outflow of life itself.

> *"Communication works for those who work at it."*
> —*John Powell*

Communication: A Spiritual Practice

The purpose of this book is to help people take spirituality from the meditation cushion to everyday life and ordinary events. When one's routine interpersonal communication is as holy as the prayers we chant, life then turns into one beautiful and wholesome experience. There will be no more desire to seek or a nagging feeling of lack or incompleteness. Life happens from the core of the soul and enhances everything we touch or do.

I am always amazed at the power of the words; how we can bring out the best in someone by our kind words or destroy someone's enthusiasm by our negative words. Words that we use in prayers are expected to connect us with God, and the same words, abused, can disconnect us with self and others. Communication influences how we experience relationships and the world. Just as attending weekly services is important, so too is awareness of our communication pattern and how we use this powerful energy of communication to create holy experiences for self and others. As stated earlier, communication is a creative force. In human beings, communication is a powerful and an energetic experience, affecting and changing individuals profoundly from the inside out.

I often relish moments of silence after an episode of interpersonal communication and ask myself a few questions. Who was I before this piece of communication and who am I after it? Has my speaking made me and the other one a better person? Changes and shifts that happen in the silence against the background of our acts of communication are profound. Our becoming is deeply affected by our communication. Turning my ordinary conversations into a sacred experience of prayer has always enchanted me. Once we learn the art of turning our ordinary communication into sacred prayers, we will not need extraordinary chants to appease or praise God. To make this happen in your life, make communication a conscious act. Each time you enter into a conversation with full awareness, you might come out of it transformed and fulfilled. We don't need extraordinary experiences of levitation or bilocation to experience the Divine. It happens in and through mundane experiences of everyday life activities—like ordinary acts of communication.

In the Book of Matthew (10:18-20), Jesus says: "and you will be led before governors and kings for my sake as a witness before them and the pagans. [19] When they hand you over, do not worry about how you are to speak or what you are to say. You will be given at that moment what you are to say. [20] For it will not be you who speak but the Spirit of your Father speaking through you." Jesus is letting us know that communication is a deep experience of letting the Holy Spirit flow and work through us. If you notice the mental chatter within yourself after a difficult conversation, you will notice words and phrases replying to themselves. A strange default process happens in our brains. There's some rethinking, regret, and even rewording that goes on. That happens more so when you get caught in the dynamics generated by the words and their energy. Most likely, you were not intentional in the moment to allow the Holy Spirit to speak through you. There's a subtle difference between your taking control of the conversation and allowing the Holy Spirit to take it over for you. In that moment, you become an instrument through which the communication happens from the higher power. The more you are an open instrument, the less you will experience regrets and rethinking. Because it was not you, your ego, or your wounds that had the speaking but the Holy Spirit, the higher frequency and vibration. No matter how much is said in this regard, the beauty and truth of this has to be experienced personally. You need to become aware in the moment and turn over control to the Holy Spirit. The results are amazing. The experience could be summed up with another quote from the Bible. Romans 8:26 says: "In the same way, the Spirit too comes to the aid of our weakness; for we do not know how to pray as we ought, but the Spirit itself intercedes with inexpressible groanings."

I could slightly reword this and say that when we do not know what to say, the Spirit himself speaks for us in words beyond our vocabulary.

I cared for a woman in her nineties. Although she died over a year ago, I think of her almost every day. She could turn a phrase on a dime and change the entire meaning of a situation, usually resulting in laughter. Her communication was very pleasant and attractive. During her hospitalization, the nurses would visit her from another floor just for a quick chat. She made everyone feel better about themselves. People loved having conversations with her. They said she was fun. It was very clear that her skills of communication were a joyful form of art that enchanted people. We all have experiences of getting carried away by various art forms. Communication, too, is an art form. The savvy communicator can use various forms of word strands, tone, and diction to make a situation more palatable. That's another spiritual dimension of communication to be realized and developed. Our communication has form and spirit. When both of them come alive in one human being, it takes on the form of creative force.

Buddha taught "right speech" as a way to end suffering. He said that right speech is "refraining from lying, divisive speech, harsh speech, and meaningless speech." When we approach communication as spiritual practice, we become more consciously skilled with words. We become deeply aware of the effects our words can have on ourselves and others. That creates alertness about our casual way of speaking. Our casual ways have become our habits. When we become conscious and make efforts to use words with greater awareness, we avoid speech that makes us "impure"—confused, muddy, self-evading, and unable to separate truth from untruth. Buddhist philosophy promotes four questions one should ask before speaking.

- Is it true and kind?
- Is it useful and timely?

- Is it conducive to concord?
- Does it improve upon the silence?

In *'The Discourse on Mindfulness Meditation,'* the Buddha asks: "And how is one made pure by verbal action?"

There is the case where a certain person, abandoning false speech, abstains from false speech. This is the rare person who can always be counted on to be truthful and honest; who never speaks in such a way as to cause discord and is both good at and enjoys making friendships; someone whom people routinely seek out because of his/her sincerity, kindness, good nature, and encouragement; and one who is always to the point and worth listening to. This is an image of a wonderful, lovable human being—the kind of person we would want for a friend, and also the one that we aspire to become. In mindful communication, we learn to be more disciplined and scrupulous with our words and we find ourselves becoming sensitive and better people. That's the end goal of any spiritual practice.

Approaching communication as contemplation is another way of making it a spiritual practice. Contemplation is vitally important for any qualitative communication. What I mean by contemplative communication is that it is an effort to connect our inner lives with the outcome of our acts of communication. We must take note of the effect our communication has in the lives of others and in the world. There is a question worth asking: Is good communication the fruit of contemplation or does contemplated communication produce fruitful relationships? It actually works either way. The more mindful we become, the greater the impact on ourselves and our relationships. Hence the goal of contemplative communication is to bridge the gap between heart and mouth. But how do we do contemplative communication? There is really no one proven method. We have to develop our own methods of contemplating along the way. Contemplation is the act of looking at something thoughtfully, so communication contemplation would be to look at our communication patterns objectively and devoid of emotions. Probably such a contemplation, done with a trusted friend, could give better results than doing it by oneself.

In the past few years, I have made conscious efforts to make communication my spiritual practice. It has brought me tremendous peace and increased the quality of my life and relationships. Naturally, I have a lesser need now to use my words for communication. I am beginning to rely on life as a whole that constantly communicates. My attitudes, choices, the way I spend my time, the books I read, the clothes I wear—everything communicates. At the beginning of this section on communication, I said that everything in the cosmos communicates, so also everything I am and do communicates. I have become mindful about everything large and small in my life, and I am not even near the end of this process. Every piece of communication reveals a new facet of life and transforms me into a new being. This is a wonderful way to live life! There is no boredom, even though the imposed Covid-19 quarantine period and its accompanying limitations has had an impact on our social and cultural lives. Ultimately, our communication is the way we perceive and think. Communication also is the way we connect with people and develop relationships. Since a major part of our lives is spent in communication and relationships, why not turn it into a spiritual practice and reap the fruits of it to make daily life peaceful, fruitful, and meaningful? Communication as spiritual practice fosters and releases great energy for compassion, presence, and self-evolution.

Communication is not a perfect gift. It is a skill that takes daily practice. In fact, a lot of practice and inner healing. We do not speak rightly because we are spiritual. We become spiritual by speaking rightly. Approaching communication from a spiritual stance helps us ask better questions and improves our capacity to perform self-inquiry. The right questions and deep inquiry further help us to engage life at a deeper level and delve into each other's uniqueness as created in the image of God. We are in the midst of race riots in the country. Racists are having proud parades. I cannot help but grieve about our incapacity to enjoy our differences. It is ironic that, while we enjoy variety in all other aspects of life, we fail to do so with one another. Treating each human being as communication of and from God will help us enjoy the beauty and depth of life itself. We are each indeed a word of and from God. If only we can put all the words together and create a beautiful story, it would be a fitting tapestry of praise and glory to God. However small a word is, it is an important link in the language of life.

> *"Communication is power. Those who have mastered its effective use can change their own experience of the world and the world's experience of them. All behavior and feelings find their original roots in some form of communication."* —Tony Robbins

Electronic Communication

A discussion on communication would be incomplete without considering the dimensions of social media and electronic/digital communication. Social media and digital communication have not only affected the way we communicate, they have changed the very fabric of communication. They are presently changing the very fabric of society. My intention in this section is to explore how we can enhance our skills and quality of communication with the help of electronics. For example, many people are consumed with the use of texting, tweeting, Facebooking, and making or receiving phone calls while in the shared company of another person. Since e-communication engages a considerable amount of our daily time and attention, it would be worthwhile to explore ways to make it a helpful tool in the journey of wholeness.

Personally, on average, I use electronic means of communication for about three to six hours daily. That's a lot of time! And younger people spend more time with "screens" than older people. Electronic communication has affected all areas of life, and like everything else in life, has both benefits and disadvantages. Let's see how we can make the electronic or virtual world work to enhance the quality of our communication.

- Do I text while driving, while with friends, or while engaged in any other activity?
- Do I talk on my cell phone while I am with a friend or family member engaged in a mutual activity?
- Do I tweet to degrade a person or to get back at people?
- What type of quotes, pictures, or videos do I share? What are my underlying intentions?
- How curious am I to find out and keep track of others from their social media postings?
- Do I post on social media to show off or to share?
- What rules do I have for myself when using e-communication?
- What is acceptable or unacceptable in e-communication?
- How would I react if a rule important to me is violated?

These are a few questions that you may personalize by adding more questions. I am deeply grateful for the opportunity to communicate with anyone in the world at any time. Being away from the family, it is not always possible to be present or share in person. YouTube and Facetime apps have made it easier to participate remotely in the important events of family and friends. E-communication provides immense possibilities to connect despite geographical distances. During this pandemic period, we have all become aware of the possibilities and have creatively used modes of e-communication extensively. Despite stay-at-home orders, our lives did not come to a complete halt. With the help of internet connections, we were able to carry on with many important activities of our lives. While e-communication is a great gift of our times, mindful use of it can help us enhance our quality of life in general. To use e-communication more mindfully, ask: How much time do I spend on electronics and how much do I really want to spend? There is no doubt that e-machines are not only altering our consciousness, they are also affecting our communication and relationships. I invite the readers to consider your communication choices and their impacts on you. Rather than being controlled automatically by the social and cultural choices, take time to think about your options. The outcome of our communication is beyond our control but making mindful choices is pretty much within our control. Let's exercise it to our benefit.

I personally prefer texting or emailing to communicating directly, especially when everything is not alright with the person with whom I am communicating. That helps me to choose my words, reflect, and re-read before sending it. Whereas, when the relationship is going fine, I enjoy spontaneous voice or face time. Usually I prefer a personal meeting and chat when we have to find a closure on a particular topic or relationship itself. Using e-communication has its limits, especially when it comes to using words to communicate emotions. In a one-on-one chat, we require fewer words because our presence communicates beyond words, but e-communication has a great potential to help us find our voice and become the voice to the voiceless. Let's be intentional in our use and choices of our means of communication.

Communication is a complex and evolving tool that takes newer shapes and expressions. If we are not careful, head can take over the heart in communication. Watch out when the mind starts weighing pros and cons, analyzing motives, and predicting unknown results. When conversations happen totally from the head, there can be an internal debate and argument going on. The chat goes something like this: *Did I say the right thing? Did I say it clearly? Did I defend myself enough? Could I have said things differently? Maybe this word or phrase would be better than that one.* There may also be some fear and anger attached to this inner debate. Each time I become aware of such mental chatter, I make an intentional effort to feel my heart. There's a total shift when I feel from the heart. The head wants to argue and prove, but the heart wants to listen and understand. The outcomes of conversations happening from head or heart are very different. When you speak from the head, you are most likely to be logical, protective, alert, guarded, to the point, defensive and fearful. In a conversation that happens from the heart, you might be irrational, emotional, crying, laughing, open, listening to understand, and vulnerable. One or more of these traits could overlap in either type of conversations, so I am not holding one over the other. We need one or both levels of communication in different situations. The ideal we need to strive for would be to align the mind with the heart. Traits of such communication would include staying open to emotions in rational conversation, being present, listening, and being vulnerable. It is equally important to be aware of our filters and strive to listen without them. The magic of heart and head alignment in communication is that you will ultimately feel loved, understood and at peace.

> *"To effectively communicate, we must realize that we are all different in the way we perceive the world and use this understanding as a guide to our communication with others."*
>
> —*Tony Robbins*

Forgiveness: Releasing the 'Me' From the 'I'

In 2011, I formally left the religious life for good. At the time, the job market seemed less promising in India than in the United States, and I wanted to return to the U.S. to find employment. I requested that the sisters not cancel my travel visa until I found a job and visa sponsor. Although they agreed to this request, both of us knew, they would indeed cancel the visa—and they did so the day after I left the convent. I was deeply hurt and angered by this, and I also felt helpless and imprisoned in a state of limbo. I simply did not know what to do. What they had done preoccupied my thoughts. No matter what I did, I could not get the nuns and their actions out of my mind. I was experiencing an internal war with them, furious and fuming over the justifications, blame and judgments that were constantly running through my mind.

Fortunately, all of this occurred during Holy Week. While I was participating in the Good Friday liturgy, something shifted deep within my soul as they read the Gospel passage from Luke 23:34, where Jesus said, "Father, forgive them, for they do not know what they are doing." Even in the face of his impending death, even in a moment of utmost suffering while hanging between life and death, Jesus could summon the sensitivity, compassion, and courage to say those words. This was certainly not coming from Jesus' human side. Jesus was channeling His divinity, the God side of Himself. As I heard those words, I knew in my heart that forgiveness was the divine presence within me, and I was a channel to release it to the world, especially when I was hurting. I was able to forgive the nuns following that moment of revelation, and ever since have been mindful about channeling forgiveness. Each time I have an opportunity to share forgiveness, I consider it a privilege, to give God a chance to flow through and dwell in my life. Who am I to stop God from working in my heart? Each experience of extending forgiveness releases and reveals the divine in me and through me. Words cannot do justice to this experience. It simply cannot be explained. It has erased my inner resistance to difficult life experiences. Individuals must experience it within the depths of their being. Sometimes we need to get out of our own way, in order to let the higher power work in us.

From analyzing and understanding my own experience, I can confidently claim that any hurt is a mirror of a strong I. How could they do this to me? They were not respectful at all! Look at what I did for them and see how they repaid me! How dare they do this! Where is the solidarity of the sisterhood they professed all these years? Does sisterhood go away the day after you walk out of their doors? What kind of a Christian witness is this? All of these, and many more such statements, kept swirling in my mind, spurring emotions such as hurt, anger, and resentment that were clearly the voice of my hurt ego and pride. From my years of service in the religious life, I had cultivated a somewhat privileged image of myself and harbored a sense of entitlement to be treated with some favor. When I did not receive the favor I sought, I was fearful and shattered, and I took comfort in all types of negative emotions. The negative emotions in me, made me feel that I was right and they were wrong. Later I came to realize that any such strong emotional experience acts as a mirror to the "I" in me. If we ever hope to live from a higher ground, the holy ground, we need to move from "I" to "Me," from ego to true self. Moving from I to me in this case would mean to acknowledge that the hurt I was experiencing was the result of my hurt emotions and not the actions taken by the nuns. They were covering their backs and their institution, by withdrawing the sponsorship of a member on her departure. Totally justified. Could I acknowledge this when the event actually happened? Certainly not. I have definitely learnt that things don't happen without a reason, they happen to teach you something.

"If you are hurt by people, you must keep in mind that they are not hurting you because you are you. They are doing it because they are them". Quote taken from Not salmon.com

Every human being knows what emotional pain or hurt feels like. It is a raw feeling—like being punched in the face by an attacker. Our heart races, lips clench, eyes rage and fists tighten. We feel as if we may burst out of our own body and flow out in a river of pain. The common understanding around hurt is that it occurs when someone does or says something hurtful. I am not sure if that entirely captures the nature of hurt, because the pain is not external. No matter what someone does, hurt and pain are experienced inside the person who is feeling it. Hurt manifests as a response to a trigger provided by someone else's behavior.

But do we have to be triggered? Consider the story of a sage who owned a fabric store. This wise man was known for his divine qualities of love and compassion. Once, a young lad decided to test his patience. He went to the store and inquired of the older man.

"How much does this shirt cost?" he asked, holding up a garment.

"That will be ten dollars, my boy," replied the sage.

The boy tore the shirt down the middle. "How much would this half-shirt cost?"

"It would still cost you ten dollars," replied the sage.

The boy tore the shirt even more and said, "If a full shirt costs ten dollars, You can have all four pieces for $2.50 a piece," responded the sage.

"That's alright, my boy. You can have all four pieces for $2.50," responded the sage.

The boy wracked his brain but could think of no more ideas to goad the sage. He bowed down and touched the man's feet, finally believing that the sage was indeed a compassionate man.

Why did the sage not respond or react to the young boy's action? If the truth is that we feel pain or become hurt by another's behavior or words, why did he not?

Hurt, anger, and bitterness originate from the wounded I. Acceptance, love, and understanding come from the peaceful Me. The more one lives from this sense of the divine Me, like the sage in the story, the more one is not easily hurt by others' deeds or words. Forgiveness becomes second nature to wise men such as this, just as it was to Jesus on the Cross.

"Pain is inevitable. Suffering is optional". Haruki Murakami

From my own experience of having forgiven the nuns, I have come to realize that forgiveness is not created by me. I am merely a channel allowing forgiveness to flow through my being. The more I extend forgiveness, the more peace dwells within me. Forgiveness is more a gift to the giver than the receiver. Forgiveness in this case has connected me with the nuns and with my own true, inner self. I have no idea how the nuns feel about it, but I have grown in my capacity to forgive ever since. This capacity has had a tremendous effect on me and opened me up to new graces and miracles from God. I will be sharing some of those as we go along. It is my woundedness that makes me block the forgiveness from flowing in and through me. Each time I experience negative emotions or find it difficult to forgive, I must stop and let go of the I so that I can free the Me. When I start living from the Me, my emotions and thoughts are very different. When the 'I' is in charge—that is contracted part of myself connected with frozen past. When I am hurt, there are a variety of tapes that play in my head: Everyone is human, we all make mistakes, people want to cover their backs, they are afraid, it will all work out. But Me is an expanded, vast self, always living in the present. The internal tapes, the restless "monkey voices," remain quiet. There's an experience of peace, forgiveness and love.

The 'I' survives and finds its identity in a collection of emotional insults; it carries its personal bruises as the fabric of its very existence. 'I' actively collects hurts and insults, even while resenting them, because without its bruises, it would be, literally, nothing. I will forgive you if you apologize to me. I never thought you would do that to me. Look how insensitive you are. Such are the interior conversation patterns of I that will forgive only when the other one acknowledges his/her fault. This is a sort of win/lose game for the I. Forgiveness undermines the existence

> *Forgiveness is more a gift to the giver than the receiver.*

of the I. According to *A Course in Miracles*, forgiveness is the way I let go of myself and remember that I am Me—the Divine in human form.

Derek Lim's story, "The Tao of Forgiveness," illustrates the essence of how forgiveness allows us to release the "Me" from "I."

> *Once there was a sage who asked his disciples to carve into potatoes the names of the people they cannot forgive—one potato for each name. Then the disciples were asked to put all of their potatoes in a sack and carry it with them at all times for one week.*

The longer time went by, the heavier the potatoes seemed to have become. To make matters worse, those carved potatoes also started to rot and smell bad. It was such an unpleasant experience for the disciples.

At the end of the week, the master asked, "So, what did you learn?"

At once the disciples told the master that they now realized that holding onto grudges only brought negative things to them. Asked how they should go about correcting it, the youngsters said they should strive their best to forgive everyone who had ever crossed them and made them angry.

The master then asked, "What if someone crosses you again after you unload this present collection of potatoes?"

The disciples suddenly felt terrified at the thought of having to start all over again with new potatoes, week after week.

"What can Tao do if there are still other people crossing us? We cannot control what other people do to us!" they asked in fear.

At which point the master replied, "We haven't even reached the Tao's realm yet. So far, we only discussed the conventional way to approach forgiveness, that is, to strive to forgive. Striving is difficult. In Tao, there is no striving."

Seeing the disciples completely at a loss then, the master further suggested, "If the negative feelings are the potatoes, what is the sack?"

> *The disciples finally grasped it, "Ahh, the sack is something that allows me to hold on to the negativity. It is my inflated sense of self-importance!"*

And that was the lesson of this story. Once we learn how to let go of the sack—our inflated sense of self-importance—whatever people say or do against us will no longer matter. The Tao of forgiveness is the conscious decision to get rid of the sack (self) altogether, not just the potatoes (negative feelings).

Derek Lin concluded that, by recognizing that there is no "self" to be hurt, we could bypass the frustration arising from our constant striving to forgive others. This is because we will not become angry with them to begin with!

With the understanding of Tao/Zen, life suddenly becomes effortless, elegant, and natural. Get rid of the sack, and there will be no more rotten potatoes. Do you want to be able to get rid of your sack? How many potatoes are you holding in it? Is your burden heavy?

Forgiveness is a Gift

Forgiveness is the most important and yet most difficult aspect of living a loving and healthy spiritual life. We forget that forgiveness is not for the other person but is primarily beneficial for one's self. Loving is not possible without forgiveness. Forgiveness brings deep healing to the person who gives it and to the one who openly receives it. Forgiveness is giving up the hope that the past could be any different. It is accepting the past for what it was. Forgiveness brings total inner freedom and is something that I do for my own good.

A preacher once said, "Non-forgiveness is like holding a burning piece of charcoal under your arm and wishing the other one experiences the burns." It has also been said that holding a grudge is like drinking poison and hoping the other person dies. Many people do not realize that when they cannot forgive, they really harm only themselves. They block miracles and abundance with anger, bitterness, and resentment. These negative emotions deflect love from entering and poison the mind with toxic thoughts. People who hold grudges suffer because they carry around the weight of this emotional pain. They are not open to new and better experiences. But all along, at any time, it is possible to mend hurt and negative emotional pain with forgiveness, and to set that negative energy free. The choice is yours!

Most of the time, we do not get closure to a painful experience in relationships. That is because the two people are in a totally different place in their lives. I have learned from my own experience that to forgive someone, we do not need

> *Forgiveness is a gift to yourself because it prevents the past from reaching out to hurt you in the present.*

an apology or closure. Most people who are hurt themselves don't recognize that they are hurting someone else. They can't see past their own pain to see that they continue wounding others because they are victims to their own unhealed wounds. "Hurt people, hurt people" is an old saying. When I am wounded by someone who is wounded, then the whole vicious cycle starts all over again—like Covid-19 spreading through the population. It is transmitted in every human interaction. I know for a fact from my own personal experience with family members, they could never see my pain, they could only see theirs. They viewed and presented themselves as victims and remained emotionally disconnected. I do not expect an apology and have not tried to have any family reconciliations or resolutions. I have done my part and it was this: allowing forgiveness to flow through me which gave me the freedom to be Me. Some of my family members who have gone before me, may have taken their hurts to their graves, but I have broken the cycle for myself and made forgiveness a way of life. As a result, I experience the freedom and peace that comes with it. Forgiveness is a gift to yourself because it prevents the past from reaching out to hurt you in the present.

Self-forgiveness is a Miracle

It is easier to forgive other people than it is to forgive one's own self. In fact, while forgiving others is a gift to self, forgiving self is nothing less than a miracle! Forgiving yourself has the power to transform every cell in your body. Having said that, it should be noted that there are people who find it easier to forgive themselves than to forgive others. For myself, it is much more difficult to forgive myself because I am harder on myself, and it takes a good deal of courage to forgive my own failings. That is why, I consider forgiving others as a gift and forgiving self a full-on miracle. When you forgive yourself, you accept yourself, your past, and your failures. You have taken the plank from your own eyes and can then see others more clearly. When you cannot forgive yourself, you are viewing others through those unforgiving lenses.

Why do I find it difficult to forgive myself? The first thing that comes to mind is my inner conflict. I never intend to hurt anyone or cause pain, but when my words or actions cause pain, I struggle to forgive myself. Second, when I do an act of kindness or service with the intent to help others, sometimes it turns out to hurt them, and again, I cannot easily forgive myself. Finally, I find it difficult to forgive myself because I am constantly judging myself using the judgments others have used on me. Learning to forgive myself has taken me longer than learning to forgive others.

It is interesting to observe the big "I" hidden underneath my difficulty to forgive self. I am such a kind person—how could I hurt others? I am such a good caretaker—how can I be capable of doing something hurtful? I am a person with only good intentions for others—and yet I have hurt others. How could I do something horrible to hurt someone's feelings? The "I" takes multiple forms and shapes to survive. At such times, I have to change the words of Jesus from, "Forgive them, for they know not what they do," to "Forgive me, for I do not know what I am doing." This does demand some humility on my part, to accept my failings. It also offers me an opportunity to feel the tenderness and love of God, that can in turn enhance my tenderness and kindness towards others. Only when I live from the Me state, can I easily forgive the weaknesses of the egotistical "I" that is not as much aware as Me. Me is the inner awareness and plays a greater role in forgiveness. If forgiveness flows through me so does hurt. I need to allow both of these to flow...but not allow them to make a home in me.

To some extent, forgiving others and self are two sides of the same coin. By forgiving others, I stop focusing on their faults and focus instead on their well-being. In return, I stop not only punishing others, I stop punishing myself as well. My increased ability to let go of others' faults helps me let go of mine. The energy of forgiveness releases the frozen, negative past in me and frees new possibilities. The past controls me only when I hold onto it.

With all that is said, I do not have a proven method to share on how to grow in the capacity to forgive. Each person has a unique way of accomplishing it. Some people can decide to forgive and—*boom*—it is done. For others, forgiveness is a process, something that is not just one decision, but many small choices to remind one's self to forgive each day, each moment. As Jesus noted, forgive seventy times seven. From my own perspective, I pray for the grace and the miracle, where we will be touched and opened by the healing power of forgiveness.

Some have said that praying for the person you need to forgive helps, and I believe it does. Either because the person you pray for starts to behave differently or you don't care about the hurt anymore because you have rewired your brain, your heart and your soul. So…pray, pray, and pray, for the gift of forgiveness of self and others.

> *"People hurt each other. It happens to everyone. Intentionally, unintentionally, regretfully or not. It's a part of what we do as human beings. The beauty is that we have the ability to heal and forgive".* Adi Alsaid

Borrow a Heart, Mind, and Ears

Holding onto hurt, blame, anger, resentment, or hatred is a heavy emotional burden that not only occupies our mind space (and time!), but also shrinks our heart and minimizes our overall capacity to conduct life. Deep emotional wounds compromise our overall capacity to handle everyday life in a fruitful way. For example, when I was upset with the nuns for cancelling my visa, they were in my mind and heart every minute of the day. No matter what I did they were right there. They were living in my head rent free, and my behavior reflected this. I became easily irritated and upset, and even withdrew from others. I did not realize that one event could paralyze all other areas of my life so intensely. No matter whom I met, I wanted to tell them how unfair the nuns had been and secretly strengthened my 'I' by presenting myself as a victim. I was literally so stuck in those emotions that I was not able to see life beyond those feelings. It was through the grace of God that I was given the gift to forgive.

Many times, in the past, I have gone through similar situations, to a greater or lesser degree, when I needed to forgive. I have noticed this compromised capacity of self in each of those instances. What has helped in such times is a good listener, an open mind, and a loving heart to process the need to forgive. Since my own capacities were compromised, I trusted either a good friend or a spiritual director to listen to me, to think for me, and to process my emotions in their hearts. I have never regretted enlisting someone else's healthy ears, mind, and heart to help me process my "stuck-ness". I am grateful to family, friends and counselors for being my strength, when I was at my weakest. We all have people around us who we can depend upon and who willingly will lend us their whole self to help us process our lack of forgiveness. Build a bank of "forgiveness friends" and turn to them when you need them. Be one yourself for others, in their time of need.

Healers Heal

Operating from hurt or resentment affects all other areas of life— work, relationships, and the choices we make. It even affects our thought and sleep patterns. The tension of unforgiveness lives in the nervous system and controls all other functions of our being. As noted earlier, forgiveness is a gift to self. It heals one from within and once healed, we, in turn, become healers. We don't have to undertake any active healing activities. The way we connect, listen and conduct our lives carries the healing that we experience within. Unforgiveness is a frozen energy that indirectly controls our life in general, a sort of anesthesia—numbing us from feeling life and its depth. We might go through the motions of life but cannot enjoy its pleasures. Unforgiveness is also a form of negative, dormant energy that can be triggered at any given moment when someone does or says something that sets it off. When you are healed from your unforgiveness and you learn to channel the power of forgiveness, you experience a higher capacity to relate, and every interaction becomes a joyful possibility in which to experience the riches of life. Unforgiveness is a wound that festers inside. Forgiving heals, and the healed heart will channel healing to everyone and everything. I once heard it said, "Feel your way into forgiveness. Do not think your way into forgiveness." Let us learn the art of forgiving and experience inner healing by practicing how it feels to forgive.

The Healing of a Prisoner Who Practiced Zen

Following is a story of a prisoner in the Branchville Correctional Facility in Indiana.

> *There was a man serving time in the prison who took up the study of Zen Buddhism. He even took ordination precepts as an inmate and became known by his ordained name as Brother Ananda Abhaya Karuna. Over time, Brother Ananda found himself being able to forgive and achieve so much more in life through the spiritual practices of Zen Buddhism, most notably through Zen meditation.*

> *Having been a long-term prisoner, he said he has come to know anger intimately. The prisoners, according to Brother Ananda, are conditioned to see themselves as unforgiven. In this frame of mind, anger arises and there is a notion that forgiving others is a weakness. Society does not forgive, they reasoned. Why should they?*

> *One lesson that Brother Ananda learned is that resentment is always about the past, but it takes place in the present. It also intensifies over time, every time we relive that experience in our mind. To deal effectively with the anger present in the here and now about things and people that existed there and then, Brother Ananda said we must examine and challenge the usual pattern of how our thoughts create anger in our mind.*

Once realizing that we are merely punishing ourselves by continuing to fight imaginary enemies (thoughts of past events) in our mind, we would come to realize that the cause of such punishment is simply because we refused to forgive.

Brother Ananda discovered that when a prisoner does not let go of resentments and anger through the act of forgiveness, the prisoner becomes his own keeper. That, according to Brother Ananda, is certainly one way of defining the pain of the unhealed self.

When you practice forgiveness, you upgrade your inner software and increase your chances of downloading freedom, peace, and joy at a greater speed.

Forgiveness is a Spiritual Practice

How did all my prayers and spiritual practices enhance my ability to forgive? This is a question I often ask myself. If I have resentment and anger in my heart, it would be useless to say beautifully worded prayers, chant holy mantras, or read the sacred scriptures. Forgiveness is taught by many spiritual teachers. Let us look at some of the biblical parables of Jesus to explore his teachings on forgiveness.

In the Gospel of Luke (15:20-24), the story of the prodigal son, when the son returns home, his father does not wait for an apology or acknowledgment from the son. Neither did he hold any grudges for the behavior and actions of the son. The father unconditionally forgave the son. He harbored no resentments, no anger, no judgments—offered only forgiveness, acceptance and celebration.

How can we forgive someone who has done harm not only to ourselves, but also to others and themselves? Would that not be encouraging the wrong behavior and enabling a person to do more harm? Will my unconditional forgiveness help the person grow up? We all might have questions such as these, but it is not up to us to map the life journey of others. Instead, we are called to forgive and accept people. People learn and grow up in their own way and at their own time. Forgiveness is not about what the other one is doing. It is about who I am. Forgiveness defines me, and it gifts me with an inner consistency that increases my capacity to hold another person's fragmented self—just like the father in the prodigal son parable. Our minds can provide us with fine mental arguments about whether to offer or withhold forgiveness. Jesus is clear in his lesson from the parable: The power of forgiveness that comes from a father's heart is more powerful than the temporary sinfulness of the son.

There is another parable in the Gospel of Luke (7:36-50) that speaks to forgiveness. In the parable of the two debtors, Jesus says in verse 47, "So I tell you, her many sins have been forgiven; hence, she has shown great love.[c] But the one to whom little is forgiven, loves little." This is quite shocking to most of us. The one who is forgiven more, is able to love more. The ability to love is directly connected with our ability to forgive and be forgiven. The more I love, the more I forgive. There are many debates going on internally, as I equate the ability to love with forgiveness. It would be very selfish to love and forgive in order to grow in your ability to love and forgive. And what about the other person? What if the other one takes forgiveness for granted or abuses it? What if the other one never grows up and continues to hurt me or other people? Would I be responsible for the other people being hurt? These are serious questions and serve as a framework of reference in thinking about forgiveness. Let me explain through an example. Suppose you have a young college aged son living on campus. You are financially supporting his studies and come to know that he is not attending his classes and is blowing away the tuition fees on parties and drugs. You forgive him, continue to love him, but stop the financial support. Love and forgiveness have nothing to do with a certain pattern of behavior. While your love once meant to provide financial support, the same love decided to withdraw the support. In the parable of the two debtors, Jesus uses the example of the prostitute to illustrate the power of forgiveness. We have no idea why the woman chose to do what she did, but Jesus manifested total acceptance and extended forgiveness that potentially gave rise to pure love and transformation within the woman. Forgiveness helps us to love better, though the way we manifest forgiveness may be expressed differently in each situation we encounter.

Earlier in this chapter, we referred to forgiveness as being a decision and an ongoing process. In the Gospel of Matthew (18:21-25), we find the parable of the unmerciful servant. The parable opens with a question from Peter. *"Then Peter came to Jesus and asked, 'Lord, how many times shall I forgive my brother or sister who sins against me? Up to seven times?' Jesus answered, "I tell you, not seven times, but seventy-seven times."* This means we must forgive unlimited times. Forgiveness is unbounded and abundant. Only my attitude and perception can limit me from extending it. As the parable proceeds, Jesus talks about the king who settles his accounts with his servants. Each servant owed the king in different measure, and he forgives everyone's debts. The servant who was forgiven wholesale is not able to forgive the debt of his servant, who owed a much smaller amount than what he himself had owed to the king. The lesson from this is that none of us is exempt from owing forgiveness. We all need forgiveness at one time or another to a greater or lesser degree. It is important to realize this and remember it. Perhaps today I might not need forgiveness as much as my friend, but sooner or later, I will need it. We must keep the flow of forgiveness ongoing. May forgiveness flow freely from one heart to the other. In such a free-flowing state of forgiveness, there will be less trauma, pain, and suffering.

In the Gospel of Mark (11:24-25), Jesus exhorts his disciples to pray and forgive. "Therefore, I tell you, all that you ask for in prayer, believe that you will receive it and it shall be yours. [25] When you stand to pray, forgive anyone against whom you have a grievance, so that your heavenly Father may in turn forgive you your transgressions.".". As we noted earlier, unforgiveness is nothing but stuck energy, affecting all areas of our lives and limiting our capacity to have fulfilling relationships or to conduct the affairs of our lives in a meaningful way. Jesus makes it clear that if we have unforgiveness in our hearts, our capacity to connect to God in prayer will be compromised. Clear that stuck energy by forgiving, and God will easily live in and flow through you!

> *And forgive us our debts, as we also have forgiven our debtors.*
> *—Matthew 6:12*

As we noted, no one is exempt when it comes to forgiveness. We all need to extend it or to receive it at one time or the other. And if we have not needed it until now, we will need it soon. No matter how grave the offense, all of us are capable of bestowing forgiveness. We have all heard stories about horrible events and people's ability to forgive and let go. If one person is able to do it, why not you and me? We all have the capacity.

Consider this true story:

> *On October 2, 2006, a mentally ill gunman entered a one-room Amish school in West Nickel Mines, a part of Lancaster, Pennsylvania. The gunman, Charles Roberts, shot eight out of ten girls in the schoolroom, killing five, and then shot himself. While stunned and grieving, the Amish community chose to forgive the man. They offered*

love, prayers and support to Roberts' wife and children, dropping off toys and food even showing up to attend Roberts' funeral. Much was made in the media of this compassionate response to a terrible act of violence, and many even questioned the Amish community's sincerity in the face of an unspeakably evil act. The West Nickel Mines school was torn down, and the community built the New Hope School at a different site. The Amish chose to forgo vengeance for past acts and to move toward a better future. Movies, books and even plays have been written about the Amish community's "power of forgiveness."

Here is another true story of a woman who let forgiveness flow through her:

On January 22, 1999, Australian missionary Graham Staines was burned alive along with two sons, Philip (aged 10) and Timothy (aged 7), by a mob led by the <u>Bajrang Dal</u> *activist* <u>Dara Singh</u> *in* <u>Odisha, India</u>. *Shortly after the sentencing of the killers, Gladys Staines, the widow of Graham Staines issued a statement saying that she had forgiven the killers and had no bitterness towards them. Rather than return to Australia, Staines said that she had decided to stay in India where she and her husband had served lepers for 15 years, keeping her daughter Esther. "I cannot just leave those people who love and trust us. I have high regard for the people of India and their tolerance."*

If Gladys Staines can offer such forgiveness, what prevents you and me from doing the same?

Let's consider another real-life story. On June 17, 2015, in Charleston, South Carolina, a 21-year-old man named Dylann

Roof joined a Bible study group at Emanuel African Methodist Episcopal Church, an historically Black church, and stood up and shot and killed nine African Americans as they participated in the Bible study. Among the nine church members killed was the senior pastor, Clementa C. Pinckney. Three people survived. The shooting shocked the nation and came to be known as the Charleston church massacre. Roof had a web-based history of racial hatred and was associated with white supremacy and neo-Nazi groups whose purpose is to ignite a race war. He knew, before targeting the church, that the church had been a site for community organizing related to civil rights. The Charleston church shooting survivors, while acknowledging their pain and loss, chose to forgive the shooter. "There is no healing with hatred," said one survivor. "We must love each other. That's what we're taught and that's the right thing to do. You have to forgive others for you to be forgiven. There is tremendous power in forgiveness."

In summary, Jesus' teaching on forgiveness is:

- Forgiveness comes from who I am and not what the other one does.
- The ability to love and forgive are interconnected.
- We all need forgiveness. Everyone is a giver and a receiver.
- Unforgiveness affects every area of human life and limits our capacity to live life fully.
- Forgiveness is the Divine spirit waiting to flow through us to heal our humanity.

Forgiveness practice is a spiritual ritual that helps liberate our own wounded feelings and find meaning in the worst of life's events. Forgiveness practice is a powerful way to be free of the inner violence of rage and pursue right action. In fact, forgiveness practice offers a clear vision that allows us to use skillful means in bringing sustainable peace.

Please make forgiveness practice a daily ritual. For your own sake, do not become locked in anger, fear, and resentment. Resentment hardens your emotions, narrows your options in responding to life, and clouds your judgment. Resentment keeps you from experiencing the flow of life, shifts your attention from those who matter to you to those whom you scorn, and deadens your spirit. Why would you choose to live in this manner? It gives those who wronged you an even greater victory than their original act! Forgiveness practice, as an act of selflessness, helps to stop the endless cycle of hatred in the world. Hate has never been erased by more hate. Only love ousts hate. In every event of hurt, let's hold the truth of our interdependence and refuse to participate in the cycle of hatred. Doing so will heal the wounds of the world. Jesus said, "If you love those who love you, what credit is that to you? Even sinners love those who love them. But if you love your enemies, do good to them, and lend to them without expecting to get anything back, then your reward will be great." A conscious forgiveness practice is not a weakness but a strength. It is not about bowing out of a difficult situation, but it is about learning to hold the difficult moment in your heart and heal it. It is a way of living your spiritual life in and through daily events.

Forgiveness is Letting Go of the Pain "I" Feels

The pain that comes from others' behavior is real. It can be touched, experienced and intense. In no way am I downplaying the devastating pain we go through in difficult times in our relationships, especially during tough experiences. I am reminded of a quote I read long ago: "Tough times do not last, but tough people do." Life is a web of relationships, and we are bound to experience misunderstandings and conflicts. The gift of forgiveness is a valuable gift from God to help us work through these tough experiences of life without getting destroyed by them. Imagine what would life be like if we had no ability to forgive or let go. Life would be one continuous experience of pain and suffering. Let's gratefully claim this gift and see how we can fully use it for our well-being and for that of the whole world.

The Me has to rise up to free the I from the pain it feels. It calls for a deep and closer examination of hurtful experiences. While on one hand I learn to acknowledge and live through the pain of an actual experience, I also open myself to accept that the "negative" consequence to the wrongful acts were really what I made it mean to me. Once I am able to learn to accept the reality of what happened, I am able to see that the experience took place in my mind and not in the reality of the external words or actions. Once I accept this truth, the pain is released and forgiveness starts to flow.

Without forgiveness, we become victims of the past and carry pain that destroys the joy of the present. Forgiveness is the ability to regain control over the part of ourselves that has become a slave to the past, a servant to the pain.

> *Forgiveness is the doorway of clarity that helps heal the confusion of a troubled mind. —Byron Katie*

We have all lived through experiences of betrayals whose memories may still cause us suffering, while those who betrayed us are free from this pain. But it is more painful to hate. Without forgiveness, we continue to perpetuate the illusion that hate can heal our pain, that grudges can protect us from ever being hurt again. Anger, hate, and vengeance do not heal us. It is only in forgiveness that we can let go and find relief.

In Buddhist spirituality, forgiveness is understood as a means to end suffering, to bring dignity and harmony to one's life. Forgiveness is fundamentally for our own sake, for our own mental health. It is a way to let go of the pain we carry. This is illustrated by the story of two ex-prisoners of war who meet after many years. When the first one asks, "Have you forgiven your captors yet?" the second man answers, "No, never." "Well then," the first man replies, "they still have you in prison."

With each instance of forgiveness, we strengthen the sense of Me and weaken the I. Unforgiveness is a clear indicator of the strong presence of I. The Me sees wisely and it willingly acknowledges what is unjust, harmful, and wrong. The Me bravely recognizes the sufferings of the past and understands the conditions that brought them about. The Me finds peace and strength in forgiveness, while 'I' strengthens itself by holding tightly to grudges, pain, and suffering caused by an unfortunate experience. When we forgive, we release the past and resolve not to carry bitterness and hate in our heart.

Here is a story told by Bill Clinton on what he learned from Nelson Mandela about forgiveness. In one meeting with Mandela, Clinton asked, "I wonder what you must have felt toward your jailers when you were walking out of that prison after those 27 years. Weren't you angry at them?"

"Yes, I was angry. And I was a little afraid," answered Mandela. "After all, I've not been free in so long. But when I felt that anger welling up inside me, I realized that if I continue to hate them after I got outside that gate, then they would still have me."

With a smile, Mandela concluded, "I wanted to be free, so I let it go."

Forgiveness Starts with Me

No one likes to go through painful experiences, but there is wisdom and growth in pain. Only in and through painful experiences can we learn to release and grow in love, understanding, acceptance, and forgiveness. Once the unforgiving pain of the "I" is released, the Me starts gaining greater ground within our being. All the I's pain and hurt become raw material for the Me to gain greater ground, so in a way, the I provided us needed substance to grow into Me.

Understanding the difference between I and Me and developing a strong and healthy sense of Me is a pre-requisite for forgiveness, because forgiveness has little to do with what the other does and everything to do with my reaction or response. Forgiving self is as important as understanding self. We can live from the sense of I or Me. Most of our emotional pain originates and dwells in the sense of I, but this is simply a mental image, a constructed reality. Upon deep examination of any instance of hurt, we will find that it comes from the pain caused to that mental image of self. For instance, if offended by a friend, I may think, "I was good to her—how could she betray me?" In this case, all my good actions for the other person have helped my "I" form an internal impression that I am a good person. When the person for whom I did so much betrays me, damage is caused to my ego-based belief that I am a good person because I have done so many good things. My interior self-image is what gets hurt. My "I" has a little nervous breakdown. If we can operate from the "Me" and understand the difference between the two, our souls become fertile ground in which seeds of forgiveness will grow and multiply.

Let me confess that I still need to walk my talk. I catch myself red-handed all the time. Recently I received an apology from a friend who had broken an agreement we had made. My first reaction was… *well, it took her years to realize what she had done to me.* But then I recognized my reactions and their source and told myself that the gracious God keeps sending events and circumstances to help me strengthen my forgiveness muscles. Until I learn to respond from the loving and understanding Me, I will keep getting these lessons. I do not know if any one of us will finally arrive at the final stage. One thing I can certainly say is true is that, with every added experience, we grow one step closer to the Me. Reliving the experience of leaving the convent helps me release the divine power of forgiveness in me and with additional experiences, it takes a shorter time to figure things out, to let go of my pain, and to forgive.

> *"To forgive is the highest and most beautiful form of love. In return, you will receive untold peace and happiness".*
> *Robert Muller*

Understanding How Forgiveness Liberates Me From I

Let us conclude our reflections on forgiveness with a story from the life of Buddha taken from upliftconnect.com and contributed by Sofo Archon:

> *The Buddha was sitting under a tree talking to his disciples when a man came and spat in his face. As the Buddha wiped his face, he asked the man, "What next? What do you want to say next?" The man was a little puzzled because he himself never expected that when you spit in someone's face he should ask "What next?" He had no such experience in his past. He had insulted people and they had become angry and reacted. Or if they were cowards and weaklings, they had smiled, trying to bribe him. But the Buddha had not reacted in either of these ways. He was not angry, nor in any way offended, nor in any way cowardly. But just matter-of-factly, he said, "What next?" There was no reaction on his part.*

But Buddha's disciples became angry, and they reacted. His closest disciple, Ananda, said, "This is too much. We cannot tolerate it. He has to be punished for it, otherwise everyone will start doing things like this!"

Buddha said, "You keep silent. He has not offended me, but you are offending me. He is new, a stranger. He must have heard from people something about me, that this man is an atheist, a dangerous man who is throwing people off their track, a revolutionary, a corrupter. And he may have formed some idea, a notion of me. He has not spit on me, he has spit on his notion. He has spit on his idea of me because he does not know me at all, so how can he spit on me?

"If you think on it deeply," Buddha said, "he has spit on his own mind. I am not part of it, and I can see that this poor man must have something else to say because this is a way of saying something. Spitting is a way of saying something. There are moments when you feel that language is impotent: in deep love, in intense anger, in hate, in prayer. There are intense moments when language is impotent. Then you have to do something. When you are angry, intensely angry, you hit the person, you spit on him, and you are saying something. I can understand him. He must have something more to say, that is why I am asking, "What next?"

The man was even more puzzled! And Buddha said to his disciples, "I am more offended by you because you know me, and you have lived for years with me, and still you react."

Puzzled, confused, the man returned home. He could not sleep the whole night. When you see a Buddha, it is difficult, impossible even, to sleep anymore the way you used to sleep before. Again, and again, he was haunted by the experience. He could not explain it to himself, what had happened. He was trembling all over, sweating and soaking the sheets. He had never come across such a man; the Buddha had shattered his whole mind and his whole pattern, his whole past.

The next morning, he went back. He threw himself at Buddha's feet. Buddha asked him again, "What next? This, too, is a way of saying something that cannot be said in language. When you come and touch my feet, you are saying something that cannot be said ordinarily, for which all words are too narrow; it cannot be contained in them." Buddha said, "Look, Ananda, this man is again here, he is saying something. This man is a man of deep emotions."

The man looked at Buddha and said, "Forgive me for what I did yesterday."

Buddha said, "Forgive? But I am not the same man to whom you did it. The Ganges goes on flowing; it is never the same Ganges again. Every man is a river. The man you spit upon is no longer here. I look just like him, but I am not the same, much has happened in these twenty-four hours! The river has flowed so much. So, I cannot forgive you because I have no grudge against you.

"And you also are new. I can see you are not the same man who came yesterday because that man was angry and he spit, whereas you are bowing at my feet, touching my feet. How can you be the same man? You are not the

same man, so let us forget about it. Those two people, the man who spit and the man on whom he spit, both are no more. Come closer. Let us talk of something else."

Every man is like a river.

This story powerfully brings out the message that the hurt and wounded part of me is only an image created in my mind or in the mind of the other. Ananda had an image of Buddha as a saintly figure, who should not be spat upon by a stranger and that made him feel hurt and react. His reaction does show Ananda's love for his master. However, his reaction comes from the mental image of his master that he had created. Buddha, on the

> *The enlightened mind has nothing to forgive.*
> *—Anonymous*

other hand, was clear that the spitting had not been done to Buddha, but only to the mental image the spitter had in his mind. Buddha was acting from the sense of Me and the spitter and Ananda from the sense of I. This story accurately captures my perspective, and the lesson it teaches is tremendously beautiful and important. May the power of forgiveness flow and reign in and through the hearts of every human living.

The Co-Creative Power of Work

Over the course of my thirty-year career, I have had the privilege of working in a variety of positions—as a teacher, leadership trainer, social worker, pastoral coordinator, spiritual counselor, and now as a caregiver. I began caregiving not out of choice, but out of need. Though I joined the convent and became a nun to bring Jesus Christ to the world, a major portion of my time was engaged in various service projects. I was not even aware how and when my zeal for the kingdom of God had turned into a career, and my work had begun to provide me satisfaction and identity. Most of my waking hours were engaged in work and a few hours a day in prayer exercises. Work was—and is—very important to me. Since work is one of the major activities of human life, I thought of exploring it as a spiritual practice. Research shows that, over a lifetime, the average person spends 90,000 hours at work, which is 24% of the typical number of years in the workforce, which is 50. These numbers almost certainly refer to paid or professional jobs alone, but my frame of reference is not limited solely to paid work, but to the work we pursue around the clock. We continue working at home, we work while we are in school, and we work in our communities as well. If we spend so much of our time at work, why not make it a source of happiness and meaning?

In the convent, I never needed to worry about finding a job or negotiating a salary. The community had its own prestigious institutions and additional programs, and these offered a variety of work assignments; for example, I taught during the day, and in the evening, I helped students at the residential school to complete their school and home work. No missionary lacks work—there is always an abundant harvest and few laborers! After leaving the convent, I had to conduct my first job search. Fortunately, I fell into a job without much effort—working with a lay community for people with disabilities—and I see that as God's way of reaching out to me, by showing me how to reach out to others.

Seeking out employment takes many pathways. Some people are so desperate to find a job, they take whatever comes their way, because they want to make a living. In other cases, people carefully choose their direction and find the right job with fair pay. There are people who feel pushed or pressured into a job, not by their own choice, but to satisfy family expectations. Sometimes, by circumstance, there are limited choices—for example, if a town has a coal mine, most of the town's residents will seek a job there. In this age of COVID-19 and it's havoc, most people are grateful to have any kind of job. Not every job leads to a sense of joy or fulfillment. Just imagine spending the greater part of life not out of choice, but in surrender to life's limitations. Work then becomes a source of frustration and unhappiness and can take a great toll on an individual's physical, mental, and emotional health. When work, paid or unpaid, is done "just for the heck of it" and your whole self is not in it or you are not enjoying doing it, daily life can be painful and burdensome.

Sometimes in a community setting, you do not have enough space to be yourself. Something deep within me, nudged me to move on from working with the lay community and find another job. I sent out hundreds of résumés and job applications and went for several job interviews, always returning home with the feeling that I had given my best. Although I hoped to get called back, I was sorely disappointed. Spending weeks and even months looking for a job and sending applications and interviews in vain is not fun. I enlisted help from friends to work on my résumé and practice interviews. In one situation, I was given books to learn the "right" answers for the interview. Many of those answers seemed redundant or trite, but, hey, I wanted that job! I memorized the answers and dutifully repeated them like a parrot, yet still had no luck. I wondered if I was doing something wrong. Why was I not getting job offers? Was there hidden racism, as I am an immigrant from India with creamy brown skin? When you are in a new country with another skin color, not everything goes well for you. One of my friends reviewed my résumé and said that

I was overqualified for the entry-level jobs. No one would want to hire someone with a master's degree to do what a high schooler could do. So I deleted all but the most basic credentials from my résumé and sent my applications with high school records. Surprisingly, that did bring some results! After having searched extensively for jobs that would match my qualifications and aptitudes, I was ready to do anything, I mean anything, just to make a living. Having always been a self-reliant person, the fear of no job and potential dependence on others was not only scary, it dropped the ground from beneath my feet. It was an experience that words will never be able to describe or memory will never be able to erase. I guess when you are in such a position, you tend to think little and worry more. Most of what you do does not come from a reasoned, right thinking mind as much as it comes from a fear-driven, worried place in you.

From such a worried mental state, in 2012, I applied for a job on Craigslist and received a call within an hour. The call came in at about 9:30 a.m. and I had an interview scheduled by 3 p.m. The job was to serve as a live-in caregiver to a 98-year-old woman. Her son said he had received 60 applications for the position. He had chosen ten candidates whose résumés seemed to indicate a good fit, and he scheduled eight interviews on that day. The woman saw me at the interview and told her son that I was the one she wanted. That was it! I was hired on the spot and was asked to start work the next morning. My heart raced with fear and joy on the way home. I had no idea what caregiving involved, and I was afraid of not being able to do my job well. As soon as I arrived home, I looked up the job description for a caregiver and breathed more easily. I was able to do all those things. But while I was ecstatic and grateful for the job, I could not share my joy with family or friends. Caregiving jobs in India are considered menial jobs. They are not for the educated, and only an illiterate person would take up such tasks. I feared that people who knew me would mock me for the type of job I had chosen for myself. So for the fear of being ridiculed or made fun of, I kept this information to myself. I had always taken pride in my multiple diplomas and two master's degrees and had never intended to underutilize myself. I confided my embarrassment about this to the woman with whom I shared caregiving duties, and she suggested that it was not necessary to offer details to others, especially if I felt ashamed. Ultimately, I decided to tell friends and relatives that I worked for myself. This provided me with some temporary relief, but I continued hiding my job for nearly a year, and the act of keeping it hidden ate me from inside.

Despite my misgivings, I enjoyed every moment of caregiving, and that was the best year of my life! This phase of my career was a wonderful time and an utterly fantastic experience. The woman I cared for was very motherly and she, in turn, cared for me deeply. We became the best of friends, and I even began to feel that I was working with a living saint. For the first time in my life, I was living with a person with whom I had no fear of judgment or criticism. My friend was grateful for every act of service and in return was deeply caring towards me. I had no need to pretend or show off; all I had to do was be genuine and offer sincere care. Working with one person gave me a lot of time and silence to reflect, pray, and think about self. It was a time of deep healing from within. I felt loved, cared for, and at peace. While I experienced much peace and fulfillment at work, I was still afraid to reveal it to my family or friends back in India. After a year of struggle with this fear, I finally said to myself, what the heck! I realized that I was happy with my work and that it mattered to me as well as to the family I worked with. For the first time ever, I found myself happy with my work and it brought me healing and peace. From that point on, I decided that I would always tell people what I did and would not care about what they thought or said. With that freedom, I have continued working as a caregiver and I enjoy every bit of it. I have grown by leaps and bounds in my capacity to genuinely care for and love people. What a gift! To think that I had been ashamed of revealing my vocation! People now seek me out as a good caregiver. I never have to look for a job, and I receive more offers of employment than I can accept.

When seeking new assignments, it is very important that I enjoy the person I work with, and so I have become quite selective in choosing my elderly friends. I take a few days or a week to determine if I will work well or not with a certain person. Some of my friends critique this approach, saying I expect too much out of my work. Why not? I ask. I spend almost twelve hours a day at work, and I want it to be an enjoyable experience for all. I do not want to be stressed out and keep looking at the clock or phone until the time that I can run home. After holding all sorts of jobs, I have found caregiving to be my thing. I get paid to love and care for people! What more could anyone want from life? Had I not joined the convent for the same reason and gotten off track? Now work is life and life is work. I engage myself in a variety of activities during the day, and through all of them, my life is one whole unit. I do not have to "wait for the weekend" and dread Monday. For me, it is TGIM!

Mahatma Gandhi said, "Work is worship." Indeed, work is my worship and my living prayer. As 1 Corinthians 10:31 notes, "So whether you eat or drink, or whatever you do, do everything for the glory of God." Who I am and what I do, is all to bring honor and glory to God. This is a good reminder that there is no distinction between the secular and the sacred. All of life is sacred. In this section of the book, I want to explore how our mundane, everyday work can become the source of deep joy and meaning.

The Zen of Working

Buddhist meditations developed in Japan are known as Zen. "Being **Zen**" is essentially a state of being at peace with one's own thoughts and becoming self-aware of your place within the universe. Zen's approach to work is very inspiring. Let's look at the Zen of working with the following story:

A young boy became a monk. He dreamed of enlightenment and of learning great things. When he got to the monastery, he was told that each morning he had to chop wood for the monk's fires and then carry water up to the monastery for ablutions and the kitchen. He attended prayers and meditation, but the teaching he was given was rather sparse.

One day he was told to take some tea to the Abbot in his chambers. He did so, and the Abbot saw that the boy looked sad and asked him why.

He replied, "Every day, all I do is chop wood and carry water. I want to learn. I want to understand things. I want to be great one day, like you."

The Abbot gestured to the scrolls on shelves lining the walls. He said, "When I started, I was like you. Every day I would chop wood and carry water. Like you, I understood that someone had to do these things, but like you I wanted to move forward. Eventually I did. I read all the scrolls, I met with kings and gave council. I became the Abbot. Now, I understand that the key to all wisdom is that everything is chopping wood and carrying water, and that if one does everything mindfully, then it is all the same."

Here is a slightly adapted version of the same story (from an internet article by Kyle Kowalski, titled "On Enlightenment: 3 Meanings of the 'Chop Wood, Carry Water' Zen Quote," www.sloww. co/enlightenment-chop-wood-carry-water/).

The novice says to the master, "What does one do before enlightenment?"

"Chop wood. Carry water," replies the master.

The novice asks, "What, then, does one do after enlightenment?"

"Chop wood. Carry water."

Being spiritual is nothing more than continuing to live our everyday lives—but with a new perspective or an added quality. One of the illusions most of us have about spiritual life is that we must meditate or pray all the time. Certain activities in life are considered spiritual—like chanting prayers, performing religious rituals, and attending church. Work, raising family, and pursuing studies are supposed to be secular activities. When work becomes worship, the whole of life turns into worship. The whole of life becomes seeking and finding.

> *When work becomes worship, the whole of life turns into worship.*

"When you are doing any work, do not think of anything beyond. Do it as worship, as the highest worship, and devote your whole life to it for the time being". Swami Vivekananda

All of us would agree that at work, we often face stressful situations, dreadful projects, irritating co-workers, frustrating bosses, and an overwhelming number of tasks and messages. Work becomes boring or stressful and we don't enjoy it. There's a saying about "being on company manners," where we feel that we must watch what we say and how we say it, lest we hurt others or ourselves at work. Therefore, we nervously watch our words and actions. Such efforts cause stress, and no wonder we wait for Fridays to let off the steam! In reality, it is never the work that causes stress. Work is deeply satisfying and an enjoyable activity. It is the surrounding environment at work and the systems created around it that cause stress. The zen of working therefore is nothing more than becoming aware of my reaction to work and to people working with me. Our bodies can feel physically tired over long periods of work, but frustrations, stress, anger, irritation, feelings of overwhelm—all are caused by our ideas and minds. Zen teaches the art of mindfulness, which allows us to see how these thought processes cause us pain. It allows us to delve into the negative baggage we are holding onto.

Mindfulness also helps us return to the present moment, so that all those things running around in our heads can fade away, and we are able to live in what is actually happening right now.

Work and the Bible

How does the Bible treat work? The first mention of work in the Bible occurs in the story of creation. Genesis 3:19 notes that Adam would die and be buried in his workplace because of his sin: "By the sweat of your face you shall eat bread, till you return to the ground, for out of it you were taken; for you are dust, and to dust you shall return." Today no one believes that work is punishment for sins. Work is not only creative and lifegiving, it adds meaning to our day and our lives. The work that God does for a week is all creative. God creates the whole cosmos and then humans. After completing his creative work, he observes the result of His work. We are told that it was all very good. God further entrusts the care of everything he created to human beings. In fact, he creates human beings to help him take care of what he created. That is the first work humans had—to take care of the creation. If God entrusts us with the precious work of tending to creation, why does the Bible present the dichotomy that we are co-creators, but work is punishment?

Is the Bible trying to say that work is evil? Not at all. Most of the Bible presents work as good. In effect, God designed work so that it might be a blessing to us and to others. Work is good because the wages we earn help us meet our financial responsibilities to support our families. The New Testament disdains people who can work and have the opportunity to work, but don't work because of laziness. Here are some Biblical teachings about work.

- **Everyone should work if they are able to.** "In fact, when we were with you, we instructed you that if anyone was unwilling to work, neither should that one eat.'" *(2 Thessalonians 3:10)*
- **Work for God's glory and not for personal motivations of money, power, or fame.** "...So whether you eat or drink, or whatever you do, do everything for the glory of God." *(1 Corinthians 10:31)*
- **Work with all your heart.** "Whatever you do, do from the heart, as for the Lord and not for others." *(Colossians 3:23)*
- **Set aside the Sabbath to rest from your work.** "Remember the sabbath day—keep it holy.[a] 9 Six days you may labor and do all your work, 10 but the seventh day is a sabbath of the LORD your God. You shall not do any work, either you, your son or your daughter, your male or female slave, your work animal, or the resident alien within your gates. 11 For in six days the LORD made the heavens and the earth, the sea and all that is in them; but on the seventh day he rested. That is why the LORD has blessed the sabbath day and made it holy." *(Exodus 20:8-11)*

The Bible makes it clear that work is important, necessary, and good. It even promotes the idea of rest because we get tired and need rest to recover our energy for more work. The verse from Colossians says, "Work with all your heart, as if you were working for the Lord and not human masters." We have human people who either hold a position of supervision or employ us. Looking at the work as coming from God and giving our best is a reward in and of itself. I have grown to enjoy the work and be fully present at work, whether I am watched and appreciated or not. My work and my total best efforts bring me much deeper satisfaction and happiness than approval or reward from human bosses.

I am reminded of a story about a man who visited a construction site and found three workers all doing the same task, but each viewed the work very differently.

> *A man came upon a construction site where three people were working. He asked the first, "What are you doing?" and the man replied: "I am laying bricks." He asked the second, "What are you doing?" and the second man replied: "I am building a wall." As he approached the third, he heard him humming a tune as he worked, and asked, "What are you doing?" The man stood, looked up at the sky, and smiled, "I am building a cathedral!"*

All three workers were doing the same job, but each held a different vision of what their work was about. Vision becomes the fire that provides fuel and energy to work. Working for the Lord brings out an unknown quality in us and in the work itself. This is the quality we call spirituality—life that vibrates at a higher frequency. We can all create that higher frequency by our intentions and attitudes.

Does my work energize or drain me?

Cooking is hard work, or at least I always thought so, but I lived with a nun who, when tired after the day's activities, would relax by going out to the kitchen and creating a delicious meal. Why did cooking relax her and exhaust me? This is a question I always wrestled with, and now I have a glimpse of the answer. I always marveled that my colleague never needed a recipe—she just pulled things from the pantry and played with the ingredients until she produced amazing end results. Cooking was a creative act for her. It surprised and delighted her and added joy when everyone enjoyed the dish. Just as interesting, there was an undefined, unexplainable quality and flavor to everything she cooked. I always followed a recipe to the line, worrying about whether the dish would turn out well and my fellow nuns would be happy to eat it. Too much caution and worry about the outcome and the need to please others drained me, and at the end of the cooking hours, I would be tired. But the other nun had none of those worries. For her, cooking was a creative play!

The same notion can be applied to all other works in life. Children enjoy playing and it energizes them overall but tires them physically. The same also goes for every type of work. Like my companion nun, if creativity is one of your strengths, the more work you do, the more it flexes your strength, joy, and excitement muscles. The positive emotions experienced from energizing work benefit the worker, work, and employer in many ways. Imagine a firm where all the employees are energized by their work. This would increase their performance, focus, enthusiasm, and mental and physical strength, and might also help to build a strong, satisfied, happy customer base.

There is a subtle difference between learning frontline business etiquette to keep the customers happy and engaged, and the product that speaks for itself and does not need additional charm to keep the clientele. This is not to say that client etiquettes are not needed. But when the product carries the quality of the worker's passion, it attracts the customer by its inherent energy. We all have had experiences in our lives where we have traveled far and wide to find and buy a particular product. My intention here is to emphasize that when work becomes a source of additional energy, there is something divine going on: the creative power of the universe is at play through the human mind and hands. We need to create such an experience for ourselves so that work, in and of itself, becomes a spiritual experience.

What, exactly, do I mean by a spiritual experience? My first lessons in spirituality came from home, where I went to church regularly as a young child. Then, at the age of 12, I was schooled in the Catholic faith as preparation to receive the sacraments. Later as a nun, saying additional prayers, observing a time of silence, reading spiritual books, attending retreats—all of these were expressions of spirituality in addition to viewing my full-time job as a service to mankind. All of this is good and helpful, and these practices are a means to become present to self, world, and the divine energy all at the same time. When that coming together of all elements happens in the integrity of our being, we bring quality to everything we touch.

The intuitive experience of spirituality need not be a random moment in our lives. It can permeate every aspect, every minute of life even while working, an activity that consumes almost 65% of our waking hours. Separating spiritual from temporal life does two things. First, the spiritual life becomes a ritual to be performed at a certain time of the day, and second, work becomes a draining experience. Our lives become disjointed and compartmentalized, and we keep running between the two experiences. When all of life becomes spiritual, no matter what happens, everything acquires an inherent quality that cannot be expressed in words. Life becomes a meditation, even though there is a need to move between different tasks, needs, and activities, and through this meditation, all of them have that spiritual, divine, creative energy running through them.

For 18 years, I was involved full-time in parish community organization programs. I was coordinating 30 small communities at one time—a responsibility that kept me busy not only during my waking hours, but also when I was asleep! I had dreams in which I was either planning, organizing, or solving problems. The work did wear me out physically, but it energized me to the core, and I wanted to get right to it when I woke up each morning. This task offered me an opportunity to fully express my creativity, gifts, and talents, and people responded in kind. In fact, I became known for building small communities and was invited to visit several countries as an expert in the field. I plunged my entire being into this work and derived complete satisfaction from it. While this was my inner experience, I faced another reality and problem from those observing my work. There were many negative reactions and efforts to keep me humble. My fellow nuns thought that I had a great need for popularity and my hard work was nothing other than an effort to gain popularity. They grew worried that I was growing more concerned with doing rather than being. As a result of this feedback, I did question my own experience, and to please them, did compromise on my quality of work. The lesson I learned from these experiences is: *you need to keep doing your part no matter what others think, say or react.* When work becomes a spiritual experience and provides inner fuel, one can work longer hours, produce better results, and make a greater impact. This may not go well with coworkers who are not at the same place. Our social nature wants to be in harmony with others, therefore we might revert to functioning from a lower frequency. It would be worthwhile to become aware of our inner dynamics and choose to live from the higher frequency so that no matter what we do, it will energize us, and we, in turn, will be able to bring quality and passion to every task. That is spiritual living and spiritual work. You have heard the phrase "high on life"? You might describe this as being drunk on work.

> *"Your work is going to fill a large part of your life, and the only way to be truly satisfied is to do what you believe is great work. And the only way to do great work is to love what you do. If you haven't found it yet, keep looking. Don't settle. As with all matters of the heart, you'll know when you find it". Steve Jobs*

Workaholism Versus Work Drunk

Workaholism is a word we have all heard, maybe because it was used to describe ourselves, a friend, or a family member. The term is generally used to describe someone who spends almost all waking hours at work and does not engage in any kind of relaxing or leisure activities. Let's use a case study to decode the word.

Micha manages an American tech company and is a good and responsible leader. His work routine is quite disciplined. Although no one is watching, he arrives at the office usually a before 7 a.m. and leaves no later than 5 p.m. He engages his weekends in different types of activities. He lives a block away from his parents and works an average of 45 hours per week. Though he leaves his office on time, he has a problem "switching off" his mind from his job. He makes himself available on the phone 24/7 and constantly checks his email. He worries about his work and thinks the success of his company and new contracts totally depend on him and his performance. Though he is in his early forties, Micha has been diagnosed with high blood pressure and cholesterol. He is on medication and at high risk for a heart attack.

Mira is a referral specialist at a highly rated home care company. She works 12 to 15 hours a day. Though her office hours are usually from 9 to 5, she must be on call in case the caregivers cancel at the last minute and she needs to arrange for a substitute. She is a young mother with three children. Even after she puts them to bed, she often sits up for another three hours, not closing her laptop until midnight. She sometimes also works on weekends. Though Mira works 60 hours or more per week, she can "switch off" when she needs to, and she still feels energetic every day. She does not have any health issues.

We could safely call both Micha and Mira workaholics. In my own case as a community organizer, the onlookers thought I was a workaholic. That was not the case when I looked within, even if it appeared that way. I was not workaholic but work drunk. I was led by an inner energy to give more. My work created more of that energy within me. When you are work drunk, you are under the influence of this energy and are guided by its force. We see a glimpse of that in Mira, and external onlookers might not pick on that inside experience. Work is a very personal experience, and only individuals who are attuned to their inner life will be able to tell the difference. The fruits of the work are a witness, to the spirit of the work and the worker.

In today's high-stress culture, we are all certainly working longer hours, and we not only carry work home, we carry it wherever we go. Yes, working too much is bad for one's health. The inner compulsion to work and its intent are very personal and different from being forced by external forces to work longer and harder. The people who take part in reality shows such as "American Ninja" or "America's Got Talent" work almost 16 to 20 hours a day to improve their performance. Their bodies may become tired, but their zeal to reach the competition's next level drives them onward. They are driven by their intention to win and they are, to some extent, not workaholics but simply drunk with their work.

Like Mira, a work drunk person can switch gears from work to other activities and a workaholic cannot. There is a fine line between being passionate about work and consumed by it. Does work hold you hostage as with Micha, or can you mentally detach from it, like Mira? That is the difference between being workaholic and work drunk. From my own life, I can see how I have crossed in and out of workaholism and being work drunk. I have worked just to please or to seek approval. There have been times when I worked for money and status, and times when I worked just to reach out to people in vulnerable situations. Through every experience of work, I have grown to be the person I am today.

Self-Evolution Through Work

Life has a default system to take us from one phase to the next. We are led to evolve through a series of mysterious happenings and events. Few people are born with a clear vision of their life purpose and vocation. Perhaps some extraordinarily gifted people might have a clear sense of purpose; for example, a person with an exceptional voice becomes a singer. For most of us, we tend to move through various jobs and situations to find our bliss, but we must realize that each experience is an important part of the whole picture. We might move through jobs and each of them prepares us for the next step in the journey of life. Some of us might remain in the same job throughout our working years but may have different bosses or a shifting cast of colleagues. We evolve through these kinds of changes, too.

What I mean by evolution here is using a given moment or situation at work, to stretch toward the highest level of our abilities. Work becomes an opportunity to allow the true expression of the emerging self. We *become* in and through our work. Self-evolution becomes an art form in the same way that a composer creates music, or an artist develops and creates a painting. Through work we can make our person and its multifaceted expression of self a masterpiece. How does one let this evolution happen at work?

At work there are two types of difficulties. One comes from interpersonal relationships with the boss and colleagues, power dynamics within the hierarchy, and mutual affiliations upon which promotions and salary increases depend. The second type of difficulty comes from work itself—either the work is not energizing, is difficult, or is not suited to the worker's tastes. Whatever might be the source of such difficulties or problems, these can become a steppingstone for self-evolution. Instead of blaming someone else or the work itself, we could use it to stretch our capacity to handle life situations. In my twenties, for example, I was working for a diocese which had a board comprised of over 20 members. I found their communication style very complex. They made suggestions that they did not follow through with or they proposed them just to undermine someone else's ideas. In my view, there were many discrepancies and inconsistencies, and I did not expect a team to function in such a dysfunctional manner. I remember approaching one of the senior members in the group and sharing my concerns. He said, "You'd better grow up. In a metropolitan city, people are complex and so is their communication and work style. They will not conduct themselves as the people in small villages do. They have been here working together for several years. You either get on board or return to work in a small rural setting." Whoa! That was a direct slap in the face. I remember replaying the conversation a million times in my head, and I did accept his challenge. I started making careful observations of how people spoke and functioned. I read books about group dynamics in the workplace, and I ultimately found my place in the group. Eventually, this turned out to be one of my most successful places of work. I had grown in my ability to understand the complexity of working in groups and had successfully, with effort, carved a niche for myself. I had grown in my skills of tactfully communicating and understanding group behavior—skills that since then have been tremendously useful no matter where I went. I learned how to develop

> *We can always evolve by choosing to behave differently.*

and negotiate projects that are a "win-win" for everyone. We can always evolve by choosing to behave differently.

In the first few years of working for pay, I accepted any amount paid to me. I treated my meager wages as a gift and deprived myself of even the smallest legitimate need just to save my pennies for the future, even to the extent that I would go thirsty to spare a dollar on a bottle of water. I eventually realized that I was being paid sub-standard wages, and I decided to work only for those who paid me fairly. On the other hand, there were times when I volunteered to take a salary cut when my clients ran out of money. By then I knew that they valued me and respected my services, and I chose to work where I felt better about myself and loved my work. Money was one important aspect of working, but more important was that I was recognized as a person and given dignity and respect as a caregiver. Though some of my friends said that I was expecting too much from my work, I felt justified in my expectations. When I made my expectations clear about what I needed from a job and what I wanted to give in return to my work, coincidences started happening. From out of nowhere, I ran into people who attached dignity to every form of labor. I enjoy my work and my clients likewise enjoy my services and person. There is a dignified quality and relationships established about my work and the people I work with. This growth in and through work has changed my life perspectives, and I am able to bring those fresh perspectives to my clients and their families.

> *"You and I possess within ourselves – at every moment of our lives, under all circumstances, the power to transform the quality of our lives. Knowing that you can choose, that you have the power to transform the quality of your life – at every moment, and in all circumstances – is what the work is all about. And the transformation happens in an instant." ~ Werner Erhard*

Who am I becoming in and through my work?

Sometimes work can become mundane and routine. We arrive at work and get at our list of tasks, complete them, and head home to relax and regain our energy and purpose. Not all time spent at work is a source of peace, pleasure, satisfaction, and creativity. When I initially started caregiving as a job, my close friends told me I could do better.

What they really meant was that with my educational background, I could pursue better opportunities in the job market. But I had found my bliss in caregiving. I was loving people to make my living. What else did I want? With each passing day, I am growing in my ability to channel love and this has impacted all other relationships in my life. I have come to understand life a little more deeply, along with life's natural process and cycle. Death does not scare me anymore. I am now able to handle the sacred cycle of life and to assist people to embrace death as much they welcome the arrival of a new life. I view myself as a midwife assisting people in their heavenly birth.

One of the most common desires I encounter in families when they hire a caregiver is, they want the caregiver to stay busy and keep their loved one involved in various activities. Once I was interviewed for a position as caregiver to a person with Alzheimer's disease. The family had created a huge box of activities with games, puzzles, and all sorts of creative art material. They had taken great pains to draw up a schedule of activities. Despite this, the person would become bored within a few minutes of involvement in any of those activities. I felt pressured to keep the person engaged and tried all my tricks to entice the person to do those activities. Eventually, I realized that the client with Alzheimer's could not remain focused and had very little interest in those activities. I felt this was a torture to the person and the caregiver, and so I shared my experience and perspective with the family members. They wanted to keep their loved one's mind engaged so that it would not deteriorate further. I thought the person wanted more "peace time" than activities. We all want some time of meditation to find our peace, but we do not value peace when it comes naturally to someone else. We have a deep need to keep the mind active. I asked the family member what they thought the result of keeping the mind active would be when the person is clearly showing desire for quiet and silence.

The human brain in seniors naturally connects with the mind of the universe and initiates itself into the process of the next life. This is not understood or valued by most people. They want to keep busy for the sake of keeping busy. Having learned this at work, I question similar traits in my own life and make choices to engage myself in those activities that bring me meaning and purpose. I have accepted that I might not fit into the so-called normal cultural practices of the people around me. I am fine and comfortable with being different. I do not have the need to conform or stand out. There is a peaceful depth from where I can draw from life's energy and flow with the cycle of life.

Years of caregiving have helped me to become more loving, caring, accepting, empathetic and understanding of life and its cycles. I observe seniors who have very little sense of social obligation, are much more their real selves and want to live attuned to life itself. Their life is a constant reminder of what is essential and necessary. As a result, I have questioned my own choices of essential and necessary things and relationships in life. In my adult life, friends hold an important place and rightly so. Watching how families rally around their elderly loved ones, has brought me to prioritize my time with family and friends. I have become a different person in and through caregiving.

I once worked with a man who met with a terrible road accident on the way to dinner, on the evening of his retirement at age 62. The accident left him immobile from neck to foot, and he became an angry man. When first hired, I was told that he was abusive in his language and angry by nature. I decided to give life a chance and work with him for a week before deciding to continue or move on. On the first day, I asked him to tell me more about himself and his disabilities. He shared with me about the accident episode and briefly about his life. I could not help but cry at his story. How could he *not* be angry and use the only tool he had on hand to react to the tragedy of his life? Some extraordinary empathy was born in my heart on hearing his story. His anger and abusive language never hurt me. I was able to be kind to him even when he experienced anger. He would often apologize for using curse words. I told him that he had a right to feel as he did. He did not curse me—rather, he cursed the accident or the driver who caused it. He once joked that if I needed to, I could learn some of his favorite curse words and join in. That was the last day I heard him curse. That man chose to bless me with his death. I was out of town for three weeks and thought he would die before I returned. He waited, and the day I returned, I had the privilege to share the last 24 hours of his life and help him make the transition to his next life. I realized that, unlike other caregivers who took his curse words personally, I was not offended since I did not have the history of growing up with those words. I was also able to see and understand his pain rather than his reactions to the pain, and I realized that this was an important component of empathy.

Another woman I worked with was very sweet and almost a living saint. She was the first person in my life who never wanted me to be any different than who I was. I never heard a word of criticism from her. She was grateful and appreciative for every act of service I offered. I became so much at ease in her presence that, for the first time, I started to appreciate myself and simply bonded with her very deeply. I had lived more than 40 years constantly being criticized for this or that and being told when I was right or wrong, and this had taken a toll on my personality. She was able to redeem me by allowing me to let my true self shine. What a gift and a blessing! I had moved from simply having a job to loving to work with her. We both were able to channel love to one another, and the two-and a-half years caring for her, were a period of bliss and inner healing.

Outside of caregiving, I have grown through other jobs, too. As noted previously, one of my jobs was organizing communities. Handling 30 communities at one time called me to become more organized and attentive in developing leadership programs and leaders. Listening to people's experiences, reflections, and stories caused a shift within, and I grew into a "person cultivator." I became better able to see the potential in people and create training and opportunities to help them to move to that next level in their lives.

Growth comes from the positive experiences as well as the difficult ones. While I was working as a community organizer, my immediate boss took credit for every initiative I had undertaken. He would make it look and sound as if these were *his* initiatives and programs. Though my initial reactions were ones of resentment and passive aggression, eventually this led me to do some soul searching, and I recognized my own need to be known and recognized. I believed that I had the gifts and talents deserving of recognition. It took me years to let go of this need, more out of helplessness than choice. When one is in a subordinate position, there is limited opportunity to assert one's self. I did ultimately learn to let go of this ego-driven need and grew comfortable in my own skin. As long as I knew what I had achieved, that was enough for me and much more important than others patting me on the back. As a result of this experience, I have also grown very sensitive about recognizing people and making them feel appreciated for even their smallest contributions.

While we look at the monetary returns, benefits, and work conditions of a given job, it is also important to pay attention to work dynamics and the people with whom we work. We grow from each experience and become the person we are meant to be.

Accessing Greater Truth and Values of Life Through Caregiving

When I started caregiving, I had no idea that I could come to love someone so deeply. The capacity to love and care for a stranger have surprised me. What's happening here? My experiences have questions without answers. I have no need to know. It is enough for me to love and let go.

I am reminded of an experience of working with a woman who asked me to hold her. After ten minutes, I asked her about five times if that was enough holding, and she replied that it was not enough for her. So, at that point, I told her that I was going to hold her as if she were my own mother. I closed my eyes and imagined that this woman was my Mom. Lo and behold, I truly saw it was no longer her, but my Mom! The feeling of holding her was literally the same as if I had been holding my own mother. The skin, the face, the smell—everything about my client had turned into my Mom. I will never forget this experience. This was truly a moment when the feeling of being distinct, different human beings had vanished. I could see how we were all one humanity. In motherhood, I did not see these two women as being different. They both had six children. One happened to have me, and the other had me to care for her. That experience of the vanishing of human body boundaries, has transformed me profoundly. I see everyone as connected and can love everyone equally. Why should my love be of a different quality just because someone is not related to me biologically? This has brought my job of caregiving to a totally different level. People I work with feel truly cared for and I feel cared for by them in return. Sometimes I wonder who is taking care of whom. In experiences like these, there is more life and love.

Caregiving has become love in action, and I have grown by leaps and bounds in my ability to love. You become what you practice. Loving people I work for and with, has increased my ability to love. I am as comfortable as I am in

> *People I work with feel truly cared for and I feel cared for by them in return. Sometimes I wonder who is taking care of whom.*

my own home. This has dissolved boundaries between "my people" and "not my people." Between "us" and "the other." Every human being on earth feels the same to me, as my own flesh and blood. The biological boundaries created in my mind encourage me to ration my love to particular people, but caregiving has helped me break open those boundaries and extend my heart to everyone.

Caregiving has also changed my perspective about death and aging. This, in turn, helps the people I work with to develop a healthy attitude towards aging, loss, and dying. I can help them to see that this phase of life need not be a sad process, but rather, that it is a natural process where we can help one another through the transitions. The whole of creation is set up to renew itself, and death is how it brings this renewal to fruition. We can all help the renewal of creation by embracing death as something that not only happens at the end of human life, but as something that is a reality of everyday life. Our bodies die cell by cell, bit by bit, over time, and so do our ideas, projects, and dreams. There is no more fear about death. Death and birth are just two aspects of the same cycle. I experience this within me and can bring this perspective and peace to my clients. Death is not an end, but simply a shedding of a tired and fully used human body so it can be returned and recreated as a new part of the cosmos.

Caregiving thus becomes the practice of honoring the miracle and cycle of life and death. In fact, there are many similarities between caring for a newborn and an aging person. In both, we see life from two ends of the same spectrum. Since I see the whole of humanity as one and life as one, death is just one part of going back to the earth to let life and humanity continue. The fear surrounding death is only fear of the vanishing of self. The self that was created by society will disappear with the disintegration of the human body, but human life will continue, and the self will emerge with every new experience. When death is viewed from this lens, there is no more fear. The more I have been involved in ministering to the aging, the more I am in touch with death and the more I become comfortable with it and am better able to share that comfort with my clients and their families.

In my experience, another great gift that comes from caregiving is the gift of vulnerability. By nature, most adults are proud and value their independence, and it is difficult for them to relinquish their self-reliance as they become more fragile. But when people openly accept the vulnerability that comes with aging and allow themselves to be served, a tremendous desire to care for the person is released in the caregivers. Whenever people are open and vulnerable, the love and care flows naturally. When people are too self-dependent and think life is entirely in their control, it is often difficult to figure out how to relate to them. Love is at its best when you are around a little baby, because the baby does not assert its independence. The infant is open and vulnerable, and we do not expect a baby to do things for itself. Similarly, we need to be around people who are old and sick. When they cannot do things for themselves, instead of ridiculing them or making them feel smaller, you can use their vulnerability to release greater love and compassion in your heart—a gift you can offer to them and to yourself!

Slowing down and being in the moment are gifts of aging. Because the physical body has less strength and speed, the aging person slows down, and this helps them to relish and enjoy simple moments of life. We move from quantity to quality of life. When I initially began caring for older persons, I had hard time slowing down to match their pace. I was a multitasker by nature and took pride in my ability to do several things at once. When I started working with the seniors, I had to slow down. Thank goodness! Slowing down has helped my inner growth tremendously, allowing me to catch myself and pay attention to those areas of life that were neglected by my multitasking. Slowing down to accompany my clients has in turn helped me to deepen the inward spiritual journey.

The joy of assisting another human life is a tremendously rewarding experience. There is a Chinese saying that says, "If you want happiness for an hour, take a nap. If you want happiness for a day, go fishing. If you want happiness for a year, inherit a fortune. If you want happiness for a lifetime, help somebody." Many great thinkers confirm that happiness is found in helping others. I am not saying that giving away one's self is easy, especially when it is one sided. When it is one sided, it can be a depleting experience. In caregiving, two people rise from mere job to sharing of life. The woman I worked with would not eat until I sat down and was ready to eat myself. That spoke to my heart and I knew that she cared, too. When care is reciprocal, it is much easier. And care is not the number of things one does or the other cannot do. The one with more physical strength can do more than the one who has less energy, but the mutual care has equal strength no matter how it is expressed. For me, that one incident of waiting was enough and spoke volumes and in turn made me give my best and entire self.

Work to me is a source of mysticism. In and through work, I am trying to create more beauty or beautiful experiences. Mysticism has traditionally been thought of as an experience of ecstasy, and work does have the potential to create such experiences. What makes work or life mystical is the attitude and quality we bring to what we do and how we do it. It is how we approach something or someone and understand or respond. It is, as Mother Teresa said, doing many small acts with great love. Or as a nurse friend who worked in the emergency room said of her work, "It is cutting the filthy, urine-soaked clothes off of a homeless person and not letting them see that you find it disgusting." When work becomes a source of mysticism, it becomes a place of learning new manifestations of God. Work acquires new perspective and direction and we hold it in awe and gratitude. The flow of

> *We make a living by what we get; we make a life by what we give —* Winston Churchill

energy and attention is total. The outcome is beautiful. People can know and feel the difference you bring to your work. Work becomes a sacrament and means of God's grace. You look forward to getting to work and are fully present when engaged in the activity. The work is no different when it is done for money or done at home for no pay. The essence of all activities remains the same. Caregiving is my job and is not limited to my clients alone. How I take care of myself, my other relationships, things at home and even my car or other inanimate objects are all expressions of the same spirit that flows through all things. Every single moment and every single activity are a sacrament. They are moments and means to experience and share God's grace.

Work without Desire – Nishkam Karma

Nishkam Karma is a central theme in the Hindu Scripture, the "Bhagavad Gita." It is an important concept about work and human action, it means to act unselfishly, or without personal gain in mind. When acting out of Nishkam Karma, an individual is acting without any expectation that good will be returned to him/her. In Sanskrit, *nishkam* means "action without motive," "work without desire," or "desire-less." It is a call to perform any action purely for the sake of the action and not for what one will get out of it or in return. This is another way of describing the mysticism of work. When you enjoy the activity in itself and by itself without the desire for an end result, it takes on a new frequency. It has the capacity to energize you and everyone engaged in it.

Nishkam karma is selfless action without expectation for returns. It is non-attachment to the result of one's actions. One gives fully to the action and is not affected by the result it produces, whether positive or negative. Another aspect of nishkam karma is that you give yourself fully to those activities that are meant for the sake of others' welfare and not for self-benefit alone. Jesus said something similar in the Gospel of Matthew (25:40): "And the king will say to them in reply, 'Amen, I say to you, whatever you did for one of these least brothers of mine, you did for me." Humans are transactional. Usually, there is a common feeling that 'I' did this or that for someone. We expect a response because we did a favor, while the truth is that we are only an instrument executing the energy and motivation provided by God. In each act of service or doing, we are only doing what God asks of us. This takes an inner understanding of life and God. The more we realize and live as instruments or channels through whom life is flowing, the more we will live from Me and not I. 'I' is only temporary, and when it has achieved what the 'Me' is meant to, it will disintegrate and vanish.

Selfless actions in today's capitalist economy might sound redundant. Negotiations are expected. "I will do so much if I am paid so much." Everyone needs to make a living. We live in a society where very few individuals will voluntarily offer a return for what they got freely. We are in a system where people only recognize their own needs. We do not see that everyone else has similar needs. If I deserve fair wages and a good lifestyle, then all the others do, too. Being part of a culture where everyone primarily looks out for their own personal gain or needs, we are forced to be proactive in giving selflessly. Even when external circumstances are not *nishkam karma* friendly, it does work. There are millions of stories and accounts where, in every act of selfless giving, people experience amazing power and transformation, both of self and others. We might all desire and work to reform social and economic structure of oppression. Very few, like Mother Teresa, realize that selfless service is the immediate solution to an unjust system. Here's a story from her life in her own words: "One day, in a heap of rubbish, I found a woman who was half dead. Her body had been bitten by rats and by ants. I took her to a hospital, but they had told me that they didn't want her because they couldn't do anything for her. I protested and said that I wouldn't leave unless they hospitalized her. They had a long meeting and finally granted my request. That woman was saved."

Every time Mother Teresa saw a person suffering on the streets of Calcutta, she realized the desperate need for a home to care for those who were dying alone. She requested a place from city officials and was given a building next to the temple. She called the new home for the dying "Nirmal Hriday" which means the "Pure Heart." Millions of people before Mother Teresa had observed the dying people on the street, but it took a special heart to move into selfless action and create a worldwide chain of care for the homeless and dying. There is tremendous power in every selfless act. One such act by Mother Teresa led her to establish homes all over the world for the dying, the sick, orphaned children, lepers, the aged, the disabled, and AIDS victims. Mother Teresa saw beauty in all these individuals who had been abandoned or rejected by others. There are people who have critiqued her and questioned her religious motivations and goals as the reason for her acts of service, but one cannot deny the role and goodness of religion that provides fuel to the desire to serve.

> *"Be faithful in small things because it is in them that your strength lies".*

> *"Spread love everywhere you go. Let no one ever come to you without leaving happier".*

> *"It is not about how much you do, but how much love you put into what you do it counts". Mother Teresa*

Religious affiliations and faith are deeply tied to giving and sharing. There are studies showing that the highest contributions to charity, both in money and

There is tremendous power in every selfless act.

service, come from people who have faith and follow a religion.

That does not mean that we can deny the role and contribution of philanthropy, non-governmental organizations (NGOs), and individuals with a heart to serve. Every little bit counts. The values of giving are deeply rooted in the texts, traditions, and practices of many faiths. In the Gospel of Mathew, Jesus directly tells the rich young man to sell all his possessions and give the proceeds to the poor. Pursuing these values, a long monastic tradition has seen men and women taking vows of poverty to give themselves in acts of service to all humanity. Similar values are promoted in almost all religious traditions. For Muslims, giving is one of the five pillars of Islam. "Zakat" (meaning to grow in purity) is an annual payment of 2.5 percent of one's assets, considered by many to be the minimum obligation of their religious giving. A majority of Muslims worldwide make their annual zakat payment as a central practice of faith.

The Practice of Mysticism at Work

When one approaches work from a mundane attitude of earning a living, it produces ordinary results. For example, John is in his early twenties. He has successfully completed a graduate degree in software engineering and gotten a job in a prestigious tech company through a campus placement program. He works hard to prove himself and earn a promotion. His dedication and hard work pay off, and he rises from being a mere tech to the leadership position in his company. John can provide material comfort to his family and engage himself in luxurious activities like international vacations, fishing, and hunting. By most definitions, he is a successful man at work and at home. He has a beautiful family of four and all of them are happy as they have everything, they need to enjoy life.

Peter is a successful software engineer. Like John, he has managed to find a well-placed job in a tech company. He is very hard working and innovative. He notices those traits not just in himself but in his colleagues. When he was offered a promotion, he declined the offer as he had noticed more worthy candidates for the position among his other colleagues. Teamwork was very important to Peter and so was the mission and work of his company. He always stuck his neck out for those colleagues of his who were victims of discrimination, a trait that was not particularly appreciated by his superiors. Dignity of work and rights of the workers were important to him. He treated all ranks of workers with equal respect. He even had friends among the housekeeping staff. Some of his values and choices kept him in the same position for years, but it really did not matter to him. He enjoyed his work and contributed his best. His colleagues loved him, and he never felt that he was in competition with anyone.

Which of the two individuals practiced mysticism at work? Mysticism looks different in each situation. Mysticism is not confined to religious experience alone, where one is able to establish a direct connection with God through meditation and thinking. In Peter's case, meditation is how he observes work, life, success, and others. He establishes connections with every human being who shares similar experiences, needs, and desires in their daily life. Connecting with life and its experiences and opening our eyes to the situation and dynamics around us can be as sacred as closing our eyes in meditation and thinking about God or spiritual issues. The very attitude of working as co-creators with God to create more beauty and goodness through work, is no less valuable than any spiritual ritual. Work that consumes most of our time, energy, and attention is a gift and a powerful means of mysticism. Each time we connect with our work from the depth of our heart, we create mystical experiences for ourselves. Every artist will attest to this experience. Some call it "being in the zone." At concerts or on the singing shows, you notice the singer closes his/her eyes and connects with that inner self and gives him or herself totally to the singing. The result is a soulful voice that not only creates pleasant music to the ears, it also stirs our spirits and hearts. Work done with such deep sense of connection can be a transforming experience. Instead of work stressing and exhausting you, and instead of watching the clock until your shift is over, when you come to view your work in this way, you can become a new person with each work shift.

Finding Your Passion and Bliss at Work

Should I choose a profession that is most in demand and would be very lucrative, or should I choose something that fulfills my heart? When it comes to choosing one's profession and life's work, this is a dilemma people all over the world must face. Some people are fortunate to find a job that fulfills both their passion and their need for money, while many must wage a lifelong struggle to find a compromise between the two needs.

How passionate am I about my work? Does my work satisfy me well enough? Does my happiness depend on the amount of money I make or the joy of co-creating with God and adding beauty, goodness, and value to the creation and human life? Obviously, there are no readymade answers and no secret formula that will tell you how to draw your passion and bliss from work. We can, however, come up with some tips that might help us to make good choices. For most people, it does take years to develop skills and find the fulfillment we seek through work. As for me, I never knew that caregiving was my passion, until I bumped into it through sheer luck and realized that this was my place.

If moneymaking is the goal, then one could easily overlook other important factors and end up in a compromising situation. Life's needs keep changing and so does the need for income. For example, individuals might begin their working career by prioritizing earning capacity but may eventually learn to value passion and bliss over money. Most people value the pleasure and security that ample money can bring, and a smaller number of people move on to find meaning and passion.

How do you know if you have found passion in your work? To discern this, here are some helpful questions to reflect upon:

1. How energized do I feel at work?
2. Am I always preoccupied with issues other than those pertaining to work?
3. Do I find my work boring?
4. Am I waiting to get out and relieve the pressure I experience at work?
5. How connected and engaged am I at work?
6. Do I experience a sense of loss of time and self when busy at work?
7. Do I see how my work is contributing to making human life meaningful and beautiful?
8. What moves and excites me at work so that I want to do more of it?

You know you are passionate and blissed out by work when:

- Time will simply fly by during work.
- You will look forward to going to work and feel satisfied at the end of your work shift.
- You do not mind any pain and tiredness that comes from work. Rather, you feel good for having worked hard and are willing to put in more to accomplish the task.
- You are not constantly looking for another job or client.

Overall, the quality of life that you experience within and the quality that you bring to work creates a deep connection within you and fosters a feeling of being fully alive. When this happens, you will not be working for personal gains alone but for the greater good. That feeling and experience in turn becomes the source of bliss and passion. It can also be called spiritual and mystical. The truth is that extraordinariness of life is integrated into the ordinary happenings of everyday life. Chopping wood and carrying water—the ordinary man's purgatory or the enlightened sage's bliss. We do not have to go to special places or do out-of-the-ordinary things to find greater purpose and meaning. These are right in front of our faces in the daily tasks and responsibilities of life. When we have a greater sense of life (which I call Me), daily life becomes a school of unfolding that greater Me. Living from the small sense of I contracts the world to limited goals and poor use of our gifts. Living from "ME" leads to a fuller participation with the world and expands our sense of self and connection with the higher self.

The Gift of Work

"Not all of us can do great things. But we can do small things with great love". Mother Teresa

During this time of pandemic, many people have been laid off or have permanently lost their jobs. Some say that their job loss has led them to fully realize the value and gift of work beyond a paycheck, and they appreciate the jobs they had more now that they are unemployed. As Joni Mitchell sings, "Don't it always seem to go, that you don't know what you got 'till it's gone." Work is a gift not just for its monetary returns, but also for its many other

> *Working hard for something we don't care about is called stress and working hard for something we love is called passion. –Author Unknown*

blessings. Work helps us to grow in creativity, organization, patience, dependability, dedication, flexibility, teamwork, communication skills and so many other values and virtues. Work gives us something to do and helps us cultivate a sense of pride and achievement. Work exercises our physical and mental stamina. Many of these gifts are natural byproducts of work. Imagine what life would be like without work. In my personal experience, I find a day at work makes me feel more accomplished than a day off work. Even though time off helps me rest and enjoy some necessary leisure activities, my sense of accomplishment is higher on days I work. I am also able to achieve much more on the days that I work, because I plan the day around work.

In and through work, I have become my own person and learned to value my gifts that enhance my work. This even gets carried over into understanding the value of my skills and negotiating salary. I used to think that negotiating pay for works of service was rude. I worked with people with disabilities and deep in my heart, I viewed that as pure service to humanity. I did not want to equate the deep meaning of this service with a monetary return. However, eventually it became clear that if I continued with this attitude, I would probably be a beggar in my old age! I needed a decent paycheck and employment in order to plan for my retirement. I started accepting my needs and acknowledging them openly. This was a big step in my life! I was trained to deny my own needs and only think of others. Through years of family conditioning and service in the convent, talking or thinking about my needs was believed to be selfish. Even today, I feel some residual guilt for thinking about myself and my legitimate needs. Each time I discuss pay with a client, I must give myself a "pep talk" to ensure that I will advocate for fair compensation. But the point is, it is possible and healthy to evolve to view life and one's needs in a much more healthy and holistic way. When you grow in one area, it affects the rest of your life and attitudes.

Work has thus aided my becoming and evolution. I have grown to view work from its impact on me as a person rather than from the lens of external grades and monetary value attached to it. Caregiving in general is not a lucrative job. There is high turnover in any retirement community or nursing home. But I have found it to be the most satisfying and rewarding experience. I tell people that I make my living by learning to love. Isn't that cool? Indeed, I have grown in my ability to love people who do not belong to my biological family and who are not related to me. This is such a gift. And because I work in a private home care setting as opposed to an institutional facility, I am spared the hierarchical supervision and black and white roles and rules. Each day is new and this helps me to become fully available to seniors wherever they are on a given day—happy, sad, angry, joyful, lethargic, energetic—wherever they are! Work like this has accelerated my inner journey by leaps and bounds. Work is a gift in that it becomes a means to transform the world into a better place and to infuse God's spirit into the world.

Lifegiving work is a blessing and means for growth and transformation, but there are bad jobs. Sometimes work does not enhance personal growth, and as noted before, it is important to discern whether your work is lifegiving or soul-sucking and to act accordingly. In some of my earlier jobs, I had to play roles and pretend to be who I am not. There are jobs that make you feel dishonest by making you create a false image just to sell a particular product or service. Sometimes these dynamics are out in the open, but often they are subtly hidden. People in these types of jobs suffer from within and it takes a toll on their overall health. It is essential to be aware of the impact of such work on one's physical and mental health—and to take steps to remedy the situation.

The Biblical Parable of the Talents

The book of Matthew offers one of Jesus' most important parables regarding work. Matthew 25:14-30 tells the story of a rich man going on a journey who delegates the management of his wealth to his servants. He gives five talents to the first servant, two to the second and one to the third. All three of them are aware that one day the master will return, and they will have to render him an account of their management. The first two servants go out and make use of their money, doubling their investments. The third servant buries his talent in the ground. Upon his return, the rich man rewards the two servants who made good use of their talents and punishes the servant who did nothing.

A "talent" was a term used in the bible to describe a measure or unit of money, and it was considered quite a lot of money. How interesting that today the term "talent" also describes our skills and gifts! Each of us are blessed with a wide variety of talents and gifts. The more we use them, the sharper those skills become. When not properly used, our talents can stagnate, like the treasure of the servant who hid it in the ground. One thing that is clear from this parable is that whatever gifts we have are given to us by our creator, and we are only stewards of these gifts. How we manage, invest, or make use of those gifts will shape our lives and our becoming.

Have we used our talents wisely? We are not talking exclusively about money here. Some might complain that they have fewer talents than others. But perhaps we should be grateful for whatever we have and to go and create opportunities to use even one talent. I am reminded of a personal story shared by a bishop. The bishop had a late vocation to the priesthood. While his fellow seminarians were in their early twenties, he was in his late thirties. He described how he would often feel sorry for himself when he saw the younger men playing sports or employing dramatic skills that he lacked.

He would complain that he had no talents. After reading the parable of the talents one day, he reflected upon his own plight. He realized that he did have three gifts. The first was the gift of teaching. He then asked himself how he could best use that gift. The bishop had observed that there were fellow seminarians who were not good at the English language and he decided to teach them. His professors noticed his desire to teach and appointed him to teach religion in a parish school. He kept receiving many offers and opportunities to teach people. He became so busy teaching in different settings that he forgot what the other two gifts on his list even were! He went on to be appointed a bishop and he continues teaching to this day.

As stewards, we are called to employ our gifts in the service of humanity. It is true that we all have differing gifts and a different number of gifts and why that is so, we will never know. But our gifts are not our personal skills alone. They include family connections, social positions, education, experiences, and available opportunities. What is clear from the parable is that how we produce results by using our gifts is important. Our gifts are directly related to the work we do. Our gifts are the capital we invest at our work—our knowledge, love, joy, right attitude,

> *What you are is God's gift to you. What you become is your gift to God. —Hans Urs von Balthasar, Prayer*

connections, savvy, experience. Investing my gifts is not a selfish act. Growing and multiplying my gifts is my duty as a steward of God's gifts. And like the servants entrusted with treasure, I must also multiply the gifts I am entrusted with in the workplace. I work to grow as a person and my work grows as I do this.

You are only required to invest the gifts that you have. You need not compare your gifts with others'. You do not have to cry over what you do nor try to acquire what is not yours to pursue. This would be a waste of time and energy. Work is a great source for our becoming and seeking self and God. If you ask yourself, "What am I seeking in my work?" you will understand your seeking. This search will reveal where you are in your life and will help you set a new direction if you decide to, and that new direction will lift you to new heights in your work and in your quest to live life at a higher frequency and with a deeper sense of purpose and meaning.

The Graces of Daily
Spiritual Practice

Author's Note: Just as artists work with canvas and paints, personal experiences serve as tools to teach us to learn more gracefully, think more clearly, and form the most beautiful picture of the essence of our lives. This chapter presents a framework for using personal experiences to shape the narrative—the pottery, the artwork, the creation—of our lives so that we may live in grace.

Everything that happens in life is grace. The grace and presence of God flows in and through our everyday life experiences. The little nudge that we feel inside to make better choices and raise the quality of our ordinary daily events are called grace. Grace flows constantly from its source. What is not constant is our openness to receiving grace. We must practice opening ourselves to become effective recipients of grace. Practice connects our physical exterior to our spiritual interior, and allows them to work in harmony. If we seek to transform our lives, then we must develop a daily spiritual practice and ritual.

Like rain from the sky, grace flows freely and abundantly, but it is spiritual practice that helps us access and use it in daily life. If grace is available and dependent on my capacity to tap into it, what can I do to access it more abundantly? Practice, practice, and practice! What I mean by practice is to grow in one's capacity to listen to the inner voice and discover deep-seated values by which life is unconsciously guided. Once you develop that skill and become sure of that foundation, you will be able to provide new direction to your life by setting the values you want to bring forth and live by. You will also be able to unleash these values to bring new life to the world. Discerning those values only happens through grace. Sometimes we take our own inner processes so much for granted that we do not recognize the difference between activities of our mind (the I) and the higher power that is at work in us (the Me). We sometimes fail to recognize the presence of grace in our lives. What is it, exactly? Grace is experienced as an insight or deep inner understanding. Some people describe it as "a revelation." Grace may make you feel as if suddenly an inner eye has opened, and you begin to see something ordinary in an extraordinary way. According to Dallas Willard in his book, *The Great Omission*, grace is God acting in our lives. Grace is a pure gift. It can never be rationed and is available to everyone at any time. It requires us to approach life beyond the conditioning of our minds.

You will also be able to unleash these values to bring new life to the world. Discerning those values only happens through grace. Sometimes we take our own inner processes so much for granted that we do not recognize the difference between activities of our mind (the I) and the higher power that is at work in us (the Me). We sometimes fail.

Let me share some spiritual practices that have helped me and have the potential to help you to create an openness needed for grace to manifest itself in your daily life.

1. Developing Right Perspectives as a Spiritual Practice

Recently, at a group prayer meeting, one of the members spoke of being distraught by her nine-year-old grandson's refusal to participate in family traditions and follow the family's faith. I recalled another friend who had described a similar experience that he had been through with a daughter who had refused to attend church. He and his wife were troubled by this, and had tried in vain to convey the importance of church and a belief in God. Nothing made sense to the young woman and she simply refused to accept their explanations. Exhausted by all their efforts to explain their faith to her, the father finally asked her if she loved them, and if so, whether she would be willing to do something for them. The daughter was willing to do anything for the love of her parents. They asked the girl to go to church. She returned to the church without further resistance and grew up to be a very faithful adult Catholic, eventually raising a faith-filled family of her own. The group debated whether this man's approach was correct. They observed that his tactics seemed more like emotional manipulation than allowing the girl to follow her own mind and heart. In my opinion, the parents' approach worked out well for all concerned, and it is not necessary to morally evaluate or grade his approach to the situation. That is just my perspective—and all of life is a matter of perspective. Developing the right perspective is therefore important and should be a part of one's daily spiritual practice.

Developing a new or different perspective can be a powerful, life-transforming experience. It has been said that when you change the way you look at things, the things you look at change. I am more than convinced that we do not see life as it is, but as we are. In small Bible-sharing groups, we often ask the question: How does Christ see our situation? We then attempt view the situation based upon what we know about Jesus' life and teachings. We realized that often we are blinded by our own perspectives because we are emotionally invested in them. In fact, our perspectives appear to be part of who we think we are and they become the default system through which we live and view our lives and the lives of

> *We do not see life as it is, but as we are.*

others. Because of this tendency, it can be helpful to step back and distance ourselves from our default perspectives so that we may evaluate them and work to develop healthy perspectives.

In developing new perspectives as part of daily spiritual practice, it is important to understand that one's perspective is subjective and that it can be altered and improved. Become aware of your perspectives and examine their roots. Educate yourself by reading or researching what others think about a given issue, situation, or event. Consult sacred scriptures, theology, wisdom traditions or diverse faith philosophies to gather other available viewpoints. Test your perspectives against life experiences and decide which seem the most concrete and life-giving to you and others. You may find it helpful to maintain a perspective mindfulness journal.

One of my friends recently asked me about my perspective on the immigration policies of the current government. I responded that it depends upon how you view the issue. If you see immigration from the perspective of the human quest for a better life, you will evaluate human mobility from that perspective. If you view the issue from your identity as an American, then you may see others as outsiders, who are encroaching upon and trying to take what belongs to you.

At this time of pandemic and social unrest, it seems we are all becoming victims of other people's subjective perspectives as well as perspectives provided by cultural forces and political parties. How many hate crimes have we witnessed during the COVID-19 pandemic period? People with Asian features are being spat upon, ridiculed, and called racially charged names since the virus originated in China. Citizens fear walking in public places because they do not know who may view them as an enemy and pull a trigger at any given moment. People are running away from the sneeze of a stranger in public places. This sickness, in perspective, is causing fear, destruction, chaos, and death. If humanity is to evolve or even survive, developing healthy and informed perspectives about life and everything concerning life, must

> *"Life is all about perspective. The sinking of the Titanic was a miracle to the lobsters in the ship's kitchen." — Anonymous*

become a sacred ritual and a spiritual practice. My personal perspective is that I did not choose to be here and neither did you, but now that we are here, and knowing that we are not going to be here forever, let us see how we can help one another to get through this journey called life. How do I view human life, creation, work, relationships, gender roles, money, health, family life, politics, and every other aspect of life? Do these views help me live fully, peacefully, and wholly as a human being? Do these views help me live my best possible life?

2. Explore Your Unique Person and Purpose

Our being is the raw material with which we come into the world. It is a gift given to us by God, and what we make of it is our gift to God. Our innate abilities are part of that gift. The choices we make to use those abilities are our collaboration with life and its purpose. The human community, in the name of civilization, has created an understanding of life and provided definitions for success, safety, happiness, good, bad, and many other aspects of life. Instead of trying to fit ourselves into those pre-defined boxes and perhaps feeling that we have to join the "rat race," we forget to delight in who we are. We do have the freedom to take our own inner pulse and question those social definitions. In doing so, you might turn inward and ask yourself: *What are my gifts? What makes me happy? When and how do I feel alive? What draws me and my attention? What brings me energy and light? What provides me more energy—and when do I feel lost?* We can live life more creatively when we discover our personal gifts and use all the additional skills provided to us by education and training. We can undertake this journey of self-exploration alone or seek out and use resources that are available professionally, in the community, or within our circle of family and friends.

Finding one's purpose is considered one of life's greatest quests. How do you discern your purpose? Is your purpose continually emerging, peeking out here and there, hinting at itself, or has it always been clear to you? Many people notice a unifying theme running through their lives beginning at birth. Some stumble along with no clear purpose, only reacting to life's events as they come. Others may have a hunch or intuition. Reflect on your life story and pay close attention to any recurring themes in your life. You may notice a pattern of engaging life and using your gifts, opportunities, and experiences in a specific way. When you review your activities and history and reflect upon what, when, and where you were most happy, you will likely discover your person and purpose. If you write down questions or themes that connect all the dots presented through your life experiences, a picture of your life's purpose may emerge. You might want to look at various life story journals available in the market or create one to suit your own unique needs. You may also consider joining a life story support group to explore your story and life's purpose and help others to explore theirs as well.

In my own life, I have struggled to find and redefine my life's purpose. It has changed every few years. In my twenties my purpose was to be a holy person. In my thirties it was to establish social justice. As I moved along from my 40s to 50s, it became clear that my life purpose is to bring light to others. In whatever form or shape, I am here to bring the light.

3. Honor What You Love to Do and Do That Which Energizes and Excites You

In simple terms, the above advice could be phrased as "stop self-abuse." When we do things out of a sense of social obligation or just to please others, or when we engage ourselves in activities and relationships that we hate, we are abusing ourselves and wasting our good energy and precious time. These moments in time can never be replaced. As the folksy saying goes, "You're burning daylight."

For almost 45 years of my life, I did things out of a sense of guilt or obligation. I was brainwashed to take care of others before self. I had always been taught that caring for self was purely selfish. I was forced to constantly relate to people who drained me of my good energy. This was called Christian charity—to be loving to all. I worked even when I did not like my work. I was forced to do jobs, just to learn lessons in humility and understand the pain of those who were doing certain types of work. These experiences certainly held intrinsic meaning and had formative value, and I am grateful for them. I certainly learned compassion for others and the dignity of work. I also learned to discern if I was doing things out of guilt, social obligation or to release past conditioning. Although I learnt some beautiful lessons from such experiences, I did not live my best life during these years, because I was not engaging my gifts and talents in a fulfilling and purpose-driven way.

After years of inner work and healing, I still occasionally engage in activities that could be described as "self-abuse." I may find myself playing computer games for long hours, eating junk food that harms my health, engaging in negative or judgmental communication, or polluting my mind with an overdose of political news. And I abuse myself not only by what I do, but what I do not do. Some of my omissions or failures include not giving myself one hundred percent to the present and not assessing my energy level while engaging in work or relationships. Another phrase that describes such ongoing self-scanning is "mindful living." The more mindful I am about small things in life, the better I feel within, and as a result, I can accomplish a great deal. When I live mindfully, I have the energy to do things even after eight to twelve hours of work. This more mindful, self-aware approach to life and related activities, is truly a spiritual practice and turns life itself into an ongoing meditation and living prayer.

When you honor what you love and what energizes you, your life's purpose will, like a potter's work of art, take shape and emerge. You will be able to redirect your good energy and live life with meaning. Start honoring your own needs and values. Redraw your boundaries. Feel free and safe to tell your friends how you feel when you meet with them. Let go of anything that makes you feel ashamed or fearful. Stand your ground and become a person who demonstrates self-worth, self-esteem, and self-confidence. Once you find the bravery to do that, the positive qualities within you that bring a sense of meaning and purpose, will be amplified and will shine more brightly. That is the essence of spiritual practice; a transformed life through daily life experiences. In Matthew 5:14-16, Jesus says, "You are the light of the world. A town built on a hill cannot be hidden. Neither do people light a lamp and put it under a bowl. Instead they put it on its stand, and it gives light to everyone in the house. In the same way, let your light shine before others, that they may see your good deeds and glorify your Father in heaven."

Freeing yourself from self-abusive pursuits is a powerful way to claim your authentic identity and to multiply your energy level. But forgive yourself if you fail from time to time. Most people engage in self-abuse to one degree or another, and it is important to become aware of how much of our lives, we are frittering away on meaningless or even harmful activities. It might be helpful to create a chart and log how you spend your time, energy, and gifts on a day-to-day basis. This will help you assess where you are and plan steps to get to where you want to be. In keeping a journal, it is always easier to observe exterior sources of self-abuse (for example, gorging on junk food, drinking alcohol to excess, watching mindless, meaningless TV shows, etc.), but try to become mindful/aware of interior sources of self-abuse as well (for example, negative self-talk, engaging in angry thoughts to experience that "rush" of adrenalin, continually judging others, etc.). To be who you are and honor your true self, you will need to let go of what others told you to be.

4. Turn Religion into Mysticism Through Self-Observation

Jesus observed ordinary life interactions and drew out their deeper spiritual meanings. He continually observed life around him, and most of his teachings came from what he saw and reflected upon, in everyday life. In one of the Gospel accounts, we are told that he sat near the wall at the entrance to the temple and watched people enter the temple to make their offerings. Among other visitors, he observed a humble widow who offered a paltry two cents while other wealthy citizens made lavish contributions. He noticed the widow and appreciated her offering, because he knew that she had given all that she had while the others had given only a small portion from the great wealth they held. At another time, Jesus was keeping company with a family as they cooked a meal. As he watched the women cook, he used the analogy of salt and light to teach them about life. Life is like salt, he told them, and it loses its worth if it loses its saltiness. He pointed out that a lamp must be put on a lampstand so that its light can shine, and exhorted his friends, "*You* are the light of the world." Jesus always observed ordinary people going about their daily lives—for example, the shepherds in the pasture, the sower in the field, the women in their homes—and pointed out the deep spiritual quality of these activities. He used the literal example of sowing seeds and connected this with the energy of the spoken word, comparing the real-life example to its metaphorical meaning, to show his followers how the principles of creation operate in human relationship dynamics.

There were times when Jesus became overwhelmed by the demands of his followers. When Jesus wanted to deepen his connection with the Father, he withdrew into the desert for a period of prayer and inner reflection, and there he was able to summon the strength to resist worldly temptations and align himself with spiritual values. Besides Jesus, there are similar examples of more contemporary figures who retreated into the desert and returned transformed through the strength of self-observation—David Henry Thoreau, Thomas Hubl, Sadguru and others. Please note that I am not comparing Jesus with the people mentioned. I am merely seeing a similar pattern in their life's journeys. After their journey into solitude and self-observation, each one returned refreshed with new perspectives to transform the world. That is the power of connecting with one's self at a deeper level. When individuals integrate not only the teachings of a community, but also the spirit of those teachings, their lives become powerful and they become mystics. There are mystics in all religions and traditions, who have paved new paths and whose lives have positively impacted many.

I have noticed that when I began observing my inner self in detail by studying the patterns of my own actions and reactions, my spirit began to heal, and I gained new confidence. I was much better able to face life and its challenges, than when I remained stuck in and operated from years of conditioning. While it is a great blessing and gift to have a strong family and community to provide support and a foundation during one's growing years, the same family and community can become a barrier when they refuse to let you fly and discover yourself. When they seek to block you from expressing your spirit and your unique purpose in life, they can do the greatest disservice to you. When you embody the values and teachings of your community, to the extent that you begin to live by the spirit enshrined in them, you turn into a mystic. I therefore strongly recommend studying self as a means of living out deeper spiritual values.

Many of us who practice a given religion or faith tradition, study the scripture, theology, and history of the community to which we belong. After studying these, we sometimes become zealous or fanatical, even willing to defend those ideas with our lives. Are we supposed to sacrifice ourselves in defending these ideas, or should we instead use them to realize the deeper purpose and meaning of our lives? In my view, our study of scripture and theology should aid in our becoming, or else it is meaningless. We experience God in our lives and transform ourselves through self-study and self-observation. This process is comparable to keeping a vigil with self, not unlike the beautiful Catholic tradition called "Lectio Divina," a practice of maintaining a vigil with the scriptures. Those who practice Lectio Divina sit quietly with the scriptures or meditate upon them in such a way that the words of scripture turn in their hearts, the way a plow turns soil to welcome the seed for planting. In an atmosphere of vigil, the words take root and bear fruit. Similarly, when we keep vigil with self and observe our innate tendencies— seeking God's help to act from the best place in ourselves, —we produce sweet fruit. Why is it important to practice the interior study of self? During my years as a spiritual counselor, I have led numerous bible study groups and have noticed that, for any given scripture passage, participants tend to have very diverse interpretations. No two insights are ever the same. Why would two people reading the same passage of scripture offer such differing insights? We each read the scriptures from where we are. I am sure we all have had similar daily life experiences in this regard. Someone writes a letter and we read it not from the heart from which it was written, but from the heart *we* have. As noted, a bit earlier in this chapter, we tend to see things not as they are, but as *we* are. If both hearts are not on the same page, there could be differing interpretations or even downright misunderstandings. The important thing to remember is that, individuals experience life uniquely, and because of that, it is essential to study self along the spiritual path of life.

Ancient Greek philosophers had a phrase, "know thyself," an aphorism that simply means "know thy measure." Know the measure of yourself. Study of self as a subject can be practiced by reflecting on self. Each of us have different tendencies, interests, and ways of reacting to and approaching life events. You can choose from a variety of means to study yourself and your tendencies, as long as you keep in mind the goal to "know thyself." The market is filled with resources such as the Enneagram, the Myers-Briggs Type Indicator, and other tools that can offer a glimpse into our inner workings, our woundedness, and our motives for behaving in a particular way. In my spiritual study groups, we have used role playing to learn about self, for example, by placing one's self in a biblical character from the scriptures.

Becoming your authentic self and developing your unique capacities is a powerful spiritual practice. Being who you are is a way of honoring God who created you and living that creation fully. From intentional self-observation, I became acquainted with my strengths, weaknesses, addictions, behavior patterns, and reactionary tendencies. Through the process of self-discovery, I remained nonjudgmental and decided to parent myself in a nurturing way, so I could become a mature adult. As a result of this practice, I was able to accept my wounds, heal them, and learn new ways of acting and conducting myself. It has taken about ten years to fully embrace the study of self as a spiritual practice, and I am nowhere close to the finish line, although I am grateful to be on this journey. Along the way, I have noticed that accepting my limitations and strengths has made me more compassionate with myself, and that helps me show greater genuine acceptance and compassion towards others.

> *Becoming your authentic self and developing your unique capacities is a powerful spiritual practice.*

Self-observation and inquiry helped me to trace the origin of my behavior and wounds. Through this process, I began to realize that people who hurt me, acted from their own woundedness, while I kept collecting their hurts as my own wounds. Over time, I gained the insight that no one had intentionally done things to hurt me. My own inner woundedness made me collect wounds of and from others. I was able to let go of all unhelpful tendencies with gratitude and without blaming anyone for their past actions.

The role of spiritual director has been an important one on this journey of self-study. Over the past thirty years or more, I have been blessed with many good people who have served as mentors and guides. I am equally grateful to some of my friends who have played a valuable role in accompanying me on this journey and sharing with me their struggles to become better versions of themselves. Finding people who can help you know who you really are, is a great blessing and a gift!

Mysticism is nothing more than the inner adventure and exploration for which our spirit yearns. Religion offers us dogma, doctrine, community rituals, and faith codes. While these are not solely intended for external observation, when we remain at the external level of religious practices, our inner mystic—our spirit—is left to starve. This is one of the reasons why some people find that religion becomes boring and rote. Mysticism helps us tap into the heart of divine wisdom and compassion. While the mere practice of religion can make us moralist and self-righteous, mysticism transforms the person from the core and enables them to embrace life with inner wisdom and compassion. Judgment of others is more common among individuals who scrupulously follow religious tenets and dogma. Judgmental attitudes weaken the inner core of the person, because these blind us from seeing life in all its myriad beautiful expressions. The goal of mysticism is essentially experiencing the real self, the self that is created in the image and likeness of God. Once you touch upon that self, all else becomes relative. In the light of that real self, all of life's passing events become temporary, and they do not drain our creative and good energy. While religious practices can offer help in enduring pain without being destroyed by it, the mystic approach views pain as part of human life and not something that needs to be overcome by the practice of religion. According to Japanese writer Haruki Murakami, "Pain is inevitable. Suffering is optional. Say you are running, and you think, 'Man, this truly hurts, I can't take it anymore!' The 'hurt' part is an unavoidable reality, but whether or not you can stand anymore is up to the runner himself." While Murakami is talking about physical pain, the same can be said about emotional or spiritual pain. While we run the race of life, we will encounter and experience pain. The mystic can choose to suffer—or not.

At some point in life, almost everyone will be faced with fundamental questions such as: *Who am I? What do I want? What is the meaning and purpose of life?* Questions like these have set many individuals on a path of self-exploration. This journey into the self is a mystical journey, whereupon meeting the real person inside, an inner transformation occurs. The needs of human life do not change, but one's inner disposition does change. The transformed human being is then able to tap into the mystical energy that guides them to fulfill their purpose, as life fulfills their individual needs. On this journey of transformation, a few things that have helped me are self-observation, self-study, inquiry, and intuition. When you are led to meditate and study self, the process usually culminates in a deeper understanding of your innate tendencies and this, in turn, leads to healing your inner wounds. The actions and perceptions of a healed self are more life-giving to everyone. In our culture, psychotherapy does a good job in helping people gain this inner glimpse. But why wait until hitting "rock bottom" and seeking out a psychotherapist? Self-study as a spiritual practice, provides us with tools to find inner peace and meaning in our life.

Metaphorically speaking, many people spend their whole lives trying to avoid looking in the mirror, because self-observation is a direct experience of dealing with one's self. It is a serious discipline to sit quietly with and reflect on what's inside, looking into one's heart, examining one's motivations, even picking at one's emotional scars. Sometimes it is easier to avoid getting in touch with one's inner self, but everyone has the basic human capacity to do so. Some religious traditions promote the practice of mindfulness for self-observation. In my own experience, self-observation means bringing my attention to the experience of the self in the present moment. Just as observation is important for insight, self-observation leads to self-insight. Spending quiet moments of silence and solitude are the foundation of self-study. Devote some silent time daily for meditation and self-examination.

> **Romans 12:2** — "Do not conform yourselves to this age but be transformed by the renewal of your mind, that you may discern what is the will of God, what is good and pleasing and perfect."

5. Kabbala Body, Christ's Heart and Buddha's Mind

Taking due and deserved care of body, mind, and heart is an essential and mandatory spiritual practice in our day and time. In his book, *God in Your Body: Kabbalah, Mindfulness and Embodied Spiritual Practice,* Jay Michelson says, "Your body is the place where heaven and earth meet." Our human body is a wondrous vehicle with which to experience life. While our culture obsesses over body care and maintenance, there is also a great abuse of the body as a means for pleasure seeking. Michelson acknowledges that "The greatest spiritual achievement is not transcending the body but joining body and spirit together. But to do this, we have to first break through our assumptions and perception of the human body as a temporary material thing and wake up to the body as the site of holiness itself." Our bodies are a guide to the Sacred. We need to learn how to use our bodies to experience the presence of God. Michelson's book is a guide to cultivating an embodied spiritual practice, to transform everyday activities— eating, walking, breathing, washing—into moments of deep spiritual realization, uniting sacred and sensual, mystical and mundane.

When he reached the age of 96, jazz musician Eubie Blake reportedly said, "If I'd known I was going to live this long, I'd have taken better care of myself." If you wear out your body, where will you live? The body is a partner and container for the soul and a gift which makes the divine journey possible on earth. Jesus says that the body is a temple of God and the Holy Spirit. The body and soul need to work together to make the presence of God real in daily life. If we separate these two elements and treat them differently, then the very purpose of human life can be lost. The Kabbalah and Hindu traditions recognize energy centers in the human body that make divine action possible. This means that simple activities which sustain the body are as important as any spiritual ritual. I personally think saving the Amazon rainforest is as important as preparing and eating a healthy lunch. Spiritual practices such as consuming healthy food, getting exercise and keeping the body fit will help us maintain the body and along with it, the soul.

The very name of Jesus Christ calls forth ideas of love, compassion, and healing. Christ is associated with the human heart and worshipped under the title of the Sacred Heart. Our hearts perceive the world through feelings and are thought of as the seat of all emotions. We perceive life not only with our minds but also with our hearts, and when we perceive with the heart, we perceive with love. A heart full of love sees and approaches

> *When we perceive with the heart, we perceive with love.*

everything with love. Such a heart can create transformational energy that brings happiness and peace. Heart, as lived in union with Christ, is a spiritual organ. Often in our lives we have heard others say, or said ourselves, *my heart does not agree to do that.* What we are conveying through this phrase is that the heart is an instrument, finely attuned to life's choices. As toddlers and through adolescence we do not think, but feel our way into the world. Heart refines and redefines the choices suggested by our head. When our heart must carry the baggage of negative emotions, it becomes muddled and dysfunctional and is unable to make loving choices and decisions. When we think with our hearts, we think under the influence of love and often are able to make good choices.

Many people experience difficulties in making major life choices. The brain offers rational, logical information about why one choice would be better than others. For example, if there is a choice between two jobs, your mind will support one over the other with many explanations. Perhaps one job features a better salary, perks, benefits, working environment, and ethics. But somehow your heart keeps nudging you to go in another direction, even though your mind has supported the first job. What is that heartfelt nudge? One of my friends who had been pursuing the study of law, went to Europe and fell in love with food. She took culinary classes, opened her own restaurant, and never went back to another semester of law school. She told me that she had completely followed her heart in this career change and had no regrets. You may choose one thing, but as life happens, you notice life grabs your attention through mysterious coincidences. Growing in the sensitivity of the heart and learning to feel that nudge is an important skill that can be cultivated as a spiritual practice. First, clear the heart space from all negativity and wounds of the past. A

> *"All that we are is the result of what we have thought. The mind is everything. What we think we become." —Buddha*

clean and healed heart will better receive life-giving messages. Through loving deeds, thoughts and letting go, we exercise our heart muscles and grow stronger as people of the heart. We are then able to enter another's world with empathy and see the world as they see it. Once we do that, we become much more sensitive and make a difference by becoming instruments of peace and healing. Just as we clean filters on our cars or household appliances, we need to examine our heart and its dynamics from time to time to clear the emotional toxicity that accumulates through life experiences. This periodic cleansing process helps us grow as loving human beings.

It may not seem necessary to discuss the value and importance of the human mind in developing spirituality. We have all known its blessings and its curses. People often talk about cultivating the Buddha mind. What Buddha taught was to observe the nature of the mind. His teachings are all about how to cultivate the mind. We human beings have a great capacity and powerful potential to develop ourselves, if we focus our attention and energies in that direction. Our mind is like fertile soil needing to be tilled, fertilized, planted and harvested. Many people become victims of their conditioned mind and live as slaves to racing thoughts. They run on autopilot, serving the chattering "monkey brain." Cultivating our minds becomes a powerful spiritual practice that helps regulate our world and all its aspects.

> "*Eventually you will see that the real cause of all problems is not life itself. It is the commotion that mind makes about life that really causes the problems*". Michael Singer

What, exactly, is mind cultivation as a spiritual practice? In our ordinary experience, we often become overwhelmed by life situations and find ourselves inadequate in coping with them. During such times, we turn to God and surrender our situations to the mind of God, to handle it for us. In cultivating the Buddha mind, we train our thoughts through the practice of meditation, to prepare our minds to welcome every experience in life without becoming overwhelmed. This mind training/cultivation becomes a spiritual practice, when we maintain a state of continuous mindfulness. All actions and words then flow from that state of awareness, providing a sense of total fulfillment. We are completely present to life as it happens, and choices made from that presence are fulfilling and life-giving. This is an experience of conducting life from the mind, liberated from all negative impressions and compulsions. It is a form of training the mind to respond to life in the present moment, and these responses are creative, fresh, new, and full of the life force.

The fields of science and physics have made great strides in harvesting different forms of nature's energy, naming them and even grading them. While we may talk about spiritual energy as being separate from or more valuable than natural energy, the truth is that the two are intimately connected. Life is all about the dance of spirit contained in matter. Taking care of our body, heart, and mind, and cultivating their potential and power is a spiritual practice.

To grow and develop your spiritual practice, consider the following exercises in practicing mindfulness: awareness, silence, meditation, and physical activities that require your total attention.

6. Release Love's Power

The human heart is always on the run. It continually seeks, and the questing heart often finds temporary rest in things or relationships. After a bit, the heart continues on again, seeking further until it finally comes to rest in true love. This is not a kind of romantic love and is not found in any material thing or any relationship. True love is the highest form of energy in the universe and is found in one's own capacity to love truly, totally, and unconditionally. Once the human heart touches it, there is no more racing or seeking, and it comes to rest. True love then starts creating, transforming, and renewing the world. Each human being has the capacity to love in this way and to remake this world by unleashing the power of the heart. We might all have differing energy levels and abilities, but we are all immensely blessed with the capacity to love. Once we learn to release the power of that love, nothing can make us desire anything less worthy.

The word "love" has been very well used and abused. Each person holds a subjective understanding and definition of love beyond what words can describe. This plays out in our relationships through demands, expectations, and dependence on the other. Based on our understanding of love, we interpret one another's actions and respond accordingly. While our capacity to love is marred by the wounds we collect from life's painful and negative experiences, we can choose to grow in our capacity to love by healing these past wounds and nurturing ourselves to the extent that we are able to love purely. What does this mean? Pure love is powerful love. It is love that has no demands, no expectations, and no dependency. All too often, we depend upon family and friends to make us happy and what they do for us, makes us happy or unhappy. That dependency is manipulative, and we may misinterpret it as love. When I do not depend on someone else to make me happy, or depend on their approval of me, I am free to give love. Love does not flow because of what the other one does; it flows freely when we create a reservoir of love within. Building this inner reservoir of love. is a spiritual practice par excellence. As it is said in 1 Corinthians 13:1-3, we might offer profuse prayers, but if we have no love, we are but an empty vessel making noise. "If I speak in human and angelic tongues but do not have love, I am a resounding gong or a clashing cymbal. [2] And if I have the gift of prophecy and comprehend all mysteries and all knowledge; if I have all faith so as to move mountains but do not have love, I am nothing. [3] If I give away everything I own, and if I hand my body over so that I may boast but do not have love, I gain nothing."

Practically speaking, how can you unleash your power to love? Define what love is for you and make a concrete action plan to do things, that will help you turn your definition into actual expression. Become aware of your fears and desires and do not allow these to affect how you share love. Love because you simply want to love. Consider creating love experiences as memories. Love transforms the person from within. Loving self, life, and others for the sake of love puts an end to all the running, and your soul will find rest. It is like wildfire contained in a person. When it is unleashed, it will find its own direction and it cannot help but affect everything and everyone it comes in contact with. Once love finds a home in one's heart, it simply pours itself out. Love is by nature unconditional and pure. All the limitations that we place on love come either from our conditioning or inner wounds. Becomes channels of love. Let love flow freely in and through you.

7. Welcome Everything as It Is

Earlier in this book we talked about letting experiences flow through us. This is a serious spiritual practice that requires focused effort and consistency. It means welcoming everything as it is and welcoming everyone as they are. Life happens, and we have very little control over things that happen. You may, for example, plan how many children you want to have, but you cannot predict how they will turn out. Even when we think we have everything the way we want it to be—to have it all—so to speak, sometimes unexpected things happen. "Life is what happens to you while you're busy making other plans," said John Lennon. Much of our pain and suffering occur when we want things to happen the way we think they should. Unfortunately, life has its own inherent flow, and until we learn to flow with it, we will see life as problematic and full of difficulties. When we sense the direction of the flow and learn to go with it, our struggles ease and life becomes more enjoyable. Swimming against the current is always difficult. We label things as good or bad, happy or sad, and go through life's experiences attaching emotions according to those labels. It is human nature to want only good and happy things to happen, and we try to avoid the bad and sad things. But by doing so, we waste a great deal of effort and sometimes end up experiencing even more pain. The truth is that none of us is spared from life's negative experiences. True wisdom lies in noticing the way things happen and learning to welcome whatever life brings and flow with peace. When you learn to allow things and people to be, you will notice a change within. But if you resist what is, there will be suffering and pain. Welcome everything as it is.

Learning to welcome life as it happens is not a skill that can be learned quickly or easily. There are very few people who have practiced this spiritual skill to the extent that they are able to welcome every present moment with ease. It takes continuous practice and daily effort. Mindfulness can be a useful tool to bring attention to what is happening, as it is happening. Bring moment-to-moment awareness to things that are happening outside yourself as well as to your inner responses—the thoughts, emotions, resistance, fears, and inner sensations occurring in you at that very moment. Practicing mindfulness is not easy. In fact, moment-to-moment attention to life might create struggle and conflict in the mind. We need to learn to acknowledge the process and the struggle of the mind and then to cultivate an open, boundless awareness. With constant practice of awareness, the mind will learn to be aware and be in the present without struggle. Developing or cultivating the mind and inner awareness means allowing pleasant and unpleasant experiences to appear and disappear without struggle, resistance, or harm.

Learning to accept and let everything be as it is means letting go and giving up control. Meditation to control our thoughts must become our way of life. True meditation happens when we let go and allow God to direct our lives. Often our prayers consist of working hard to empty our minds into silence or using words to appease God. These are just ways to exercise control; for example, I might pray and ask God to keep me well and spare me from difficulties. What would happen if we allowed everything to be just as it is? There would be some fear and anxiety about, how to live life without directing our energies in a specific way. When we give up pushing life too hard and step back, life starts manifesting its own natural direction. Possibly, for a short period of time you might not have much to do. Then people and projects will start showing up. The inner light will start shining your attention on things that need to be done by you. In the inner core of your being and consciousness, things will start emerging. We are taught well to set goals and chase them with all our might. There is a time to do that. Once that race is over, we need to teach ourselves to let go of our desire for control and rest in the vibrancy of life that is waiting to emerge through you. Words will not be able to explain the simplicity of this practice: just step back and let everything be as it already is.

8. Identifying with Small Self (I)

While growing up, my family and teachers observed my ability to study concepts and solve math problems, and they told me I was intelligent. Because of what others told me, I thought and still think of myself as intelligent. That has become part of my identity. There are many other traits that have been added over time. and most of them are based on what others think of me and have told me about myself. They said; I was smart, hardworking, goal-oriented, socially appealing, and so on. As a result, I have tried to prove people right, but sometimes I wonder if I really know my true self or instead have just focused on being what what others saw in me. Identity thus can delude a person and bring a lot of pain.

Most of us give a lot of weight to this type of self-identity which I would call the "small self" or "I". After forty years of life, I began to question this identified self. The truth is, you and I are constantly changing and becoming. For many years, I have ignored the evolving part of myself and clung to the rigid sense of self, thinking, this is who I am. I have been on an emotional roller coaster for most of my life, because my identity came from what others thought of me, and I depended compulsively on others' approval or disapproval. I identified myself with the material goods I had accumulated, with friends I had made, with my feelings and abilities. Thank goodness I am now at a different place! My small self—called I—is only an expression of the greater reality called God, Consciousness or Cosmos. All that God wants to do is happening through this small self and passing through me. Emotions pass through me. Wealth passes through me. Work happens through me. I surrender myself daily to God, who wants to let things happen through me. My small self is not responsible for creating and coordinating all the small and great things that are happening in the world through me. This brings me great relief and inner freedom. I am rarely sad now. Sadness passes through me in certain situations, and I let it pass. Learning to let life pass through me, has made me a witness of life and there is nothing that I take pride in or feel low about. I give my best and at the end of the day, am happy for being an open instrument of God and life.

The more we realize that we are not the labels society has created and slapped on us, or our feelings or material possessions, we more we become pure awareness in our body, mind, and heart. We become aware of our experiences and develop likes and dislikes that eventually come to be known as our personality. When we do not abide in this awareness, we will be identified with labels, and labels will turn into sources of pain and suffering. Ceasing to identify ourselves with any labels, feelings, accomplishments, or possessions is a spiritual practice. Here are some simple tips to implement this practice:

- Maintain awareness. Be aware by continually observing.
- Witness everything that passes through you.
- Catch your thoughts and choose to live life by being in the now, rather than being lost in the world of thoughts.

- Observe silence and be present to current activities in order to relax the sense I, like children who lose themselves in the act of playing.
- Each time you catch yourself worrying or feeling anxious, repeat the following mantra: All shall be well, and this too shall pass away. Let me enjoy this journey called life.

Treat all desires and fears as human energies that pass through you to provide direction to your life. Become aware of all fears and desires and use them to determine what you want to do with them, and how you want to handle life without becoming overwhelmed by it. Become conscious of unconscious fears and desires, because they may take you on a path not intended or planned. The act of becoming conscious or aware of our inner dynamics requires seeing with the inner eye, and this seeing helps us to release our inner beauty and goodness allowing us to transform ourselves and create anew.

9. Handle Life with Prayer

When it comes to prayer, most of us turn to words or scripture. Just as we have variety in the literary world of language, there are myriad ways of using words in prayer form. There are chants, psalms, songs, quotations, beads, and other vocalized prayers. There are as many varieties of prayer in all traditions and faiths as there are approaches and perspectives on prayer itself. Prayer is a way or medium to connect with God by whatever name that God is known by. For some, prayer is asking something from God, for some it is listening to God, and some would say it is surrendering to and trusting in God. The journey of prayer has been a dynamic one in my own life—from vocal prayers to catechism to Bible study, to the study of theology and then finally realizing that life itself is a prayer. That is not to say that I don't use the abundant treasury of prayers offered to me by my family, church and community. The faces and definitions of prayer have changed consistently and constantly. At one point in my life, prayer was a commitment to serve the poor, and at another time, it was a desire to have an experience of spiritual awakening. There was a period when being honest with self was a genuine prayer; and there was a period when prayer meant growing in my capacity to seek and know the truth. Whatever form or definition we might have for prayer, it is an essential need in our lives. Life is fragile and full of the unknown. Prayer is a stable and powerful tool that gets us through life.

Practicing some form of prayer provides us an additional tool to get through life's difficulties without being permanently scarred by them. Prayer lights a path through the darkest moments of life. If you belong to some faith group or tradition, you can borrow prayer practices of that path or you can create your own. Fortunately, in our present times, scriptures and prayers can be accessed with the tip of our finger. Let us enjoy the richness of prayer offered by our own tradition and be open to what other traditions have to offer as well.

Prayer is a discipline requiring daily practice, so setting aside a time and place for prayer is very important; for example, I set aside the first early morning hour on a prayer chair facing the east. This has become an effortless practice. Here are some things you can do to make prayer a daily habit:

- Journal the prayers.
- Use your body in prayer with gestures or physical postures such as kneeling or prostrating. You may keep your palm on your heart as you say a prayer.
- Listen to devotional music or chants as you quiet your mind and heart.
- Prepare an altar with sacred images and books. Place some flowers or light candles around it. These simple acts create a powerful sense of spiritual presence in the house.
- Write a list of gratitude to God for all the blessings you enjoy.

- Practice intercessory prayers. Make a list of people and things you want to pray for and say some spontaneous prayers or formal vocal prayers for those intentions.
- Consider fasting, almsgiving, or penance as another form of prayer. Undertake some intermittent fasting or impose some disciplined practices involving self-denial or sacrifice. Consider offering some volunteer service.

The more we pray, the more we want to pray. Develop a taste for prayer. Let prayer become part of the rhythm of your day. Set alarms, use sticky notes, and schedule it in your planner if need be. The practice of prayer requires perseverance and discipline. Prayer trains you for the battles of life. There are some people who think their prayers will work if they do it "the right way." There is not really any right or perfect way to offer prayers. We must try different prayer modes and see where the heart finds its rest and feels most connected with God.

> *It is not the arithmetic of our prayers — how many they be;*
> *nor the rhetoric of our prayers — how eloquent they be;*
> *nor their geometry — how long they be;*
> *nor their music — how sweet their voice may be;*
> *nor their logic — how argumentative they be;*
> *nor yet their method — how orderly they be;*
> *nor even their divinity — how good their doctrine may*
> *be, which God cares for:*
> *but it is the fervency of spirit which availeth much.*
> *(Bishop Joseph Hall, 1808)*

These are just some possible practices I have proposed. You may pick and choose one or the other as they appeal to you. Practice them with consistency and you will notice the results. The quality of your life will change. You will experience greater flow and depth in all aspects of your life—your personal life, family life, and work life.

Even the way you communicate will be impacted by your spiritual prayer practice.

The greater the force of life you experience, the less you will feel the need to prove yourself to anyone. To live up to external labels that do not define who you really are is a waste of life. Instead we need to grow into becoming an instrument of God's presence. Only then will the full, abundant life that Jesus spoke of manifest in you with great force. You will become an expression of the greater reality called - God.

In his book, *Living on Love*, artist and author Klaus Joehle writes, "The universe is saying: 'Allow me to flow through you unrestricted, and you will see the greatest magic you have ever seen.'" May we all become channels for that magic, that force, that divine love.

I started this book with the story of the eagle in a chicken coop. The eagle did not know his own essence, his true nature. Because he had grown up in the chicken coop, he believed and acted like a chicken. He lived a small life. He never knew his brave and noble capabilities, and he didn't realize that he could soar. Like the eagle, we are surrounded by the things of the chicken coop—the affairs, goals, drives, and desires of the world that make us forget our divine essence, and we act from our small individual self (I). But also like the eagle, we are so much more than we know. We are whole, holy, and contain the spark of the Divine One. We are created in God's own image and likeness. No wonder we are naturally drawn to seek something more so that we can return to our true core! Acting from the small I will never satisfy us. Embracing our magnanimous self (ME), and doing our best as part of the whole, will bring rest and peace to our inner being. I hope this book has played part of the role of the naturalist, who called forth the real nature of the eagle. May it beckon forth the divine essence that you truly are.

A seed with massive potential
Goes into the ground and
Waits in darkness
For the universe to act upon.

Our would-be self
Comes to BE,
In and through complex relations
With family, friends and events.

Life is a constant dance
Of seeking and surrender
Acting and being acted upon
BEING and becoming.

Reflection Questions for Personal Growth

Chapter 1

Are you seeking anything in particular at this time in your life? what is it?

What does your seeking reveal about yourself?

Do you feel complete, satisfied, and whole today? Right as you are.

Is your life an inspiration? How?

How do you feel about this statement; "Life is not about you, but you are all about life".

Are you able to let the hard experiences pass through you?

Does your past haunt you in any way?

What beliefs and concepts do you find difficult to let go of?

Did you ever go through a Jonah-like or Nicodemus-like born-again experience in your life?

How would you re-describe your self-identity in the light of the contents of this chapter?

Chapter 2

What are some of the most important relationships you cherish in your life?

Share about one relationship that has deeply transformed you.

How did relationships help you to grow in your ability to love?

Did any relationship deeply affect your relationship with God?

How have all your relationships helped you to be the person you are today?

How would you relate differently by making relationships a spiritual practice?

Chapter 3

What things and people do you most react to? Why? How does that make you feel?

Do you see the hidden cry for help, under negative behavior of people?

What struggles do you face between being available to people and being free from their drama?

How and when do you get caught in other people's shit? How do you handle yourself then?

How can you assert your person and place by letting people go?

Chapter 4

When and why do you experience the need to prove yourself and how do you do it?

Do you experience any inner conflicts between who you are and who others want you to be?

What is the difference between concepts and real life?

Do you believe that you are whole? What can you do to enjoy that experience?

What are the threats you experience to your wholeness?

Chapter 5

How do you understand I and Me. How are they similar and how are they different?

What are the different ways you hold onto and promote the sense of 'I'?

What events or actions of others hurt you? Are these an indication of a need for inner healing?

How can you help self and others to move from I to Me?

Which traits of I and Me do you identify in yourself?

Do you want to do anything differently to put the Me in the driver's seat?

Chapter 6

What did family experiences teach you about life in general and about self in particular?

Share some of the beautiful family experiences and memories you cherish.

Do you have an image of a picture-perfect family? How does it affect your relationships?

Have you ever approached family life as a spiritual practice? Do you think it is a good idea to do so?

If you had a chance to do the family life all over again, what would you do differently?

Do you want to share how you see and experience wholeness in your family?

What are some of the heartaches you experience in helping your family to move to its full potential?

Chapter 7

How proud are you about your gifts of voice, speech, and language?

Are you satisfied with the way you have used your gift of communication?

Does your style of communication accurately reflect your inner self?

Do you communicate from your heart, head, or social norms and etiquettes?

What are the hidden filters in your communication that you need to become aware of?

How could authentic communication become a spiritual practice?

Chapter 8

Share or remember an experience of forgiveness in your life? Did it change you?

What do you need to do in order to let the forgiveness flow through you?

How difficult or easy is it to forgive yourself?

Who is the person from whom you borrow an ear, a heart, and a mind to help you move through forgiveness?

When do you find it most difficult to forgive? What do you do then?

Chapter 9

Do you enjoy your work and daily chores? What activities energize or drain you?

What are some of the chores you do not like but still do?

How proud are you about the jobs you have held in your life?

What are your thoughts about the biblical presentation of work?

Do you have experiences of getting lost in your work and losing the sense of time?

How has work transformed you and helped you grow up?

What are your thoughts and experiences about life and death?

Chapter 10

Are you willing to develop a practice ritual to help access grace in daily life?

What limitations do you experience in following up with your plans? How can you help yourself?

From your choices in the past one month, what are the hidden values you discover in yourself?

Do you want to make any changes in those values and choices?

What are the three helpful and not helpful perspectives you want to evaluate and change in yourself?

How proud are you to be 'you' and your unique self?

What is your life purpose at this time?

What things do you do out of fear or social obligation? Do you want to change your perspectives or activities?

What have you observed within yourself recently and been surprised by?

Do you enjoy catching yourself and engaging in an intentional self-observation?

Are you satisfied the way you take care of your body, mind, and heart? Do you want to do anything different or more?

Love is the power you possess. How has it transformed you and others in your circle? What do you need to do to grow in its depth?

How would you rate yourself on the scale of 1 to 10, about welcoming everything as it is?

How identified are you with your small self? How do you feel about it?

Do you have a prayer practice routine that you would like to share with others? Would you like to make some changes to it?

Did this book help you release the greater inner potential in you?

Suggested Resources

Following is a list of suggested resources for those seeking further study and reflection on spiritual development.

Books

Care of the Soul (25ᵗʰ Anniversary Ed.): A Guide for Cultivating Depth and Sacredness in Everyday Life, by Thomas Moore, 2016, Harper Perennial. In this New York Times bestseller, the author presents a powerful spiritual message for our troubled times and proposes a therapeutic lifestyle that finds the sacred in everyday activities, events, problems and creative opportunities.

Full Catastrophe Living: Using the Wisdom of Your Body and Mind to Face Stress, Pain and Illness, by Jon Kabat-Zinn, 2013, Bantam Books. This groundbreaking book, first published in 1990, now revised and updated in 2013, is considered a landmark work on mindfulness, meditation, and healing. The author discusses how stress can produce anxiety, depression, and disease, and presents a mindfulness-based stress reduction (MBSR) program to promote healing and well-being.

Loving What Is: Four Questions That Can Change Your Life, by Byron Katie, 2003, Harmony Books. After living for years with depression, rage, despair and thought of suicide, the author reframed her life's perspective to one of joy. Using practical examples, the author presents the process using the four questions that help the reader to radically reorient negative thinking and alleviate suffering.

The Four Agreements: A Practical Guide to Personal Freedom, by Don Miguel Ruiz, 2001, Amber-Allen Publishing, Inc. This bestseller reveals the source of self-limiting beliefs that rob us of joy and create needless suffering. Based on ancient Toltec wisdom, The Four Agreements offer a powerful code of conduct that can rapidly transform our lives to a new experience of freedom, true happiness, and love.

The Power of Now: A Guide to Spiritual Enlightenment, by Meister Eckhart Tolle, 2004, Namaste Publishing. In this New York Times bestseller, spiritual guru Meister Eckhart Tolle takes readers on an inspiring spiritual journey to find their true and deepest selves, to eliminate pain and suffering, and to discover truth and light.

Think Like a Monk: Train Your Mind for Peace and Purpose Every Day, by Jay Shetty, 2020, Thorsons/Simon and Schuster Publishing. Storyteller, podcaster, and former monk Jay Shetty captures the timeless wisdom of the world and packages it in a practical and relevant way. Also recommended is Jay's #1 health and wellness podcast, "On Purpose."

Movies

Amish Grace: How Forgiveness Transcended Tragedy (2010). A dramatization of the 2006 West Nickel Mine shootings in Pennsylvania which took the lives of five Amish schoolgirls and wounded three others. The film highlights the ability and power of the Amish community to forgive the mentally ill man who committed the crime and come together to grieve with and assist his family.

The Power of Forgiveness (2007). Narrated by Elie Wiesel, Thich Nhat Hanh, and Thomas Moore, researchers examine the psychological and physical effects of forgiveness across a broad spectrum of examples and situations, from petty insults to sexual assault to the attacks of 9/11.

The Power of the Heart (2016). Spiritual writers Maya Angelou, Paolo Coelho, and Deepak Chopra narrate a thoughtful documentary on the astonishing power and intelligence of the human heart. Available on Amazon and other media sources.

Websites

www.thework.com
Author Byron Katie presents resources, videos, meetings and events to embark upon "The Work," the process of freeing one's heart from pain and suffering and living a life full of joy.

www.spiritualityandpractice.com
Spirituality and practice offer resources including films, books, blogs, e-courses, and inspirational quotes to assist those seeking to integrate spirit into everyday life.